JOHN MAYNARD KEYNES

To Mirella and Indra

John Maynard Keynes

Keynesianism into the Twenty-first Century

Edited by

Soumitra Sharma

Professor of Economics and Associate Dean of the Economics Faculty, University of Zagreb, Croatia

Edward Elgar

Cheltenham, UK • Northampton, MA, USA

Published by
Edward Elgar Publishing Limited
8 Lansdown Place
Cheltenham
Glos GL50 2HU
UK

Edward Elgar Publishing, Inc.
6 Market Street
Northampton
Massachusetts 01060
USA

A catalogue record for this book is available from the British Library

Library of Congress Cataloguing in Publication Data
John Maynard Keynes: Keynesianism into the twenty-first century/
    edited by Soumitra Sharma.
        Includes index.
        1. Keynesian economics. 2. Keynes, John Maynard, 1883–1946.
    I. Sharma, Soumitra.
    HB99.7.J638   1998
    330.15'6—dc21   97–29928
                                                                                CIP

ISBN 1 85898 653 2

Printed and bound in Great Britain by
Biddles Ltd, Guildford and King's Lynn

Contents

Figures

Tables

Contributors

Philip Arestis is Professor of Economics and Head of Department of Economics, University of East London (UK). He has published widely in journals and books in Keynesian economics, macroeconomics, monetary economics and applied econometrics. He has been an elected member of the Council of the Royal Economic Society. His publications include *Post Keynesian Monetary Economics: New Approaches to Financial Modelling* (1988); *The Post Keynesian Approach to Economics: An Alternative Analysis of Economic Theory and Policy* (1992); (ed., with V. Chick) *Finance, Development and Structural Change* (1995); (ed., with M. Sawyer) *The Biographical Dictionary of Dissenting Economists* (1992); *The Elgar Companion of Radical Political Economy* (1995) and *Keynesian Policies for the 21st Century* (1997).

Ivo Ban is Assistant Professor of Economics, Faculty of Tourism and Foreign Trade, Dubrovnik (Croatia).

Zvonimir Baletić is former Professor of Political Economy, Faculty of Political Science, University of Zagreb. He has served as Minister in the Government of Croatia. Currently he is Director of the Economics Institute, Zagreb (Croatia). He is the author of many books and articles.

Đuro Benić is Associate Professor of Economics, Faculty of Tourism and Foreign Trade, Dubrovnik (Croatia). Currently he is the Dean of the Faculty. He has published many articles and two text books in economics in the Croatian language.

John-ren Chen is Professor of Economics and Econometrics, University of Innsbruck (Austria). His field of interest is research in commodity markets, economics of credit information, development economics, and economics of East Asian Countries.

Victoria Chick is Professor of Economics, University College London (UK). Her publications include five books: *The Theory of Monetary Policy* (1973, 1977); *Macroeconomics After Keynes: A Reconsideration of the General Theory* (1983); (eds, with P. Arestis and S.C. Dow) *On Money, Method and Keynes* (1992); (ed., with P. Arestis) *Recent Developments in Post-Keynesian Economics* (1992) and numerous articles on monetary theory and Keynesian economics.

E.V.K. FitzGerald is Fellow at the Trade Policy Research Centre, Queen Elizabeth House, University of Oxford (UK). He has written extensively and most of his works are in the field of finance.

James K. Galbraith is Professor at the Lyndon B. Johnson School of Public Affairs and in the Department of Government, University of Texas at Austin (US). He holds a Ph.D. in Economics from Yale University and has served as Executive Director of the Joint Economic Committee, Congress of the US.

Murray Glickman is Principal Lecturer in the Department of Economics, University of East London (UK). His major research interest is in the application of post-Keynesian ideas to finance theory. He has published a range of articles in the area.

Jan A. Kregel is currently Professor of Political Economy, University of Bologna (Italy). After studying economics with Paul Davidson, Joan Robinson and Nicholas Kaldor he began his academic career in the UK, Belgium, the US, the Netherlands and Italy. He has also worked as an economist in private industry and as a consultant to international organizations. He has written widely in the area of post-Keynesian Economics and has recently published *Origini e Sviluppo dei Mercati Finanziari*.

Kunibert Raffer is Associate Professor at the Department of Economics, University of Vienna (Austria). He was previously a consultant to UNIDO. He was Visiting Professor at the University of Klagenfurt, Austria (1986–9), a Visiting Fellow at the IDS, Sussex, UK (1989), and Honorary Research Fellow at the University of Birmingham, UK (1990–93).

John S.L. McCombie is Fellow and Director of Studies in Economics, Downing College, Cambridge (UK). After gaining his Ph.D. at Cambridge, he was a member of the Departments of Economics, University of Hull (UK), and the University of Melbourne (Australia). His research interests include post-Keynesian economics and the determinants of economic growth. He has published extensively in these areas, including (with A.P. Thirlwall) *Economic Growth and the Balance-of-Payments Constraint* (1994).

Gerald M. Meier is Konosuke Matsushita Emeritus Professor of International Economics and Policy Analysis at Stanford University (US). He has written extensively on international and development economics. Among his many books notable are: *International Economics: Theory of Policy* (1980); *Pioneers in Development* (2 vol. 1985 and 1986); *Emerging from Poverty: The Economics That*

Really Matters (1985); *Politics and Policy Making in Developing Countries* (1991); and *Leading Issues in Economic Development* (VI edn. 1996).

Malcolm Sawyer is Professor of Economics, University of Leeds (UK). He has published several books including: *The Economics of Michal Kalecki* (1985); *The Challenge of Radical Political Economy* (1989) and *Unemployment, Imperfect Competition and Macroeconomics* (1995). He has also been active in co-editing books including (with P. Arestis): *The Biographical Dictionary of Dissenting Economists* (1992), *The Elgar Companion of Radical Political Economy* (1995) and *Keynesian Policies for the 21st Century* (1997). He is the managing editor of *International Review of Applied Economics* and founding co-editor of *International Papers in Political Economy*.

Soumitra Sharma is Professor of Economics and Associate Dean of Economics Faculty, Zagreb (Croatia). He has published widely. He has edited volumes published by Macmillan and Edward Elgar: *Development Policy* (1992); *Macroeconomic Management* (1995); *Restructuring Eastern Europe: The Microeconomics of Transition Process* (1997) and *John Maynard Keynes: Keynesianism into the Twenty-First Century* (1998)

Sir Hans W. Singer is Emeritus Professor and Fellow of the Institute of Development Studies at the University of Sussex, UK. He has served in the UN Secretariat, latterly as Director of the Economics Division of the UNIDO. He was previously Director of the UN Research Institute for Social Development in Geneva. Prior to his UN career he taught at Manchester and Glasgow Universities. He is the author of many books and articles and director of various field missions.

Anthony P. Thirlwall is Professor of Applied Economics, University of Kent at Canterbury. He has written extensively on Keynesian economics and his latest book is published by Edward Elgar: *Macroeconomic Issues from a Keynesian Perspective: Selected Essays* (1997). He has been responsible for organizing Keynes Seminars for Keynes College, University of Kent on such themes as: Keynes and International Monetary Relations; Keynes and the Role of the State; Keynes and Money; Keynes and Economic Development and Keynes as an Economist-Philosopher.

John Toye is a Fellow of the Institute of Development Studies at the University of Sussex, UK and a Professorial Fellow of the University. He served as Director of the IDS from 1987 to 1997. His books include *Dilemmas of Development* (1995); *Does Aid Work in India*? (co-authored with Michael Lipton); and *Aid and Power* (co-authored with Paul Mosley and Jane Harrigan).

Pan A. Yotopoulos is Professor of Economics, Food Research Institute at Stanford University (US). His most recent book is *Exchange Rate Parity for Trade and Development: Theory, Tests, and Case Studies* (1995). He has served in an advisory capacity to governments in East and South Asia, Africa, the Middle East, and South America, as well as to the World Bank, the UNDP, the UN Fund for Population Activities and the FAO.

Martin Zagler is Assistant Professor of Economics at the Vienna University of Economics and Business Administration (Austria), where he received his Ph.D. His interests include macroeconomics of endogenous growth, new Keynesian economics and theory of business cycles.

Preface

Fifty years ago on 21 April 1946 John Maynard Keynes, certainly the most influential economist of this century, passed away. Sixty years ago his magnum opus *The General Theory of Employment, Interest and Money* created a revolution in intellectual economic circles. Anniversaries are, usually, the reminders of either great people or grand ideas or important historic events. Here we have a personality whom everybody remembers for his originality of mind and for his influence on the economic politics of the time. Even after 50 years of his death, the shadow of his influence can be felt and it seems likely that policy solutions suggested by him would probably last even longer.

Ideas of great minds are always an inexhaustible source of inspiration not only to historians of thought but to all those people who peep into the minds of great thinkers in search of fresh ideas and new solutions for current or future problems. Keynes's was definitely such a mind.

The history of economic thought comprises the accumulated capital of the discipline and its study permits both the retrieval of important ideas and conduct of analysis which places present day work in context. Studying economic thought and a quest for new ideas is a duty of all those who have an influence on the shaping of economic policy. It certainly is the duty of economists. Keynes rightly states that the attitude of economists and political thinkers is far more influential than is usually recognized, without regard to whether they are right or not. People by habit, who believe that they are beyond the influence of intellectuals, are often slaves to some old-fashioned economist. For this very reason, if one is looking for the solutions to contemporary economics, one needs to study and re-examine the ideas of this great economist.

Keynes's ideas were shaped by the course of events and problems of the time. These ideas definitely attract attention even after 60 years after the publication of his *General Theory*. Over all these years he has been thoroughly studied, criticized and pushed aside by many. Only during the past few years has there been a marked revival of interest in the personality and economic thought of John Maynard Keynes and of the impact of his theory on modern economic ideas. This revival of interest in his ideas seems to be fairly strong. In the 1970s it was almost taken for granted that academic interest in Keynes would be soon lost. But it proved to be an illusion because judging from the literature of the late 1980s and the 1990s it can be seen that a great deal of attention was focused on Keynes's historic role on the one hand, and importance of his ideas in dealing with the current economic problems, on the other. Today, especially in context of transitional economies, his arguments are being frequently used both ways, that is, either to support or to refute opposing views. Grafting of the sapling of western-style free market model, on the economies devastated by the centralized planning system in East and South Europe, has created almost an economic chaos in these countries, sparing only a few. Problems of falling output, unemployment, inflation, economic instability, and social unrest remain common to all these countries. Now, in search for a middle way economists in these countries look towards Keynes once again.

This volume presents 19 contributions in Keynesian mode, classified into five parts: theoretical contributions; global governance and the state; unemployment wage and prices; money management and miscellaneous. These contributions try to understand Keynes, as an economist whose work remains influential in both academic economics and popular economic ideas. The chapters presented in this volume have been selected out of a larger number and were originally a subject of discussion in an international meeting of economists held at Dubrovnik (Croatia) in November 1996. The event was gracefully sponsored by the local Faculty of Tourism and Foreign Trade.

The editor wishes to express his sincere thanks to the contributors and the publisher to make this volume appear.

Finally there are sincere hopes that this volume shall modestly add to the understanding of the ideas of John Maynard Keynes.

Soumitra Sharma

1 Introduction: J.M. Keynes before and after the *General Theory*

Soumitra Sharma[1]

Nobel Laureate Sir John Hicks writes:

> The historian...may well come to reckon the third quarter...as the age of Keynes. It is true that Keynes died (in 1946)...; but it is nothing unusual for a great thinker and teacher to make his greatest impact upon the world after he is dead. That surely is what one must judge Keynes to have done (Hicks, 1975).

Fifty years have passed since John Maynard Keynes (born 1883) died in 1946, and 60 years since his magnum opus *The General Theory of Employment, Interest and Money* appeared. The two anniversaries are a reminder of this influential economist's impact on the course of economic theory and policy in the twentieth century. Few economists find it easy to challenge the fact that Keynes's theory has been the 'the most significant event in twentieth century economic science' (Samuelson, 1988) or that modern macroeconomics is his creation. Initially his theory received a mixed reception but soon it became the centrepiece of macroeconomic theory and policy. The last 60 years have seen it being appreciated, interpreted, reinterpreted, criticized, re-examined and reconstructed. While opponents have tried to convince us that Keynes was fundamentally mistaken (Hayek, 1983), the Keynesians themselves seem divided between those who regard the policy implications of the *General Theory* as being moderately conservative (Tobin, 1987, pp. 1–54) and others who see it as a historic break from mainstream classical and neoclassical doctrine (Robinson, 1971).

Keynes was trained in Marshallian tradition in which economists were supposed to make the world a better place. While classical economists were still preoccupied with government failure and evils of monopoly power or too much government interference in economic affairs, preventing the price mechanism from yielding maximum national output, for Keynes writing his *General Theory* was a long struggle and escape from habitual modes of thought and expression, that is escape from the idea of *laissez faire*. In contrast to the classical orthodoxy his whole life was a struggle to show that with regard to the general level of employment and output there was no invisible hand directing social optimum.

Following is a brief analytical review of Keynes's contribution to economic theory and policy.

1

Keynes before the *General Theory*

It was not until the Treaty of Versailles that Keynes achieved fame and began to make public the theoretical system on which he based his contributions to economic theory and policy. The professional career of Keynes began with a 'solid and substantial' book *Indian Currency and Finance* (1913) which was very favourably accepted by his professional colleagues. At that time Keynes was primarily interested in achieving price stability for India and he supported his recommendations for stability which were based on purely classical insight. He suggested that India should have a gold exchange standard and that a central bank be set up to centralize the gold reserves for meeting extraordinary drains in times of crisis. He thought that his plan would provide greater stability to the Indian currency system than the strict gold standard could ensure.

At the outset of the World War I Keynes worked at the British Treasury on problems of French finance and the war reparation question. He wrote some articles on the behaviour of money markets and the banking system, but hardly anything of brilliance to attract attention.

His book *The Economic Consequences of the Peace* (1919) was certainly the best-selling analysis of the Treaty of Versailles. Keynes devoted a chapter to economic process as it led up to the war. He looked with nostalgia at the pre-war system of free trade, ample investment opportunities, capital accumulation and population growth. Keynes like any other classical economist saw the pre-World War I era as a period of stability and prosperity and capitalism being at its zenith. He cautioned against the possibilities of restrictive post-war policies which do not present a brighter perspective (Keynes, 1919, p. 11).

The post-war economic issues such as inflation versus deflation; stability of exchange versus stability of prices, gold standard and so on provided the stimulus to much of Keynes's writings. Although Keynes was always in favour of price stability, if economies had to be cured by price manipulation, he was invariably in favour of inflation against deflation (Keynes, 1924, pp. 44–5; and 1933a, pp. 105–13), recommending inflationary measures out of the three alternatives open to the Minister: levy capital tax, reduce interest rates or raise prices). He remarked, 'it is worse in an impoverished world to provoke unemployment than to disappoint the rentier' (1972, IV, p. 36). Although this was a part of his broader conception that a high level of investment is essential for economic growth under capitalism, it was not until the investment opportunities sunk low that Keynes recognized their complicated character and the necessity for vigorous measures of revival of the economic system. His desire for price stability is in line with Marshall's teachings. Keynes was unequivocal in his preference for domestic price stability over exchange rate stability, so that the monetary authority can maintain control over the domestic economy. He specifically suggested to the Bank of England to quote a weekly spot and future price for gold. These prices were not supposed to be fixed but to fluctuate as conditions warranted.

For the analysis of the problem of price stability Keynes employed the theoretical apparatus of the classical quantity theory of money. Throughout the 1920s we found him insisting on price stability with the policy measures based on the orthodox theory of money. Evidently the theory of determination of price level is based on Marshall's *Money, Credit and Commerce* (1923).

From the appearance of *Tract* to the time when *A Treatise on Money* (in two volumes) was published in 1930, there was one single, most important problem that troubled England and which Keynes was attempting to solve. In England in 1929 over one million people were unemployed and depression prevailed while other countries were fairly prosperous. The unemployment in England was largely confined to the iron and steel, shipbuilding and coal industries. The remedies suggested by Keynes for the improvement of the level of employment mostly involved monetary control and manipulation. He contended that the system was not perfectly self-adjusting and that *laissez-faire* policies do not work for recovery. In fact he defined this state of prolonged depression of the 1920s as one of pseudo equilibrium (see Keynes, 1933a). Keynes's reaction to Beveridge's contention was that overpopulation has little effect upon the level of employment. He held that a phenomenon of economic malaise arising out of such causes as transition from lower to higher price level, attempts of labour unions to obtain an increase in wages and changing external markets etc., is the real cause of unemployment.

Keynes denounced the British return to gold standard at pre-war parity because he considered it not only being a deflationary measure but also as an attempt to restore an automatic mechanism of balance of payment adjustment to which he had been opposed since the end of war. In *The Economic Consequences of Mr. Churchill* (1925a) Keynes argues that the main source of British economic difficulties is the disadvantageous parity of internal and external prices. The suggested line of action according to him was to let the sterling depreciate abroad, or to force the domestic prices and wages fall in line with the sterling. Naturally, because of the fear of deflationary effects he ruled out the latter alternative.

In the 1929 election, Lloyd George pledged to reduce unemployment through spending on public works. Keynes with D.H. Henderson examined the common sense of the pledge and argued its economic reasoning (Keynes, 1929). Keynes was optimistic about the success of his policy of public works in bringing about full employment. His recognition of the possibilities of induced effects over and above the government outlays presents the signs of his later theoretical evolutionary developments.

Everybody had eagerly awaited the long-publicized *A Treatise on Money* (1925b) which Keynes had been writing for many years. In the preface of the book he mentions that his ideas have undergone great change during the writing.

The critics, however, highlight its 'loosely knit theory with many lines of incomplete thought' (Klein, 1966, p.23). But it certainly is a sum of all the lines of his thought that covered the debates of 1920s. The *Treatise* can be considered as a book based on two theories: the business cycle theory which makes investment fluctuations the prime mover of the capitalist system; and the theory that the rate of interest is determined in equilibrium by the equality of savings and investment. The whole aim of the *Treatise* seems to be to tell us how to keep prices stable; or what is the same, to keep savings and investment equal; or what is the same to keep the market rate of interest equal to the natural rate. Thus Keynes recommends monetary control. The banks by manipulating the rate of interest would influence the level of investment until the equilibrium can be achieved with the more stable rate of savings. This would give the desired aim of price stability. If interest rate adjustments prove to be insufficient, the open market operations were suggested as the measures of control. Keynes was convinced that by exposition of his 'fundamental equations' he is providing the core of his theory.

Evidently in the early years of the 1930s Keynes had a good knowledge of the troubles in the economic system. Although he then did not have sufficient argument to formalize his theoretical frame, he supported policies that were similar to his future *General Theory*. It can be safely said that it was not his theory that led him to practical policies, but that practical policies led him to his theory. His popular writings of this period are a definite proof of it. In 1931 his radio address was a strong plea for increased spending to counteract the depression. In this address he attacked thrift because he saw the fallacy of providing large savings to be offset by investment when there were no offsets in sight.

A certain change of views can also be seen in the Keynes of the 1930s against the Keynes of the 1920s. In 1923 Keynes was of the opinion that protection could not help to improve employment. In 1931 the Addendum I of the famous *Macmillan Report*, which was strongly supported by Keynes, advocated for three alternatives of domestic monetary policy: a reduction of salaries and wages, control of imports and aids to exports, and state assistance to private enterprise and to investment. Keynes's lecture in the summer of 1931 at Chicago still reflects his old theoretical frame of mind. In this lecture he made an excellent analysis of the economic situation and suggested policy cures but the theoretical basis was still unchanged.

In 1931 an important development took place. While economists (for example Hayek, Robertson and others) were debating over Keynes's 'fundamental equations', Kahn was formulating his theory of multiplier which later had a profound impact on Keynes's mind.[2] Kahn's impact on Keynes is evident (Kahn, 1931). This is visible only in 1933 in Keynes's work (Keynes, 1933a) where he makes a strong case by providing some new arguments for his public-works policy and makes extensive use of the principle of multiplier.

Economists see the seeds of origin of Keynes's *General Theory* in his dissatisfaction with his own *Treatise* of which he speaks in his letter of 14 September 1930 to his mother, in the prolonged international slump of 1929, and in the discussions of 1931 within the 'Cambridge Circus' by his fellow colleagues (Joan Robinson, James Meade, Richard Kahn, Dennis Robertson, Roy Harrod, and Richard Hawtrey). It was only during the summer of 1934, however, that Keynes was teaching from proof sheets of *The General Theory of Employment*.

The Keynesian revolution

Although the foundations were already laid, the Keynesian revolution did not begin until the appearance of his *The General Theory of Employment, Interest and Money* published twice by Macmillan of London in 1936.

But, unlike the highly publicized *Treatise*, the new book Keynes was working on was not at all known to the public but only to a few of his close friends and colleagues. In his 1935 New Year letter to Bernard Shaw, Keynes gives only an inkling into what he is busy writing. He writes:

> To understand my mind, however, you have to know that I believe myself to be writing a book on economic theory which will largely revolutionize not I suppose at once but in the course of the next ten years the way the world thinks about economic problems. When my new theory has been duly assimilated and mixed with policies and feelings and passions, I can not predict what the final upshot will be in its effect on actions and affairs, but there will be a great change and in particular the Ricardian Foundations of Marxism will be knocked away. I can not expect you or anyone else to believe this at the present stage, but for myself I don't merely hope what I say. In my mind I am quite sure (Keynes, 1972, p. 492).

Later in the summer of 1936, he mentions about it in his letter to R.F. Harrod in the following words:

> I have been much preoccupied with the causation, so to speak, of my progress of mind from the classical position to present views, – with the order in which the problem developed in my mind. What some people think as an unnecessarily controversial tone is really due to the importance in my mind of what I *used* to believe, and of the moments of illumination which were for me personally moments of illumination...You don't mention *effective demand* or more precisely, the demand schedule for output as a whole, except in so far as it is implicit in the multiplier. To me the most extraordinary thing, regarded historically, is the complete disappearance of the theory of demand and supply for output as a whole, i.e. the theory of employment, *after* it had been for a quarter of century the most discussed thing in economics. One of the most important transition for me, after my *Treatise on Money* had been published, was suddenly realising this. It only came after I had enunciated to myself the psychological law that, when

income increases, the gap between income and consumption will increase, – a conclusion of vast importance to my own thinking but not apparently, expressed just like that, to any one else's. Then, appreciably later, came the notion of interest being the measure of liquidity of preference, which became quite clear in my mind the moment I thought of it. And last of all, after an immense amount of muddling and many drafts, the proper definition of the marginal efficiency of capital linked up one thing with another (Keynes, 1936b).

In February 1936, the book finally appeared and it was being sold for 5 shillings to encourage wide readership. It was still 8 shillings and 6 pence in 1960.

The book created a stir in the professional community. Polemical as well as favourable reviews appeared. While reviews by A.P. Lerner,[3] W.B. Reddaway,[4] and J.R. Hicks[5] could be considered favourable, A.C. Pigou,[6] F.H. Knight,[7] Gustav Cassel[8] were among the bitter dissenters. Keynes himself was aware of such reactions, as he himself writes:

> Those who are strongly wedded to what I shall call 'the classical theory' will fluctuate, I expect, between a belief that I am quite wrong and a belief that I am saying nothing new. It is for others to determine if either of these or the third alternative is right (Keynes, 1936a, Preface).

Somehow the book was not well comprehended at that time. Commenting upon reviews of *The General Theory*, Klein (1966, p. 91) remarks:

> Neither Keynes nor his immediate reviewers understood the full implications of the theoretical model. Much of the later polemical literature presented wasted paper, but by no means were all the discussions worthless...but such a lack of comprehension merely serves to emphasize the revolutionary character of the work.

While it is not difficult to find in previous literature many of the same ideas, Keynes certainly said something quite different compared to most other economists. What is true is that no single economist before him ever devised a model to solve an unemployment problem based on the propensity to consume, marginal efficiency of capital, and liquidity preference.[9]

It is widely believed that Keynes's diminished presence in professional life caused by a heart attack in 1937 left the way clear for the emergence and elaboration of 'Keynesian economics' as something quite different from the 'economics of Keynes' and the burgeoning of the *General Theory* into 'the Keynesian Revolution'. At this stage it was only a revolution on the plane of theory,[10] but Keynes would not have to wait long, as it extended speedily to the policies especially in the years following the World War II. Thus it is at the end of the war (which economically considered, as Hicks said, was hardly over before 1950) that the age of Keynes, in practice, begins.

Johnson and Johnson (1978, pp. 183–202) provide a well balanced and dispassionate appraisal of the Keynesian revolution. According to them a revolutionary theory had to depend for its success on five main characteristics.[11] Keynes's *General Theory* did possess all these characteristics.

It must also be noted that the very success of Keynesian revolution, however, ensured that someday it would in its turn become an established orthodoxy and in the mid-1950s it did become just that, just ripe for an attack in exactly the same way as what Keynes chose to call 'classical economics' and to attack in the 1930s. It has had the same two vulnerable characteristics: inability to prescribe for what has come to be considered a major social problem – inflation, in contrast to unemployment of Keynes's time – and a dependence on the authority and prestige of senior scholars which is oppressive to the young.

However the *General Theory* was successful precisely because, by providing an alternative theory to the prevailing orthodoxy, it rationalized a sensible policy that had hitherto been resisted on purely dogmatic grounds. Similarly, the monetarist counter-revolution has been partly successful only because it has encountered a policy problem for which the prevailing orthodoxy was able to prescribe only policies of proven or presumptive incompetence (in the form of incomes or guidelines policy), but for which the monetarist counter-revolution has both a theory and a policy solution.

Keynes after the *General Theory*

In 1939 Keynes was by far the most distinguished economist of his time. His public status gave him much greater access to and opportunities to influence official and unofficial opinion. During World War II Keynes did not have any official position as in World War I. He was simply an influential member of the British Chancellor's consultative council. Thus he was very much of a political economist whose influence played an important role in British economic policy. According to Moggridge (1975, pp. 177–201), Keynes's activities and influence can best be studied by looking at his role in the internal and external war and post-war finance.

From the very beginning Keynes involved himself in the problems of war finance on two fronts: maximizing the *possible* under the existing constraints and *easing* the constraints themselves. The outbreak of World War II brought a rapid response at first in a letter to *The Times* on loan policy and later in the ideas *How to Pay for the War* (1940a). Keynes had first introduced the ideas of this pamphlet in a talk to the Marshall Society on 20 October 1939. Initially the talk was entitled '*War Potential and War Finance*' but four days later he circulated the draft copies of his proposals under the heading, '*The Limitation of Purchasing Power: High Prices, Taxation and Compulsory Savings*' to the editor of *The Times*, the Chancellor and others. In order to make his proposals more acceptable both to the Labour and trade union leaders, during this period of two publications, Keynes involved himself in extensive discussions. After the publication, he continued to press privately and publicly for the adoption of his policy.

The success of the German war campaign in West Europe brought about an increase in expenditure and the downfall of Neville Chamberlain. The new Chancellor appointed Keynes into his advisory council. Now Keynes had the chance to get his proposals readily accepted in official circles. Since the outbreak of war Keynes's primary concern was the best way of transfer of resources from peacetime to wartime uses especially from consumption. According to Keynes, the government could procure additional resources from consumption by voluntary reduction in personal consumption, compulsory savings, official inflationary policies, a policy of comprehensive rationing and by increased taxation.

Soon after the war began, Keynes also became involved in discussions of external finance policy sending two memorandums: one on exchange control policy to the Treasury and the other on financial aspects of the blockade against Germany to the Ministry of Economic Warfare. Keynes argued that an effective exchange control policy is necessary to conserve British overseas assets. He favoured effective exchange control, limited sale of foreign assets, access to maximum volume of foreign resources from sterling areas and so on.

However, Keynes's concern with the post-war world did not end with a consideration of the possible post-war consequences of 'policies of war effort maximization'. Keynes used his Treasury position to ensure his position in shaping of the post-war world that would see positive steps to avoid a repetition of economic events of the interwar period.

Keynes's influence on the development of post-war internal economic policy in Britain emerged most clearly in three directions: the methods of analysis used in assessing the impact of various post-war policies, the *White Paper on Employment Policy* (1944) and *National Debt Enquiry* (1945).

Keynes's macroeconomic approach was successfully implemented in the budget of 1940/1. It also came to be used in other areas of policy formulation. However, the most frequent use of Keynesian analysis came in discussions of post-war employment policy. Keynes himself was not involved in writing the Treasury documents for the Committee on Post-war Internal Economic Problems. It was James Meade who provided the impetus. Keynes used his influence in the passage of certain proposals to be included in the *Beveridge Reports*, *White Paper on Social Insurance* (1943) and *White Paper on Employment Policy* (1944). But his most substantial contribution came in the area of monetary policy. As a member of the National Debt Enquiry Committee, Keynes continued dominating the proceedings, giving evidence on monetary and debt management policy. His proposals were incorporated in the Committee's report and among them was that of the post-war cheap money policy.

Keynes's contributions to official discussions of post-war external economic policy centred around the creation of Bretton Woods institutions, a scheme for the international regulation of primary product prices, Britain's post-war commercial policy and Allied reparations policy.

On request from Anthony Eden to prepare a statement in reply to Germany's plan for a New Order in Europe, Keynes gave some thought to the issue which resulted in his *Proposals to Counter the German 'New Order'* (1940b). His approach rested upon the following principles: friendly co-operation with the US as it was the only country to have resources; post-war international currency arrangements departing entirely from *laissez-faire* practices of 1920–33; post-war institutional arrangements for currency and demand management which would be compatible with an extensive international trade and equal access for all to world markets; and organized relief and reconstruction aid to post-war Europe.

Such a framework of ideas served Keynes in subsequent discussions on the post-war international economic arrangements. In the 18 months after these were drafted Britain produced plans for post-war currency arrangements, commodity policy and international trade. Keynes wrote the first two and the third was drafted by James Meade.

Between December 1943 and May 1944 Keynes was deeply involved in discussions on the International Monetary Fund. By the time he died in April 1946, agreement on the American Loan, the IMF and a draft outline on commercial policy had been reached.

Reactions across the Atlantic
Before the publication of the *General Theory*, Keynes had urged his ideas directly on President Roosevelt, most notably in his letter to the *New York Times* on 31 December 1933. He also visited the President in the summer of 1934, to plead his case.

However, in the words of Galbraith (1975, p. 133), 'the trumpet...that was sounded in Cambridge, England was heard most clearly in Cambridge, Massachusetts. Harvard was the principal avenue by which Keynes's ideas passed to the United States'.

While Paul Samuelson at MIT was already 'an acknowledged leader of younger Keynesians', Alvin Hansen at Harvard was one of the early converts. Hansen proceeded to expound the ideas of Keynes in books, articles and lectures to apply them to the American scene. He became the 'leader of a crusade' in which he was joined by his colleague Seymour Harris. Samuelson put the Keynesian ideas into what became the world's leading text book on economics. Lloyd Metzler applied Keynesian ideas to international trade. At Yale, Lloyd G. Reynolds gathered a younger group of economists to discuss the new trends.

Soon after the publication of the book and Hicks' seminal paper (Hicks 1937, pp. 147–59), the American economists had seized upon the IS-LM technique which was based upon Walras's general equilibrium approach, and used it as the foundation of their neo-classical synthesis. As Tobin points out (see Sharma 1995, pp. 1–20), students were told that they did not have to read Keynes's difficult *The General Theory*, but could study instead the IS-LM model which their professors assured them encapsulated all Keynes's important ideas.

In the US the neo-classical synthesis was led by Paul Samuelson and supported by such noted economists as Franco Modigliani, Don Patinkin, Robert Solow, Lawrence Klein, James Tobin and others. It was fiercely attacked by the monetarists.

The monetarism of the 1960s centred around Milton Friedman. As time and understanding of both theory and reality progressed, the interest of monetary theorists shifted from demonstrating the neutrality of money to investigating the conditions of monetary equilibrium and disequilibrium. The appropriate tool was not the 'quantity theory of money' but the so called 'dynamic equation'. Much of the work of the 1920s and 1930s was reinvented by Clower (1965) and Leijonhufvud (1968) under the brand name of 'monetary growth models'. The authors of these models, particularly Lucas (1975, 1977) and Sargent (1976), preserved the classical assumption of a system in real full employment equilibrium, and hence were constrained to treating business cycles and similar fluctuations either in terms of changes in the composition of a given full employment output, or in terms of unemployment and idle capacity that was either unexplained, or explained in terms of neo-classical mechanism of an excessively high level of real wages. It was Keynes's rejection of this assumption that led to the counter-revolution.

In the early 1980s macroeconomic theory was in disarray. The question of interest was whether the monetarist counter-revolution will sweep the board and become the orthodoxy of the future, or whether it will gradually go away. It was being challenged by the monetarists on the one hand and by new classical economists on the other. Lucas (1980) even went to the length of saying that people '...take offence if referred to as "Keynesians". At research seminars, people don't take Keynesian theorising seriously any more; the audience starts to whisper and giggle at one another'. But, towards the end of the 1980s the tide seems to have turned and the so called 'crude monetarism' of Milton Friedman died, and the new classical macroeconomics is slowly dying (Blinder, 1988).

According to Johnson, the most serious defects of the monetary counter revolution are on one hand, the abnegation of the restated quantity theory of money from the responsibility of providing a theory of the determination of prices and of output, and on the other hand, its continuing reliance on the methodology of positive economics (Johnson and Johnson, op. cit., p. 200).

The monetary onslaught against Keynesianism which was started by Milton Friedman was at its climax in the mid-1970s because this system failed to provide any workable solution to the inflation problem plaguing the world. By this time, the Keynesian revolution had invited the wrath of its critics, particularly from Axel Leijonhuvud[12] and Robert Clower, the same way the classical theory had invited the barrage of criticism from Keynes.[13]

On the policy plane in the US, 10 years after the publication of the *General Theory*, the 1946 Employment Act gave the Keynesian System qualified support. It recognized that unemployment and insufficient output would respond to positive policies. The responsibility of the federal government to act was affirmed. The Council of Economic Advisers became a platform for expounding the Keynesian view of the economy.

Arthur F. Burns, President Eisenhower's Chairman of the Council of Economic Advisers, a critic of Keynes, in his introduction to the 1946 National Bureau of Economic Research report, criticized the Keynesian underemployment equilibrium and concluded, 'the imposing schemes for governmental action that are being bottomed on Keynes's equilibrium theory must be viewed with scepticism' (cf. Galbraith, 1975, p. 140). The Kennedy and Johnson administrations continued the Keynesian policies for some time but by then the ball was already in the court of 'counter-revolutionists'. The Republican administrations of Presidents Richard Nixon, Ronald Reagan and George Bush have energetically pursued monetarist and supply-side policies which resulted in huge budget and trade deficits and slowing down of growth and employment. In the mid-1990s in US once again there seems to be a tilt towards Keynesian economic policies. Under the Clinton administration there are definite signs of revival of Keynesian ideas and policies which are reflected in government policies which have spurred growth and employment.

Keynesian policies and the future

Just 10 years after the publication of his monumental book, Keynes died in 1946. These 50 years after his death have been a period of success for his theory and policies, controversies and criticisms, revival and renewed appreciation. Until the early 1970s there was a generally accepted broad consensus in macroeconomics which revolved around the Keynesian model. By the early 1980s the conventional wisdom was shattered and was replaced by competing schools of thought.

Economic theories always have policy implications and are therefore bound with value judgements. Various schools of thought have a different set of theories and policy conclusions. The consensus of the 1960s was that the mixed economies should be regulated by Keynesian demand management policies. Since then there has been a polarization of views. Keynesian policy has been questioned both on theoretical and pragmatic grounds.

The fundamental idea behind the Keynesian approach to macroeconomic policy is government intervention. Whether or not intervention at macro level will improve the overall performance of the economy, if compared with leaving adjustments to private sector markets, has much to do with which sector is stable (or unstable). Further, whether the government intervention is necessary or not centres around the question of how well markets adjust to changes and uncertainty. In the Keynesian model the private sector is unstable and prices fail to adjust. The adjustment burden falls on output and employment, thus giving rise to a case for government intervention. The core of Keynesian policy is that by changing the effective demand the government can change the aggregate supply. As against such views in the neoclassical approach it is the other way round so that government interference produces instability and is thus least desirable.

Both in the Keynesian and in the neoclassical synthesis approach, if the output is below the full employment level, increase in effective demand increases the supply only if it reduces the real wage rate. The crucial assumption that both approaches make is that workers will accept reduced real wages if it is achieved through an increase in the price level. Expansionary fiscal and monetary policies work because they increase effective demand and reduce the real wage rate by raising price level.

The post-war experience with inflation has shown that it is difficult to sustain the assumption that workers will not seek to prevent a decline in real wages if prices rise. Under such circumstances expansionary fiscal and monetary policies will fail to increase aggregate supply except in the short run, while the expected inflation rate is less than the actual rate so that real wages are lower than they would be otherwise. Once expected inflation has adjusted to the actual, real wages return to their previous level. Those who favour the traditional Keynesian policy need to show that a reduction in real wage is not necessary so as to raise the output through effective demand or that there are people willing to work given the opportunity, that is, off the supply curve. This is shown by the neo-Keynesian quantity constrained models in which both the household and firms are rationed sellers. The marginal product of labour exceeds the real wage. Firms will employ more workers at the existing or higher real wage if they can sell more output because effective demand has increased. The neo-Keynesian analysis rests on the assumption that market fails to clear because the price adjustments do not occur quickly. Whether or not such market failure is consistent with rational behaviour of economic agents is an unresolved question.

The monetarist criticism has been directed against the presumption of the 'synthesis' that workers will accept reduction in real wages that are due to inflation. In fact, real wage reductions are only necessary if there are diminishing returns to labour. The 'new microfoundations approach' demonstrates that expansionary policies can only provide a temporary boost to output. Here too the increase in the supply of output depends on a fall in the real wage.

Use of rational expectations by the new classical economists is a rather more serious attack on the Keynesian policies. Given a new classical aggregate supply function the government can only increase output if it can create a divergence between actual and expected prices. With price expectations being rational and private sector fully informed of the situation of economy, there is no possibility that systematic fiscal and monetary policy can cause price divergence and thus affect the output.

Keynes firmly believed that economists should attempt to model the state and the real world rather than an idealized long-run unrealistic system. He did not believe in the neoclassical long-run solutions for real world economic problems. In his most frequently quoted remark, he regarded as facile the neoclassicists' claim that free markets assure long-run full employment and stable price level. He wrote:

> this long run is a misleading guide to current affairs. In the long run we are all dead. Economists set themselves too easy, too useless a task if in tempestuous seasons they can only tell us that when the storm is long past the ocean is flat again (Keynes, 1924).

The main elements of the post-Keynesians approach (see, for details, Arestis, 1992; Sawyer, 1982) can be traced back to the contributions of Keynes (providing the monetary perspective), Kalecki (the real analysis) and Sraffa (the value and distribution component). The post-Keynesians stress that it is possible to construct a coherent theoretical and policy model as an alternative to neoclassical model. They try to bring together several identifiable strands which gained much of its initial impetus from the sustained efforts to 'generalize' the *General Theory* and apply its underlying vision to such matters as growth, accumulation and distribution. The common themes in their approach are: effective demand failures, the microfoundations of macroeconomics, inflation and endogenous money. One could agree with the post-Keynesians that economic theory must deal with problems in an institutional, historical setting where uncertainty regarding future events affects current economic decisions and policies. The institutions of non-neutral monetary system and use of future contracts represent the core of a real world. The ideal neoclassical model on the other hand involves a fully anticipated statistically predicted future. Hence, according to them, money and liquidity play no important roles in determination of output and employment. It is lately argued that since in a temporal real world setting the neoclassical system cannot function even as an ideal, the results should not be used by policy makers. Keynes considered that neoclassical 'teaching is misleading and disastrous if we attempt to apply it to the facts of experience'.

To conclude, if Keynesian policies cease to offer a viable economic policy option, then this would have profound political implications. Keynesian policies promise to improve the functioning of markets by means of modest government intervention and thus offer a middle way between complete state governance on the one hand and free market forces on the other.

Endnotes

1. I am grateful to Sir Hans Singer, Philip Arestis and Tony Thirlwall for their comments on the initial draft of this chapter.
2. L.R. Klein suggests that according to P.A. Samuelson some significant developments in economic literature were taking place in 1933. Joan Robinson in February 1933 points out some subtle difficulties of the *Treatise* ('A Parable of Savings and Investment', *Economica*, Feb. 1933). It was seen as an attempt to bridge the differences between Keynes and Hayek. But in another article later the same year ('The Theory of Money and the Analysis of Output', *Review of Economic Studies*, **1** (1), 1933, reprinted in her *Contributions to Modern Economics*, pp. 14–9.) she definitely provided the first exposition of the essentials of Keynes's *General Theory*. (For detailed analysis on the subject see Klein, London, 1966, pp. 38–40.)
3. 'Mr Keynes' 'General Theory of Employment, Interest and Money'', *International Labour Review*, 34, 1936, p. 435.
4. 'The General Theory of Employment, Interest and Money', *Economic Record*, 12, 1936, p. 28.
5. 'Mr. Keynes and the "Classics": A Suggested Interpretation', *Econometrica*, 5, 1937, p. 147.
6. 'Mr. J.M. Keynes's General Theory of Employment, Interest and Money', *Economica*, 3, 1936, p. 115.
7. 'Unemployment: and Mr. Keynes' Revolution in Economic Theory', *Canadian Journal of Economics and Political Science*, 3, 1937, p. 100.
8. 'Mr Keynes' 'General Theory'', *International Labour Review*, 36, 1937, p. 437.
9. The extent of impact Keynes exercised on economics of his time is evident in A. Marget's remark: 'Indeed if one needs further proof of the "strangeness" of the Keynesian episode, one needs ask only at what other time since Adam Smith, a position avowedly presented as revolutionary and heterodox, has become for so large a number of professional economic theorists a new ("modern") orthodoxy in so short a period' (*A Theory of Prices II*, Prentice Hall, New York, 1942, p. xxii).
10. Joan Robinson comments on the significance of the revolution in the following words: 'On the plane of theory the main point of the *General Theory* was to break out of the cocoon of equilibrium and consider the nature of life lived in time, the difference between yesterday and tomorrow, here and now, the past is irrevocable and the future is unknown. This was too great a shock. Orthodox (neo-classical) theory managed to wind up into a cocoon again. Keynes had shown how money is a necessary feature of an economy in which the future is uncertain and he showed what part monetary and financial institutions play in the functioning of the real economy....In the Keynesian theory after the war this simple point is lost. The whole of Keynes's argument is put to sleep. Keynes is smothered and orthodox equilibrium theory is enthroned once more. Keynes was writing and arguing against the prevailing orthodoxy. He had to argue first and last that something could be done (Robinson, 1980, p. 121).
11. According to H.G. Johnson the following five basic factors did contribute to the success of the 'Keynesian Revolution'.

'First, it had to attack the central proposition of conservative orthodoxy – the assumed or inferred tendency of the economy to full employment – with a new but academically acceptable analysis that reversed the proposition. This Keynes did with the help of Kahn's concept of the multiplier and his own invention of the propensity to consume.'
'Second, the theory had to appear to be new, yet absorb as much as possible of the valid or at least not readily disputable components of existing orthodox theory. In this process, it helps greatly to give old concepts new and confusing names, hence in the *General Theory*

marginal productivity of capital became marginal efficiency of capital; the desired ratio of money to income – the k of the Cambridge tradition – became a minor constituent of the new theory of "liquidity preference"; and the *ex post* identity of savings and investment… became the *sina qua non* of right reasoning.'

'Third, the new theory had to have appropriate degree of difficulty to understand…Keynes' *General Theory* managed to achieve: it neatly shelved the old and established scholars, like Pigou and Robertson, enabled the enterprising middle and lower middle aged like Hansen, Hicks, and Joan Robinson to jump on and drive the bandwagon, and permitted a whole generation of students to escape the slow and soul-destroying process of acquiring wisdom by osmosis….Economics, delightfully, could be reconstructed from scratch on the basis of a little Keynesian understanding and a lofty contempt for the existing literature – and so it was.'

'Fourth, the new theory had to offer to the more gifted and less opportunistic scholars a new methodology more appealing than those currently available. In this respect Keynes was lucky both in having a receptive audience available, and to hit somewhere conveniently between the old and new emerging styles of economic theorizing. The prevailing methodological orthodoxy was that of Marshall….The new methodological challenge was coming from the explicitly mathematical approach of Hicks and Allen, an approach whose empirically and historically almost empty generality was of little general appeal. the *General Theory* found a middle ground in an aggregated general-equilibrium system which was not too difficult or complicated to work with… and which offered a high degree of apparent empirical relevance to those who took the trouble to understand it.'

'Finally, the *General Theory* offered an important empirical relationship for the emerging tribe of econometricians to measure – the consumption function, a relationship…a relationship for which the development of national income statistics provided the raw material needed for estimation, and which could be estimated with surprising success given the limitation of the available data to approximately a single business cycle' (Johnson and Johnson, 1978, pp. 188–91.)

12. Leijonhuvud remarks: 'Does the market system tend to move "automatically" towards a state where all market excess demands and supplies are eliminated?'

'But the Keynesian Revolution did not quite succeed in making a clean sweep. The older view survived and has grown in strength as the 1930s recede from memory and mass unemployment on that scale has failed to recur.'

'Clower's original venture into the uncomfortable no-man's land between Neo-classicism and Keynesianism sought to provide a microtheoretical foundation for the core concept of Keynesian theory – Effective Demand' (Leijonhuvud, 1975 pp. 27–48).

13. Robert Clower's vehement criticism (1965, pp. 406–7) is based on the following grounds. In his own words, 'But if…Keynes intended, i.e. to deny the validity of the orthodox theory of household behaviour, one can only say that he was singularly unsuccessful in providing a rationale for his attack'.

'The second item in Keynes' bill of particulars is essentially the same as the first: classical theory is charged with failure to recognize the existence of involuntary unemployment (the *General Theory*, pp. 15–18). Again, the basic question is: Are "involuntary unemployment" and "chronic dis-equilibrium" synonymous terms for the same objective phenomenon or is "involuntary unemployment" a special kind of dis-equilibrium particularly associated with the breakdown of the orthodox theory of household behaviour?'

'The third and final item in Keynes's indictment is a denial of the relevance of Walras's law (the *General Theory*, pp. 18–21). Most later writers (e.g. Ohlin, Goodwin, Patinkin) have argued either that this portion of Keynes's indictment is wrong, or that the propositions which Keynes attacks is not in fact the one he thought he was attacking. Most economists have opted for the second explanation, partly in deference to Keynes' acknowledged intellectual powers, partly because they recognize that if Keynes seriously meant to question the validity or relevance of Walras' law, he would have to reject orthodox theory of household behaviour and propose an acceptable alternative – and the alternative would have to include orthodox theory as a special case, valid under conditions of full employment.'

'The conclusion which I draw...may be put in one phrase: either Walras' law is incompatible with Keynesian economics, or Keynes had nothing fundamental to add to orthodox economic theory.'

'Thus we are caught on the horns of a dilemma. If Keynes added nothing new to orthodox doctrine, why have twenty five years of discussion failed to produce an integrated account of price theory and income analysis? If Keynes did add something new, the integration problem becomes explicable: but then we have to give up Walras' law as the fundamental principle of economic analysis. It is precisely at this point, I believe, that virtually all previous writers have decided to part company with Keynes.'

References

Arestis, Philip (1992), *The Post-Keynesian Approach to Economics: An Alternative Analysis of Economic Theory and Policy*, Aldershot: Edward Elgar.

Blinder, Alan (1988), 'The Fall and Rise of Keynesian Economics', *Economic Record*, December, p. 20.

Cassel, Gustav (1937), 'Mr. Keynes' "General Theory"', *International Labor Review*, 36, 437.

Clower, Robert W. (1965), 'The Keynesian Counter-Revolution: A Theoretical Appraisal', in Hahn and Breechling (eds), *The Theory of Interest Rates*, London: Macmillan.

Galbraith, J.K. (1975), 'How Keynes Came to America', in Milo Keynes pp. 132–41.

Hayek, F.A. (1983) 'The Austrian Critic', *The Economist*, 11 June.

Hicks, John R. (1937), 'Mr. Keynes and the "Classics"': A Suggested Interpretation', *Econometrica*, 5(1),147–59.

Hicks, John R. (1975), *Crisis in Keynesian Economics*, Oxford: Basil Blackwell.

Johnson, Elizabeth S. and Harry G. Johnson (1978), *The Shadow of Keynes*, Oxford: Basil Blackwell.

Kahn, Richard F. (1931), 'The Relation of Home Investment to Unemployment', *Economic Journal*, vol. LI, reprinted in his (1972), *Selected Essays on Employment and Growth*, Cambridge: Cambridge University Press.

Keynes, John Maynard (1913), *Indian Currency and Finance*, London: Macmillan.

Keynes, John Maynard (1919), *The Economic Consequences of the Peace*, London: Macmillan.

Keynes, John Maynard (1924), *A Tract on Monetary Reform*, London: Macmillan.

Keynes, John Maynard (1925a), *The Economic Consequences of Mr. Churchill*, London: L. & V. Woolf.

Keynes, John Maynard (1925b), *A Treatise on Money*, vols. I and II, London: Macmillan.

Keynes, John Maynard (1929), 'Can Lloyd George Do It? An Examination of the Liberal Pledge', *Nation and Athenaeum*, May.

Keynes, John Maynard (1931), *Macmillan Report*, HM Government.

Keynes, John Maynard (1933a), *The Means to Prosperity*, London: Macmillan.

Keynes, John Maynard (1933b), *New York Times*, 31 December.

Keynes, John Maynard (1936a), *The General Theory of Employment, Interest and Money*, London: Macmillan.

Keynes, John Maynard (1936b), 'Letter from Keynes to Harrod', 30 August in *The Collected Writings of John Maynard Keynes*, XIV, London: Macmillan.

Keynes, John Maynard (1939a), 'The Limitation of Purchasing Power: High Prices, Taxation and Compulsory Savings', *The Times*, London, 24 October.

Keynes, John Maynard (1940a), *How to Pay for the War*, London: Macmillan.

Keynes, John Maynard (1940b) 'Proposal to Counter the German "New Order"', Radio Talk.

Keynes, John Maynard (1972), *The Collected Writings of John Maynard Keynes*, XIII, London: Macmillan.

Keynes, Milo (ed.) (1975), *Essays on John Maynard Keynes*, Cambridge, UK: Cambridge University Press.

Klein, Lawrence R. (1966), *Keynesian Revolution*, London: Macmillan.

Knight Frank H. (1937), 'Unemployment: and Mr Keynes' Revolution in Economic Theory', *Canadian Journal of Economics and Political Science*, 3,115.

Leijonhufvud, Axel (1968), *On Keynesian Economics and the Economics of Keynes: A Study in Monetary Theory*, New York: Oxford University Press.

Leijonhufvud, Axel (1975), 'Effective demand failures', *Swedish Economic Journal*, 1, 27–48.

Lerner, Abba P. (1936), 'Mr Keynes' "General Theory of Employment, Interest and Money"', *International Labor Review*, 34, 435.

Lucas, Robert E. (1975), 'An equilibrium model of the business cycle', *Journal of Political Economy*, December, 83,1113–44.

Lucas, Robert E. (1977), 'Econometric Policy Evaluation: A Critique', in K. Brunner and A. H. Meltzer (eds), *Stabilization of the Domestic and the International Economy*, Amsterdam and New York: North Holland, pp. 19–46.

Lucas, Robert E. (1980), 'The death of Keynesian economics: Issues and Ideas,' Chicago: University of Chicago.

Marget, A. (1942), *A Theory of Prices II*, New York: Prentice Hall.

Marshall, Alfred (1923), *Money, Credit and Commerce*, London: Macmillan.

Moggridge, Donald E. (1975), 'The Influence of Keynes on the Economics of his Time' in Milo Keynes, op. cit., pp. 73–81.

Pigou, Arthur C. (1936), 'Mr. J. M. Keynes's general theory of employment, interest and money', *Economica*, 3, 115.

Reddaway, W.B. (1936), 'The General Theory of Employment, Interest and Money', *Economic Record*, 12, 28.

Robinson, Joan (1933a), 'A Parable of Savings and Investment', *Economica*, February, 39, 75–84.

Robinson, Joan (1933b), 'The theory of money and the analysis of output', *Review of Economic Studies*, 1(1) reprinted in her (1979), *Contributions to Modern Economics*, Oxford: Blackwell, pp. 14–19.

Robinson, Joan (1971), *Economic Heresies*, London: Macmillan.

Robinson, Joan (1980), *Collected Economic Papers*, V, Boston: MIT Press.

Samuelson, Paul A. (1988), 'In the Beginning', *Challenge*, July/August, **31** (4), 32–34.

Sargent, Thomas J. (1976), 'A classical macroeconomic model for the United States', *Journal of Political Economy*, April, 2, 84.

Sawyer, Malcolm C. (1982), *Macroeconomics in Question: The Keynesian-Monetarist Orthodoxies and the Kaleckian Alternative*, Brighton: Wheatsheaf Books.

Sharma, Soumitra (1995), 'An Interview with Nobel Laureate James Tobin', Asian *Journal of Economics and Social Studies*, **13** (1),1–20.

Tobin, James (1987), *Policies for Prosperity: Essays in Keynesian Mode*, Boston: MIT Press.

PART I

THEORETICAL
CONTRIBUTIONS

2 The renaissance of Keynesian econ

A.P. Thirlwall

Not so long ago Keynesian economists had the distinct feeling of being members of an endangered species, with the prospect of extinction in the face of the onslaught of Monetarism Mark 1 (the monetarism of Milton Friedman) and Monetarism Mark 2 (the new classical macroeconomics, led in America by Robert Lucas). It now looks, however, that the tide has turned. The crude monetarism of Milton Friedman as an intellectual fashion is now dead; the new classical macroeconomics seems to be dying a slow death; the empirical evidence from the behaviour of the British economy and the world economy seems to be on the side of the Keynesians, and papers are being written on the rise and fall and rise again of Keynesian economics.[2] There is also a revival of interest in Keynes the man with the publication of two new recent biographies by Moggridge[3] and Skidelsky.[4]

Keynes's *General Theory of Employment, Interest and Money*, published in 1936, still provides the backbone of macroeconomic theory, in terms of the concepts it introduced – the consumption function, the multiplier, the marginal efficiency of investment, liquidity preference and so on – but its theoretical and policy conclusions have been continually attacked.[5] However, those of anti-Keynesian persuasion always seem to me to have misunderstood the basic message.

The classical–neoclassical response to Keynes was that the conclusion of the possibility of an unemployment equilibrium depended on the assumption that money wages and prices are rigid, and that if wages and prices are flexible there can be no such thing as long-run involuntary unemployment.

Milton Friedman's response to Keynes, and the inspiration behind the doctrine of monetarism, was that 'money doesn't matter in Keynes'. For him, the *General Theory* provides an *apologia* for government intervention into the macro economy which leads to a misallocation of resources and disastrous inflationary consequences through the power of governments to 'print' money.

The response of the new classical macroeconomics of the 1970s was to say that Keynesian economics had outlived its usefulness because it could not explain the combination of high unemployment and rising prices (or stagflation), and that the rational expectations of economic agents makes all government attempts to stabilize the economy fruitless. In an article *The Death of Keynesian Economics* written in 1980, Robert Lucas went so far as to say 'one cannot find good under-forty economists who identify themselves or their work as "Keynesian". Indeed, people even take offence if referred to as Keynesians. At research seminars, people don't take Keynesian theorising seriously any more; the audience starts to whisper and giggle at one another'.[6]

There is a simple reply to each of these responses. Firstly, Keynesian conclusions concerning long-run breakdowns of effective demand and involuntary unemployment do *not* depend on the assumption that money wages and prices are rigid. The ultimate source of involuntary unemployment is uncertainty associated with the existence of money. There is no immediate or automatic nexus which unites decisions to save with decisions to invest, as there would be in an economy in which goods exchanged for goods or in which the rate of interest was the price which equilibrated savings and investment. Reductions in money wages in conditions of high unemployment may reduce costs, but equally will depress the demand for output. Reductions in prices increase the real value of money, and money balance holdings, but depress the profitability of investment. Long periods on involuntary unemployment are quite compatible with wage and price flexibility.

Secondly, money does matter in the *General Theory* in a number of ways. One of the fundamental purposes of the book was to integrate the theory of money with the theory of value; to show, in other words, that money matters for the functioning of the real economy and is not simply the determinant of the absolute price level. As mentioned above, the existence of money, and the desire to hold wealth in liquid form, is the fundamental source of involuntary unemployment. Keynes accepted the quantity theory of money that prices will rise in full proportion to increases in the quantity of money but only *if* there is full employment and *if* the demand to hold money is a stable proportion of income. What he questions is the validity of the quantity theory of money if there is not full employment, and if the demand for money changes with the supply. Furthermore, he also recognizes explicitly that prices may rise before the full employment level is reached because costs may rise for a variety of reasons associated with trade union bargaining power and bottlenecks in particular sectors of the economy. We have anticipated in Keynes what we now call cost-push and structural inflation. There is also a hint in the *General Theory*, and in his earlier work on *A Treatise on Money* (1930), that money may be endogenous to an economic system which in a Keynesian model has profound implications for the interpretation of the causal relations between money, output and prices.[7]

Thirdly, it is perfectly possible to explain stagflation in a Keynesian model if the aggregate supply function is not forgotten. The aggregate level of employment is determined at the point of effective demand where the aggregate demand curve cuts the aggregate supply curve. The aggregate supply curve shows the necessary receipts that entrepreneurs must receive to employ a labour force.

There will be a different aggregate supply curve for each level of the money wage. As wages rise, the aggregate supply curve shifts upwards producing rising prices and falling employment. If governments tackle the cost inflation as if it is a demand inflation, aggregate demand will be reduced, leading to further falls in employment. There is no problem, therefore, in explaining stagflation in a Keynesian framework. The suggestion to the contrary of the new classical macroeconomists is a measure of their ignorance of Keynesian economics and the *General Theory*.

Indeed, if we want explanations of high unemployment and of rising prices in conditions of slump, we cannot return to pre-Keynesian economics, to the classical assumptions that monetarism and the new classical macroeconomics have revived in recent years. These assumptions I take to be: that inflation is always and everywhere a monetary phenomenon in a causal sense due to 'too much money chasing too few goods', as if money is totally exogenous to an economic system, and monopolies in the product and the labour market cannot cause prices to rise without prior increases in the money supply; that all unemployment is voluntary due to a refusal of workers to accept cuts in real wages; that the rate of interest clears the goods market so that there is never any deficiency of aggregate demand, and that ups and downs in the macroeconomy are to be explained by supply shocks alone. The world in which we actually live is very different.

The interesting question arises, however, of how is it that sections of the economics profession returned to pre-Keynesian modes of thinking by embracing Monetarism Mark 1 and Monetarism Mark 2, after a broad Keynesian consensus had united the profession for so long? There are undoubtedly many explanations, but I will mention two which are related. The first is that it is significant, and not accidental, that the anti-Keynesian movement started in the US – a country historically and ideologically hostile to doctrines that suggest that the State might have a role to play in economic affairs. Keynes's use of the phrase 'the socialisation of investment' (*General Theory*, p. 378) has always tainted him 'red' in the eyes of Americans, although misleadingly as it happens, because he goes on to say that beyond public investment in conditions of slump 'no obvious case is made out for a system of state socialism which would embrace most of the economic life of the community'. The second explanation is that the way economics is taught in the US, and increasingly so elsewhere, makes economists uncomfortable with the notions of disequilibrium and non-market clearing. A heavy premium is placed in the universities on the mathematization of economics, to which the subtleties of Keynesian economics do not lend themselves.

The basic proposition that both monetarism and the new classical macroeconomics denies is that there can be such a thing as involuntary unemployment. Friedman's model of the natural rate of unemployment, and

Lucas's model of the business cycle, *start* from the assumption of no involuntary unemployment, so that with either adaptive or rational expectations, any attempts by governments to reduce unemployment by spending more will meet with resistance by workers to cuts in their real wage, which then leads to accelerating inflation at the natural rate of unemployment. Why does monetarism and the new classical macroeconomics assert or assume what, in the first instance, must be proved: that markets do clear on the basis of voluntary exchange? One explanation might be that political ideology colours theoretical judgement. Monetarists simply do not like any economic theory which seems to imply market failure, and establishes a role for the State. The historian, E.H. Carr, once said about history that in order to understand history, one has to understand the historian that is writing it.[8] The same might be said for economics.

In the early 1980s, at the height of the recession in the US and the UK, when thousands queued at the factory gates when jobs were advertised, were these men and women voluntarily unemployed? When unemployment in the UK eventually fell from 3.4 million in 1986 to 1.6 million in 1990 as a result of financial liberalization and tax cuts, were the nearly 2 million unemployed absorbed into the system voluntarily unemployed? It would be difficult to answer in the affirmative. Employment and unemployment responded to changes in the level of aggregate demand in exactly the way one would have predicted from a Keynesian model (without accelerating inflation). The notions of continuous market clearing and no involuntary unemployment were discredited by the events of the 1980s, and continue to be discredited today with unemployment in the UK at over 2 million (and in the EU at over 17 million) with most willing to work at the going money wage (and a lower real wage if necessary) given the opportunity. It is significant that the British monetarist, Minford of Liverpool University, who argued that the 'natural' level of unemployment in the UK in the early 1980s was over 3 million, now concedes that at least 1 million of the currently unemployed are involuntarily so. As Frank Hahn once said of Robert Lucas 'I wish he would become involuntarily unemployed and then he would know what the concept was all about'.[9]

Monetarism in the UK

The British economics profession was never seduced by monetarism and the new classical macroeconomics to the same extent as American economists, or to the same degree as the Conservative government when it came into office in 1979 under Mrs Thatcher. Mrs Thatcher's brand of monetarism was based on five basic beliefs. First was the Friedman doctrine that 'inflation is always and everywhere a monetary phenomenon' in a *causal* sense. This, in turn, has three corollaries: that the money supply is exogenously determined and controllable; that the demand for money is a stable function of income, and that changes in the money supply preceding changes in the price level and money national income are necessarily proof that money is the cause of price level changes and not vice versa. Within this framework of thinking, there is no such thing as cost-push inflation accommodated by money responding to the needs of trade, or variations in the velocity of circulation of money. Friedman has always denied that trade unions can cause inflation.

A second belief was that there exists a direct link between the size of the public sector borrowing requirement (PSBR) and the growth of M_3 money, as if the PSBR is never funded and private sector demand for money is irrelevant for the growth of the money supply.

Thirdly, was the article of faith that government spending crowds out private spending either directly if resources are fully employed (resource crowding out) or indirectly through rising interest rates to finance an ever-growing PSBR (financial crowding out).

Fourthly, there was an implicit (if not explicit) belief in the concept of a natural rate of unemployment, and if governments attempted to reduce unemployment below what was regarded as the natural rate, there would be ever-accelerating inflation.

Finally, it was firmly believed that unemployment was high because real wages were too high; that is, that unemployment was essentially voluntary.

The theoretical and empirical validity of each of these beliefs and assumptions might be called into question, but I will focus here on the implementation of the monetarist experiment itself, and the results. The target money supply variable was M_3 money, consisting of notes and coins, current account bank deposits and deposit accounts with the commercial banks. The instrument was to progressively reduce the size of the PSBR from over £10 billion down to less than £5 billion, and to eventually eliminate the public sector deficit altogether. This was designed to give signals to markets and economic agents (that is workers and consumers) that the rate of inflation would gradually fall, so that workers should moderate wage inflation and price themselves back into work. As it turned out, it proved impossible to control the growth of M_3 money to within the target ranges, but the size of the PSBR and the rate of inflation did come down – the opposite of what monetarism predicted. The fiscal deficit contracted and the rate of interest soared – again, the opposite relationship postulated by monetarism – illustrating the fact that interest rates are determined by monetary policy not by fiscal policy (as we also see today in the UK and the US, with huge fiscal deficits but with interest rates relatively low). The exchange rate appreciated which, together with tight monetary and fiscal policy, produced a deep slump, just as a Keynesian expenditure-income model would have predicted. Wage and price inflation moderated, but at the cost of heavy unemployment, just as a traditional Phillips curve would have predicted, showing an inverse relation between the rate of unemployment and the rate of change of wages and prices.

The announcement of targets for M_3 money had no noticeable effect on private sector behaviour. If monetarism had worked, it should have reduced the growth of the money supply, and reduced the rate of inflation, without affecting the level of employment and unemployment, by changing agents' expectations of inflation and shifting the Phillips curve inwards. There was no such movement. Friedman, in his evidence to the House of Commons Treasury and Civil Service Committee on Monetary Policy[10], blamed the failure to meet M_3 targets on the incompetence of the Bank of England. However, it was soon recognized that the only way to control the supply of money is to control its demand through raising its price, that is by high interest rates. Wage inflation was also recognized as a source of price inflation, and an attempt was made to impose a wages policy in the public sector. After only three years, the monetarist experiment was beginning to crumble, but the damage to the economy had already been done: negative growth, falling investment, the destruction of manufacturing industry, and with unemployment rising to over 3 million in 1983. Since those early years of the 1980s there has been a further boom and bust, with the economy behaving in a predictable Keynesian fashion, responding to the vicissitudes of monetary and fiscal policy. Financial liberalization, and lax fiscal and monetary policy in the wake of the 1987 stock market crash, produced an unsustainable boom, and the tight monetary policy pursued from 1989 until the departure from the European Exchange Rate Mechanism in September 1992 produced the longest and deepest recession in the UK since the 1930s. The oscillations of the British economy over the last 17 years have had nothing to do with supply-side shocks or the business cycle theory of the new classical macroeconomics, but everything to do with good old-fashioned Keynesian demand *mismanagement*.

Those who did not lose their faith in Keynesian economics have been vindicated by events in the UK, and also abroad, not least in the US where President Reagan proved (without realizing it) to be the greatest Keynesian ever to occupy the White House. This is not so say, however, that Keynesianism is enough to understand the serious conflicts between macroeconomic objectives and how to reconcile them. In most economies, both capitalist and former communist, there is growing structural unemployment to contend with which Keynesian economics does not address. It is almost certainly the case that demand management by itself cannot reduce unemployment in Britain below one million without the economy running into serious labour market bottlenecks, in contrast to earlier periods in economic history (in the 1950s and 1960s, for example) when 200 000 unemployed was a reasonable, achievable target. Secondly, and a related point, in most economies the trade-off between inflation and unemployment has worsened, which will require institutional remedies. Keynes was aware of the problems that low unemployment may pose for wage push (as well as demand pull) inflation, but offered no solutions. Thirdly, many countries, including the UK and US, have structural balance of payments

problems to contend with, which Keynesian economics *pe*
to deal with. Keynes recognized, however, the conflict th?
internal and external balance, and that the only secure
interest rates for internal balance is a healthy surplus on the curren.
the balance of payments. Hence his defence of mercantilism.[11] The long
deterioration in the current account of the balance of payments in the UK
would have worried him greatly, and would almost certainly have pushed him
in an interventionist direction, even with the exchange rate allowed to float.

The central messages of Keynesian economics

To conclude, I outline below six central messages of Keynes's vision of the
functioning of capitalist economies that I believe are still valid, and which provide
a perfectly acceptable framework for analysing macroeconomic behaviour.

Firstly, the level of aggregate employment and unemployment is determined
in the product market by effective demand, *not* in the labour market. In other
words, at the macro-level (as opposed to the case of the individual firm) the level
of employment is not a function of the real wage, but rather the real wage is a
function of the level of employment, because associated with the level of
employment there will be a particular level of labour productivity and, on
profit maximizing assumptions, employers will equate real wages and labour
productivity. Cuts in money wages (in the attempt to reduce real wages) will
not necessarily increase employment and reduce unemployment because wages
are both a cost and a component of aggregate demand so there is no way of
analysing the effect of wage cuts on employment except by analysing their effect
on the components and determinants of aggregate demand, namely consumption,
investment, interest rates and the foreign balance (exports minus imports).

Secondly, unemployment is not all voluntary resulting from a refusal of
workers to accept cuts in their real wages; that is, insisting on a higher real wage
than their marginal product justifies. There can be involuntary unemployment
defined as labour *willing* to work at or below the existing real wage, given the
opportunity.

Thirdly, the act of saving (or abstaining from present consumption) does not
lead to an equivalent amount of investment via changes in the rate of interest.
Savings and investment are largely done by different groups in society and there
is no automatic nexus that unites the two activities. The rate of interest is
determined in the money market and may bear no relation to the rate of interest
required to equate *ex ante* savings and investment which is necessary for an
equilibrium in the product market.

Fourthly, the existence of money, and the ability to hold it liquid, creates great
uncertainty for an economy because, as Keynes put it in the *General Theory*:

a decision not to have dinner today – does *not* necessitate a decision to have dinner or to buy a pair of boots a week hence or a year hence or to consume any specified thing at any specified date. Thus it depresses the business of preparing today's dinner without stimulating the business of making ready for some future act of consumption. It is not a substitution of future consumption-demand for present consumption-demand, – it is a net diminution of such demand (p. 210).

In addition money has particular properties which makes an economy which uses money fundamentally different from either a barter economy or models of an economy in which money is treated simply as another good. Money is not like other goods because it is costless to produce, so that as people switch from goods to holding money less factors of production are employed.

Fifthly, the quantity theory of money, which lies at the heart of the doctrine of monetarism, holds only under the special assumptions that an economy is at full employment and the velocity of circulation of money is stable; otherwise, there will be no direct relation between the quantity of money and the price level. Moreover, cost-push forces can cause prices to rise long before the full employment level is reached. In his Chapter 21 on 'The Theory of Prices', Keynes fully anticipated modern cost-push and structural theories of inflation.

Lastly, what drives a capitalist economy is the decision to invest. It is the sentiment and whims (or 'animal spirits' as Keynes called them) of entrepreneurs that determine both the cyclical fluctuations of economies and their long-run economic performance. Enterprise can only flourish in a stable macroeconomic environment, free, as far as possible, from uncertainty about the course of relative prices and the state of demand; but entrepreneurs must also be willing to take risks. Again, as Keynes put it in the *General Theory*:

if human nature felt no temptation to take a chance, no satisfaction (profit apart) in constructing a factory, a railway, a mine or a farm, there might not be much investment merely as a result of cold calculation (p. 150) – thus if animal spirits are dimmed and the spontaneous optimism falters, leaving us to depend on nothing but mathematical expectation, enterprise will fade and die (p. 162).

Fifty years after Keynes's death, and 60 years after the publication of the *General Theory*, Keynes's vision of the functioning of capitalist economies is very much alive and relevant as it ever was, and the evidence of retreat from the simplicity of crude monetarism and the naivity of the new classical macroeconomics can only be welcomed.

Endnotes

1. The substance of this paper first appeared in *Banca Nazionale del Lavoro Quarterly Review*, September 1993, 186, 327–37.
2. An early prescient paper was Alan Blinder's (1988), 'The fall and rise of Keynesian economics', *Economic Record*, December, 20–23.
3. Moggridge, D. (1992), *Maynard Keynes: An Economist's Biography*, London: Routledge.

4. Skidelsky, R. (1992), *John Maynard Keynes: The Economist as Saviour 1920–1937*, London: Macmillan.
5. For an illuminating discussion of Keynes's vision of the functioning of the capitalist system, see Vicarelli, F. (1984), *Keynes: The Instability of Capitalism*, London: Macmillan.
6. Lucas, R. (1980), 'The Death of Keynesian Economics: Issues and Ideas', Chicago: University of Chicago Press, Winter.
7. This idea has been developed, among others, by economists such as Richard Kahn, Nicholas Kaldor, Hyman Minsky, and Basil Moore.
8. Carr, E.H. (1964), *What is History?*, Harmondsworth: Penguin.
9. Hahn, F. (1982), *Money and Inflation*, Oxford: Blackwell.
10. Memoranda on Monetary Policy, 17th July 1980, London: HMSO.
11. This issue is explored more fully in my paper to the British Association for the Advancement of Science 1991 entitled 'The Balance of Payments as the Wealth of Nations' in J. Ball (ed.) (1992), *The Economics of Wealth Creation,* Aldershot: Edward Elgar, pp. 2–11 and in my article 'The Balance of Payments and Economic Performance', *National Westminster Bank Quarterly Review*, May 1992.

3 'In the long run, we are all dead': time in Keynes's early economics

John Toye[1]

Fifty years after his death, Keynes is still regarded by some as the greatest economist that England has ever produced. But he has been ill-served both by the majority of his disciples, who simultaneously sanctified and simplified what he had to say, and by the majority of his opponents, who dismissed his ideas in the process of rejecting these neo-Keynesian simplifications. This chapter tries to clarify how, in analytical terms, Keynes treated time. The particular focus of interest here is the treatment of time in Keynes's early economics. 'Early' means prior to the publication of the *Treatise on Money* in 1930.

I surmise that, if today one asked the average educated person if they could recall anything that Keynes had said, the most popular reply would be: 'in the long run, we are all dead.' It is hard to see quite why this aphorism should be so universally memorable. Taken at face value, the statement is banal. How can one get below the surface of the words themselves to find something more profound? For this task, I start by asking how the problem of accounting for time in economic theory had been tackled by Keynes's mentor, Alfred Marshall. I shall argue that a recent revisionist interpretation of how Marshall incorporated time into economic analysis, specifically that his period analysis was meant to refer to real historical time, requires a consequential re-evaluation of the contrast that is usually made in this regard between Marshall and Keynes.

The legacy of Alfred Marshall

At the start of the twentieth century, Alfred Marshall had already established himself as the dominant figure of the Cambridge school of economics. An important part of his intellectual contribution to economics concerned the analytical treatment of time. Marshall stressed in his *Principles of Economics* 'the great importance of the element of time in relation to demand and supply' (quoted in Reisman, 1986, p. 52). In assessing the basic influences that he exerted on economics, that of making time a major factor in the theory of value is placed 'first and foremost' by Stigler (Whitaker, 1990, p. 5). That is not, however, to suggest that he entirely succeeded in his ambition to integrate time into economics.

In his discussion of Supply in Book V, Chapter V, he elaborates a scheme of periodization within which to analyse supply responses. His four periods are

(i) the market period, or market day; (ii) the short period of a few months or a year, for which supply means broadly what can be produced for the price in question with the existing stock of plant, personal and impersonal within the given time; (iii) the long period, in which 'supply' is defined to mean what can be produced by plant which itself can be remuneratively produced and applied within the given time; and (iv) the secular period, or the course of a generation. Here, as well as in other passages, Marshall frequently refers to calendar time – a day, a month, a year or several years, a generation – when discussing his four periods.

Nevertheless, modern textbooks do not interpret Marshall as speaking about chronological or calendar time. Rather they treat his periods as representing 'operational time'. Marshall's periods are here defined to mean the time during which supply cannot be increased, or capital assets cannot be expanded, or capital formation can take place, or, finally, during which everything can vary. On this modern view, given the defining operational characteristic of each period, the chronological lapse of real time can be longer or shorter according to the operational context of different industries. For example, the lags involved in adding to plant will differ as between fishing and steel-making. So, say the textbooks, the Marshallian periods cannot refer to actual calendar time.

After his death, Marshall's periodization was interpreted as a device to present a sequence of partial equilibria. As Machlup explained it, 'there are three models (or sub-models) with separate equilibria; each equilibrium is "final" on its own terms, though "temporary" in terms of a model with more variables' (1958, p. 8). Marshall was credited with developing an analytical apparatus that explained the determination of the prices of commodities over time, by assuming that the conditions affecting demand are constant over time, and that the conditions affecting supply are discrete and separable into different 'periods'. Thus continuous time was analysed with static methods, a technique that Leijonhufvud subsequently referred to as 'pseudo-dynamics' (1968, p. 50).

But this account has now been successfully overturned (Currie and Steedman, 1990, pp. 21–8). Textbook Marshallian analysis turns out to be different from Marshall's own analysis, and the construct of a theoretical tidying-up campaign started in the 1920s. The revisionist view of Currie and Steedman is that Marshall intended his periods to be defined in ordinary calendar time, and that it was the length of chronological time that limited what was operationally possible, rather than vice versa. They interpret his periodization as an attempt to describe a genuine historical dynamic. The use of statics was, he thought, necessary but not sufficient for this purpose.

As can be seen by comparing the successive editions of his *Principles*, Marshall became increasingly dissatisfied with the adequacy of the mechanical analogy to capture his ideas.[2] In the Preface to the fourth edition of his *Principles* (1898), he argued that it is simpler than the biological analogy which he took to be its alternative, and therefore more helpful in the earlier stages of economic analysis. Yet he went on to stress 'the essentially organic character of the larger and broader problems towards which we are working our way.' By 1901, in the Preface to the sixth edition, the relevance of biology even to the foundations of economic analysis is boldly asserted: 'Fragmentary statical hypotheses are used as temporary auxiliaries to dynamical – or rather biological – conceptions; but the central idea of economics, even when its Foundations alone are under discussion, must be that of living force and movement.'

His dissatisfaction with the mechanical analogy seems to have been related to his growing concern that movement up or down his long-period supply curve was irreversible in real historical time.[3] But he made little progress in applying the biological metaphor. His treatment is ambiguous in this regard. Although one brief passage shows some influence of the ideas of Herbert Spencer, it has been argued that Marshall's use of the idea of the representative firm points in the opposite direction. It is an abstract concept that avoids the need to analyse industries in terms of the real dynamic characteristics of the many different firms that compose them (Hodgson, 1993, pp. 406–15). 'The essentially organic character of the larger and broader problems' towards which Marshall was working his way after 1890 was never given a systematic treatment by him. He never produced the second volume of his *Principles,* planned in 1887, and his remaining works made no progress in advancing the use of the biological analogy in economics. Rather, the tendency of economics generally, as well as the reading of Marshall's periodization scheme in particular, was to become ever more mechanical (Whitaker, 1990, pp. 193–222).

But not all modern commentators have taken the mechanical path. Shackle's reading of Marshall does not regard the mechanical and biological metaphors as irreconcilable. According to Shackle, 'Marshall's peculiar triumph is his creation of a unity out of the conceptions of equilibrium and evolution'. The unity of concepts is explained thus:

> Equilibrium he (Marshall) conceives in a sophisticated, profoundly thought-out form where the economic subjects concerned are not helpless weights on elastic strings but anxiously thinking humans whose conduct is governed in part by their knowledge and the stages in which they attain it and by the conjectures which they base upon it. Equilibrium is a state of adjustment to circumstances, but it is a fiction, Marshall's own and declared fiction, for it is an adjustment that *would* be attained if the very endeavour to reach it did not reveal fresh possibilities, give fresh command of resources, and prepare the way for inevitable, natural, organic further change. It is this powerful conception which is the most worth-while object of study in Marshall (Shackle, 1965, pp. 36–7).

However, in order to sustain this interpretation, Shackle has to convict Marshall of a confusion between the long-period supply curve viewed *ex ante,* and as the composite of an infinite series of short-period supply and demand curves each of a different date. There is, moreover, only one footnote in the *Principles* that alludes to the latter concept. Shackle may have understood what Marshall was groping for, but it is hard to show that it is what he actually grasped.

Marshall himself did not make much use of his own tools of short-period analysis. His illustrations of their use were deferred to the never completed second volume (Whitaker, 1990, p. 202). Marshall had little interest in the short run. Shackle is right to say that 'it was in the long period that Marshall sought the arcanum, the real nature and meaning of the economic process as part of the historical process' (Shackle, 1965, p. 39). For it was in the long period that he sought the 'normal' values of commodities. Paradoxically, he defined 'normal' values as 'the average which economic forces *would* bring about if the general conditions of life *were* stationary for a run of time long enough for them all to work out their full effect'. (*ibid.*, p. 37, emphasis added). The paradox lies in identifying the normal by means of a counterfactual.[4]

Such was the ambiguous legacy of Marshall's period analysis for those who wanted to incorporate time into economic analysis. We are now in a position to turn back to our central question. How did Marshall's period analysis influence the early economic thinking of his greatest pupil, John Maynard Keynes?

The influence of Marshallian period analysis on Keynes
To the extent that he was an economic theorist, Keynes was more an intellectual heir of Alfred Marshall than of any other. From the start of his economic work, he felt the influence of the Cambridge school and its dominant figure, Alfred Marshall. He had read the new Cambridge Economics tripos at Marshall's instigation, had had personal supervision from him and had been strongly encouraged by him to turn professional economist rather than enter the Civil Service (Moggridge, 1992, pp. 95–7). He took over Marshall's lecturing responsibilities on monetary economics, when the latter retired. There are many reasons to expect Marshall's influence on Keynes to have been powerful.

At the same time, one must be careful not to assume that, just because Marshall was the leading English economist of his generation as well as a personal friend of the Keynes family, his intellectual moulding of Keynes's own economic thinking was profound and lasting. There were some mitigating factors. Keynes took up economics rather late in his intellectual formation. As a Cambridge undergraduate he read mathematics, although without achieving a brilliant success, while his extra-curricular interests lay in philosophy and politics. His major postgraduate project was in the field of probability theory, while his first academic publication was on the statistics of index numbers. Thus economics came to him as a late addition to an already extraordinarily well-furnished mind.

Further, at the moment of his pupil–tutor encounter with Marshall, the latter was already well past the peak of his powers. Keynes later expressed this as follows: 'I think that the informality of his lectures may have increased as time went on. Certainly in 1906, when I attended him, it was impossible to bring away coherent notes' (CW, X, p. 216). This picture is corroborated by what Marshall himself wrote in a letter to the Austrian economist Richard Lieben dated June 19th, 1906: 'I practically never use any diagrams at all in lectures now, and have forgotten much that is in my own *Principles*' (Whitaker, 1990, p. 202). Keynes had of course read the *Principles*, but it is unclear how much reinforcement his understanding of its theory of value received from his tuition by the author. Gerald Shove is supposed to have said that 'Maynard had never spent the twenty minutes necessary to understand the theory of value'.

Where Keynes benefited much more from Marshall's lectures was in the field of monetary theory. With specific reference to Marshall's lectures on money, Keynes also noted that the former's 'unsystematic method of lecturing prevented the average, and even the superior, student from getting down in his notes anything very consecutive or complete'. Nevertheless, 'his main ideas became known to pupils in a general way, with the result that there grew up at Cambridge an oral tradition...different from, and...superior to, anything that could be found in printed books' at that time. Keynes also asserts that Marshall did use 'some very elegant diagrams' in his 1906 lectures on the demand for money (CW, X, pp. 189–92).

Joan Robinson said that Keynes 'carried a good deal of Marshallian luggage with him, and never thoroughly unpacked it to throw out the clothes he could not wear' (1962, p. 76). A missed opportunity to do so came just as Keynes embarked on his phase of creative economic theorizing. After Marshall's death, Keynes wrote a memorial essay. This long memoir runs to some 70 pages of the *Collected Writings* (CW, X, p. 161–231). Much of it is, quite naturally, biographical in content. But even having allowed for the need to get that kind of detail right, a remarkably small proportion of the memoir (only some 10 pages in all) is devoted to an evaluation of Marshall's original contributions to economics. About half of this is given to monetary economics, and the other half to the theory of value. The first half is Keynes's unaided work. But for the brief evaluation of Marshall's advances in the theory of value, Keynes evidently felt the need to call in the assistance of Edgeworth. The usually super-confident Keynes explained his decision to do so as follows: 'It is difficult for those of us who have been brought up entirely under the influences of Marshall and his book to appreciate the position of the science in the long interregnum between Mill's *Principles of Political Economy* and Marshall's *Principles of Economics*, or to define just what difference was made by the publication of the latter' (CW, X, pp. 204–5).

The Keynes–Edgeworth selection of six elements of theoretical novelty in Marshall has attracted criticism from subsequent historians of economic thought. Schumpeter's view was that 'none of them can be accepted without qualifying reference to the work of others, though in conjunction and as elements of a general treatise for a wider circle of readers, they were of course new enough' (1954, p. 839, n. 13). Stigler is slightly more lenient than Schumpeter, striking down only four of the six Keynes/Edgeworth claims for Marshall's originality (Whitaker, 1990: 2–10). As has already been noted, he places the introduction of time into value theory first and foremost among Marshall's achievements. In this he agrees with Keynes–Edgeworth, whose third element is that 'the explicit introduction of the element of time as a factor in economic analysis is mainly due to Marshall' (CW, X, p. 206). One conclusion to be drawn from all this is that Keynes did not feel himself capable of single-handedly unpacking the Marshallian luggage, at least in so far as it contained the theory of value. Moreover, he chose as his assistant a senior who was himself too much in Marshall's thrall to be of serious help to him in that task.

But even while praising Marshall's introduction of the element of time, through the partial equilibrium analysis, Keynes criticized it. In this instance his praise was distinctly more double-edged than it was in relation to the other theoretical achievements that he claimed for Marshall. Here is Keynes's way of putting it.

> By means of the distinction between the long and the short period, the meaning of 'normal' value was made precise; and with the aid of two further characteristically Marshallian conceptions – quasi-rent and the representative firm – the doctrine of normal profit was evolved.

> All these are path-breaking ideas which no one who wants to think clearly can do without. Nevertheless, this is the quarter in which, in my opinion, the Marshall analysis is least complete and satisfactory, and where there remains most to do (CW, X, p. 207).

Keynes, however, was not specific in this memoir about which parts of the Marshallian period analysis he thought were incomplete and unsatisfactory, or why he thought so. This seems to give credence to the claim that Keynes had difficulty in distinguishing his own ideas about time in economic analysis from those of Marshall.

The *Tract on Monetary Reform*

In Keynes's *Tract on Monetary Reform* of 1923, some clues are given to the nature of his dissatisfaction with the treatment of time in the then current methods of economic analysis. The *Tract* itself is not a treatise and does not provide the reader with a unified theoretical position (Moggridge, 1992, p. 64).

It begins with a description of contemporary monetary facts, follows on with one theoretical chapter, and concludes with a set of concrete proposals for monetary management aimed at overcoming inflation. The focus here is on Chapter III, which presents a theory of money and a theory of the foreign exchanges.

The theory of money in the *Tract* is the Cambridge version of the quantity theory of money, based on the work of Marshall, as subsequently developed by Pigou. The theory of the foreign exchanges is the doctrine of purchasing power parity (henceforth PPP) anticipated by Marshall and then restated by Cassel. As Keynes explains, both of these 'theories' can be stated in a tautological form. The cash balances equation starts off as an identity, and becomes an equation only when one or more of the variables are held constant. PPP remains a truism as long as internal purchasing power is defined to mean internal purchasing power over goods that enter international trade, the truism being that arbitrage will equalize external and internal prices of traded goods (allowing for transport costs and trade taxes) via changing the exchange rate (CW, IV, pp. 61–5; 70–75). Thus both theories need to be further refined if they are to be useful for answering the policy question that Keynes is addressing, namely, is it better for countries with inconvertible paper currencies to stabilize their economies by deflating or by devaluing?

Both theories, when refined, imply mechanisms of economic adjustment. When a country's monetary authorities print more paper money than the public and the banks wish to hold, the domestic price level rises. When at the existing exchange rate it is profitable to switch supplies from foreign to domestic markets, there will be pressure on the exchange rate of the domestic currency to fall. Both theories also imply the existence of equilibrium values of the price level and of the exchange rate, at which the process of adjustment specified within each model has worked itself out and there is no incentive for further change. In the *Tract*, Keynes wrestles with two problems. One is *precisely* how these two simple models need to be refined. The other is how to use them to analyse real life situations when their equilibration mechanisms are not time-specific.

Unlike the Marshallian theory of supply, the quantity theory of money and the PPP doctrine did not have any sequence of sub-models to serve as a surrogate for the passage of time. They lacked a historical time dimension. Keynes, in his efforts to provide a policy analysis of alternative options for economic reform, felt that lack keenly. This is the origin of Keynes's most memorable remark, that '*in the long run* we are all dead'. The fuller context of this famous quotation is a discussion of the application of the Cambridge cash balances equation to post-war reconstruction in a previous era, that of the American Civil War.

In this discussion, n = the quantity of cash with the public, p = the index number of the cost of living, k = the volume of consumption over which the public wishes to retain command in cash, k' the volume of consumption over which the public wishes to retain command by cheque and r is the cash ratio maintained by the banks.

> If, after the American Civil War, the American dollar had been stabilized and defined by law at 10 per cent below its present value, it would be safe to assume that n and p would now be just 10 per cent greater than they actually are and that the present values of k, r, and k' would be entirely unaffected. But this *long run* is a misleading guide to current affairs. *In the long run* we are all dead. Economists set themselves too easy, too useless a task if in tempestuous seasons they can only tell us that when the storm is long past the ocean is flat again. (CW, IV, p. 65)

Keynes's point (less elegantly put) is that the quantity theory is an appropriate tool to analyse the effects of a policy intervention only if one were solely concerned about its very distant effects.

This passage can be easily misinterpreted as an expression of Keynes's impatience with long-run equilibrium analysis and therefore a rejection of Marshallian period analysis. Nothing could be further than the truth. 'In the long run we are all dead' is an exaggeration which seems plausible only because Keynes had selected the American Civil War as his example of post-war reconstruction. It is a bold stroke of wit, but nothing more. The real thrust is a complaint that, while the quantity theory has a long-run equilibrium position, it does not have a short-run equilibrium, nor does it have any disequilibrium analysis.[5] To say this is not a rejection of Marshallian period analysis.[6] It is a plea for its introduction into the theory of money, on the analogy of the theory of supply. In the *Tract,* Keynes tries his hand at this. Although in the long run p is a simple function of n, he suggests that a small rise in n may not leave r unaffected; that a large change in n may not, because of its effect on expectations, leave k and k' unaffected and that the trade cycle will in any case be lowering k and k' in the boom and raising them again in the slump. In Schumpeter's opinion, 'the variability of Keynes' k and k' is in fact the main *theoretical* contribution of the *Tract'* (1954, p. 706, n. 5; p. 713, n. 22).

One could, therefore, surmise that when he came to write the memoir of Marshall in the following year, Keynes was alluding to the failure to extend the period analysis to the theory of money when he described it as 'the quarter in which the Marshall analysis is least complete and satisfactory'. He had, in the memoir, praised Marshall's 'exposition of the Quantity Theory of Money as a part of the General Theory of Value' as one of his most important original contributions on the monetary side of the subject (CW, X, p. 191). Given this step towards the integration of what had previously been a more fragmented intellectual terrain, Keynes saw the need to go beyond Marshall by introducing partial equilibrium analysis into monetary theory. However, this perception came before the tidying-up campaign on Marshall's scheme of periods had got under way. Keynes wanted to import into monetary theory the genuine historical dynamic which had been Marshall's own ambition in the theory of value.

In the long run, we are all dead was not a jettisoning, in 1923, of Marshall's long-period equilibrium. It was an early recognition of the analytical problem that Keynes went on to solve, namely the element of disjunction that remained in Marshall's scheme between value theory and monetary theory, and the particular asymmetry according to which the former featured a short-period equilibrium, while the latter did not. It was not a plea that all policy analysis should be focused on the short run. After all, as late as 1930, long-period equilibrium remained the framework for the *Treatise on Money*. The *Treatise* was a continuation of, and not a departure from, Marshall's struggle to use period analysis to represent economic processes in real calendar time.

Endnotes

1. I am grateful to Hans Singer and to Adrian Wood for comments on the original version of this chapter, and to Victoria Chick for comments and discussion at the Dubrovnik conference.
2. Jevons had already said, in the Preface to his *Theory of Political Economy* (1871), that 'The Theory of the Economy...presents a close analogy to the theory of Statical Mechanics' (quoted in Deane, 1984 (1978) p. 95).
3. The problem of time irreversibility is related to the existence of increasing returns to the firm. If they do exist, 'whatever firm gets a good start will obtain a monopoly of the whole business in its trade in its district' (quoted by Deane, 1984 (1978) p. 150). And if this can happen, then the assumption of perfect competition, on which the results of the static equilibrium analysis depend, is violated.
4. The basis for this approach was presumably Marshall's concern that his economics should be truly 'scientific'. In mechanics, air resistance has to be excluded to arrive at a true measurement of the force of gravity. By analogy, the friction caused by subsequent economic events has to be excluded to arrive at true long-period equilibrium prices. But the method of a science of inanimate objects is not appropriate to an analysis of behaviour driven by human intentions and expectations. Shackle's interpretation overcomes this problem by positing an infinite series of instantaneous adjustments to new intentions and expectations. But it is not clear that this is what Marshall was 'really' getting at, or, if indeed he was, how this analysis could be operationalized.
5. The fact that Keynes called the definition of long-run equilibrium 'too useless a task' does not, to my mind, imply that he thought that it was absolutely useless, but rather that he thought it less useful than something else, namely the definition of short-run equilibrium. It has been said that Keynes's witticism 'does not imply that the long run is unimportant...What Keynes was actually emphasising was that the study of the short run is also important...' (Granger, 1993, p. 307). I would gloss this by adding that he thought the latter was more important for practical purposes, but that he did not yet believe that he could get to the latter without having first arrived at the former.
6. However, Keynes's choice of the storm/ocean surface metaphor suggests that he may have been referring to Walras (1926). Lesson 32 of the *Elements of Pure Economics* insists that the equilibrium state is constantly changing, but that the processes of adjustment to equilibrium take time. To describe his idea of the 'continuous market', he uses the metaphor of the surface of a lake that is continuously agitated by the wind. He then remarks that '. . . just as a lake is, at times, stirred to its very depths by a storm, so also the market is sometimes thrown into violent confusion by *crises,* which are sudden and general disturbances of equilibrium.

The more we know of the ideal conditions of (sc. general) equilibrium, the better we shall be able to control or prevent these crises' (Currie and Steedman, 1990, pp. 64–5). Keynes was arguing that knowledge of the ideal conditions of equilibrium may be necessary to control crises, but it is hardly sufficient.

References

Currie, M. and I. Steedman, (1990), *Wrestling with Time: Problems in Economic Theory,* Ann Arbor: University of Michigan Press.

C.W., (1971–89), *The Collected Writings of John Maynard Keynes*, 30 vols, Basingstoke: Macmillan.

Deane, P., 1984 (1978), *The Evolution of Economic Ideas*, Cambridge: Cambridge University Press.

Granger, C.W.J. (1993), 'What Are We Learning about the Long-Run?', *Economic Journal*, **103** (417).

Hodgson, G.M., (1993), 'The Mecca of Alfred Marshall', *Economic Journal*, **103** (417).

Leijonhufvud, A. (1968), *On Keynesian Economics and the Economics of Keynes: A Study in Monetary Theory,* New York: Oxford University Press.

Machlup, F. (1958), 'Equilibrium and Disequilibrium: Misplaced Concreteness and Disguised Politics', *Economic Journal*, vol. LXVIII (269).

Moggridge, D.E. (1992), *Maynard Keynes: An Economist's Biography*, London: Routledge.

Reisman, D. (1986), *The Economics of Alfred Marshall*, Basingstoke: Macmillan.

Robinson, J. (1962), *Economic Philosophy*, Harmondsworth: Penguin Books.

Schumpeter, J. A. (1954), *History of Economic Analysis,* London: Allen and Unwin.

Shackle, G.L.S. (1965), *A Scheme of Economic Theory,* Cambridge: Cambridge University Press.

Walras, L. 1954 (1926), *Elements of Pure Economics*, London: Allen and Unwin.

Whitaker, J.K. (ed.) (1990), *Centenary Essays on Alfred Marshall*, Cambridge: Cambridge University Press for the Royal Economic Society.

4 A struggle to escape: equilibrium in the *General Theory*

Victoria Chick

For Keynes the composition of the *General Theory* was 'a long struggle of escape...from habitual modes of thought and expression' (CW, VII, p. viii). He invites his readers to join him in that struggle. All the evidence, however, is that our minds are 'so filled with contrary thoughts and notions' that we 'cannot catch the clues' Keynes was 'trying to throw' us (CW, XIII, p. 470). Contemporary habits of thought are even further from Keynes's conception than the habits of Keynes's predecessors and contemporaries, and they are vigorously defended as the only correct way to think. This chapter examines equilibrium in the *General Theory*, and portrays Keynes's concept as misinterpreted by both the mainstream and the neo-Ricardians.

Some interpreters of Keynes would argue that equilibrium is a neoclassical concept not worthy of study. I believe that equilibrium serves two purposes in Keynes's *General Theory*: it is an organizing principle, and it served a didactic purpose in demonstrating that involuntary unemployment could persist, there being no endogenous forces leading to its elimination.

As Kregel (1983) has reminded us, equilibrium was not a central concept in classical economics. They had, however, a concept of a stationary state where the system replicates itself. It is therefore a position of rest of a systemic kind, which deserves to be called equilibrium. The marginalist revolution both elevated equilibrium to a new prominence in economic method and restricted the term to the equality of supply and demand. Since supply and demand represent firms' maximization of profit and individuals' maximization of utility, this equilibrium, today known also as market clearing, is simultaneously a position of optimal choice. Hicks comments on the subject (1965, p. 23): 'There is an equilibrium when all individuals are choosing the quantities, to produce and consume, which they prefer. To a conception of equilibrium that is of this type we must hold fast.'

Matters became much worse with the mathematization of economics. This formalized the system as a series of markets each described by a demand function and a supply function. If the equations are static, they admit of only one solution, if the equations are well behaved. There is no other set of values for which the specified system is internally consistent. Therefore the solution set is the equilibrium, and that equilibrium ensures co-ordination of plans which represent optimal choices, but there can be no meaning to disequilibrium in such a system. The conflict between this concept and Keynes's conception is a major source of the difficulty of understanding Keynes today. It is the source of statements that unemployment equilibrium is an impossibility or an illogicality and that, rather, the *General Theory* should be interpreted as a theory of unemployment disequilibrium, possibly adding the idea that adjustment to equilibrium is quite slow (Leijonhufvud, 1968).

As Vercelli (1991) notes, the static concept of equilibrium, though in macroeconomics the dominant concept, is vacuous: equilibrium only has meaning in a dynamic system, where disequilibrium is possible. Part of the job of Keynesian restoration, therefore, must be the rehabilitation of Keynes's dynamic system and his concepts of equilibrium within that system.

In sharp contrast to modern usage, Keynes does not look to equilibrium to provide solution values for a model but rather, in *A Treatise on Money* (CW, V and VI) seeks 'a method which is useful in describing, not merely the characteristics of static equilibrium but also those of disequilibrium, and to discover the dynamical laws governing the passage of a monetary system from one position of equilibrium to another' (p. xvii). Again, on page 120:

> the fundamental problem of monetary theory is not merely to establish identities or statical equations relating (eg) the turnover of monetary instruments to the turnover of things traded for money. The real task of such a theory is to treat the problem dynamically, analysing the different elements involved, in such a manner as to exhibit the causal process by which the price level is determined, and the method of transition from one position of equilibrium to another.

Some believe the *General Theory* to be a retrograde step, seeing it as a return to statics after the dynamics of the *Treatise* (for example Gilbert, 1982). But I believe this is a misperception; although the *General Theory* begins with a theory which has been described as static (Kregel, 1976), even that model is dynamic in its underlying structure. Indeed, without the role of time, the problem of uncertainty, understood by all close followers of Keynes to be fundamental to the *General Theory*, has no meaning.

Kregel (1976) finds three models in the *General Theory*, 'static', 'stationary' and 'shifting'. These are distinguished by the relation between short-run and long-run expectations and the relations of these to actual outcomes: in the static model short-period expectations are met, in the stationary model short-period expectations may be disappointed but the outcome does not affect long-period expectations, and in shifting equilibrium long-period expectations too may vary. There is another way of classifying the models in the *General Theory*: there is a short-period model which takes investment as given and therefore ignores monetary factors (chapters 3 and 5), the full short-period model (chapters 8–15 and 18–21), and an exploration of the long-run consequences of capital accumulation (chapter 17). Each of these has its own equilibrium. We shall use this taxonomy and show how it relates to Kregel's.

The truncated short-period model

The model of chapters 3 and 5 is meant to introduce the reader to the basic idea of the *General Theory*. In chapter 3, expectations of aggregate demand are taken to be met (Kregel's static model). There is a sense in which this description is accurate, but the underlying system which describes the process of determining output and employment is far from static. The action takes place in what Keynes called a production period, in which the output strategy decided at the beginning is unchanged until the output is ready for market sale at the end. Merely to speak of a beginning and an end precludes the idea that this model is static in the modern sense; rather, events are perceived as proceeding through time, at different paces in different industries and overlapping in the timing of their beginnings and ends.

Let us take one such production period as typical. For the *General Theory* as a whole the capital stock and state of technology are taken as given for the purposes of determining production. A wage bargain is struck at the beginning of the period; this bargain begins with last period's wage, and wages may rise if, last period, entrepreneurs failed to get the workers they required. The wage having been settled, firms will know their costs for any level of output and be able, on the basis of their expectation of demand, to decide the optimum price and output strategy. This they do despite the fact that the mathematics of the *General Theory* presuppose the small firm. These firms are not price-takers but are uncertain of their market (see Kahn, 1989; Chick, 1992; Tamborini, 1995). The optimum output (given expectations) then determines employment. The period proceeds with workers producing output. At the end the output is sold, by assumption at the prices which firms anticipated. Expectations of sales and profits are met and the decisions made last period will be repeated next period.

It can be seen that in this model the criterion of equilibrium is the replication of the system so long as the system is not disturbed by some exogenous force. The position of 'rest' is a stationary state, a system which moves through time but in an unchanging pattern. In the *General Theory* the 'method of expectations' (Hicks, 1937) immediately suggests that fulfilment of expectations is the criterion for equilibrium, for there is then no incentive to change behaviour. The model of chapter 3 assumes the fulfilment of expectations; it is, therefore, static in that it allows nothing but equilibrium positions, yet it derives from a dynamic system, quite unlike the static representation in IS-LM.

In the chapter 5 model, Kregel's stationary model, expectations are allowed to be falsified, to make the point that it is expectations, not their realization, which determine output and employment:

The *actually realised* results of the production and sale of output will only be relevant to employment in so far as they cause a modification of subsequent expectations (CW, VII, p. 47).

Economists find it difficult to accept that only the expectations of producers matter (Kregel, 1992); whether workers expected the real wage they actually receive is irrelevant. Harrod (1935) was provoked to caution Keynes:

The effectiveness of your work...is diminished if you try to eradicate very deep-rooted habits of thought *unnecessarily*. One of these is the supply and demand analysis. ...It is doing great violence to [the] fundamental groundwork of thought [to assert that] two independent demand and supply functions won't jointly determine price and quantity (CW, XIII, pp. 533–4).

The analysis is based on supply and demand, for output at the aggregate level, but employment is determined by firms' demand for labour alone. The only importance of a supply-of-labour curve is to indicate the maximum employment available at any given wage.[1] The difference from established analysis (established then and now) is that in the *General Theory* there is a hierarchy of markets: output takes precedence over labour. This makes the parties unequal: the expectations of producers count, because producers are in a position to make, and alter, offers of employment, whereas while labour is always in a position to refuse to work on a scale involving a real wage which is less than the marginal disutility of that amount of employment, it is not in a position to insist on being offered work on a scale involving a real wage which is not greater than the marginal disutility of that amount of employment (CW, VII, p. 291.)

The position of rest thus is defined not only by a lack of incentive or desire for change but also by the power to effect change. Workers' lack of power to insist on employment or to change the real wage explains why they only have an influence on events as consumers, not as workers, up to full employment. The model is stationary because there is no change in the volume of investment (the exogenous variable). It encompasses the Chapter 3 model as the special case of equilibrium. However it does not discuss the process of adjustment to the equilibrium described in Chapter 3. Rather, the point of Chapter 5 is to show that aggregate supply and firms' expectations of demand determine output and employment whether in equilibrium or not.

Only later (1937, CW, XIV, p. 182) does Keynes answer critics expecting discussion of a mechanism of adjustment. He protests that he is not interested in the 'higgling process' by which entrepreneurs try to discover the position of demand. It is natural to expect producers to learn on the basis of disappointed expectations, but:

when one is dealing with *aggregates*, aggregate effective demand at time *A* has no corresponding aggregate income at time *B*. All one can compare is the expected and actual income resulting to an entrepreneur from a particular decision (Keynes, *Ex post and ex ante*, notes for 1937 lectures, CW, XIV p. 180).

In Chapter 3, equality of expectations and outcomes was set by assumption; therefore it could apply universally. But it would be unrealistic to understand equilibrium as the fulfilment of every producer's expectations in real life. Thus the representation of equilibrium as fulfilment of expectations of aggregate demand must be understood as a rough approximation, not a precise statement. There will be some producers who will change their behaviour, even when aggregate expectations are met. Tonveronachi (1992) makes a further point:

> In principle a significant dispersion of expectations among agents is necessary if we want to retain uncertainty in a significant way. A definition of market equilibrium which requires the fulfilment of all individual expectations cannot deal with this concept of uncertainty. We can then either abandon market equilibrium or render it coherent with uncertainty (p. 25).

Keynes's dismissal of 'higgling' was perhaps tactical, for even in those less formalistic times, the lack of precise correspondence between a market outcome and subsequent behaviour would have attracted criticism. But it is easily seen that there is no way of improving the precision without the loss of something even more important.

The full short-period model

The main model of the book 'endogenizes' the truncated model's exogenous variable: investment. This entails also bringing in money, to determine the rate of interest. The dynamic structure of the model is greatly complicated thereby, although the Chapter 3 and 5 model remains the core. The ability of the level of investment to change means that equilibrium in this model may change: it is not stationary. Nevertheless only a subset of possible causes of change in the level of investment conform to Kregel's 'shifting model': those due to a change in long-period expectations. The model may also 'shift' (require a new equilibrium), if expectations of the rate of interest change.

The dynamic structure of this model begins with the rate of interest. The rate of interest is determined, in the *General Theory*, by liquidity preference and the money supply. The three motives of liquidity preference have different time horizons, the shortest of which is speculation; speculators can change their expectations of security prices, and act on those expectations, with great rapidity. The other two motives are assumed to react in a stable fashion to changes in aggregate income, which by definition changes rather slowly (because production and sale are time-consuming processes). Two conclusions follow:

firstly, the expectations of speculators at any given time dominate the determination of the rate of interest; secondly, the rate of interest so determined will inevitably alter as investment and income change in turn. What does not follow is that the investment previously decided on will be altered in response to subsequent changes in the rate of interest; investing entrepreneurs will be insensitive to these because they have already made their debt contracts.

There is a concept of equilibrium relevant to the rate of interest itself: the rate of interest is stable when there is a balance between the differing expectations of 'bulls' and 'bears'. This difference of view strikes a neoclassical economist as deeply peculiar. For them there is always only one rational 'choice', the only possible reasons for divergent expectations being irrationality or ignorance. This unease with Keynes's conception was a key criticism in Tobin's now famous reformulation (1958). But not only is a difference of view a perfectly reasonable outcome under uncertainty (which Tobin transformed into probabilistic risk), but such differences are absolutely necessary if there is to be a market in existing securities at tolerably stable prices.

The rate of interest so determined then, in turn, along with long-period expectations and the supply price of capital, determines the volume of investment. Once this is determined, surprises in short-period demand are, by construction, not allowed to affect the investment decision; the long-time horizon of investment is not to be disturbed by more immediate, and perhaps transitory, changes.

Once investment is determined, actual aggregate demand will be determined by the expectations of entrepreneurs, through their decision to hire and produce, and the marginal propensity to consume. The story goes through as for the truncated model with one troublesome exception: we must revisit the money market. (Messori, 1991 calls this process 'monetary retrodiction'.) Recall that in our dynamic story the rate of interest was determined by speculators, the level of income having been taken as given at 'yesterday's' level. Now to establish equilibrium, either we must return to yesterday's level of income or a change in transactions and precautionary demand must be compensated by a change in the rate of interest. This sounds incompatible with equilibrium, but it is not. The rate of interest has already done its work in determining the level of investment, and all we are interested in here is the existence of an equilibrium, not the approach to it. The rate of interest is free to take whatever value is now necessary to give us that equilibrium.

This description may feel uncomfortable. If so, it only reflects the fact that full short-period equilibrium in the *General Theory* shares the property of all static equilibria, that one cannot get into them; one can only be in them, from the 'Fall of Adam' (Robinson, 1978). The difference between this description and, say, equilibrium of supply and demand, is that here the difficulty is transparent, not least because we have started with a dynamic story. There is no way to win, really: either static equilibrium is not part of a dynamic story and is therefore vacuous, or the derivation of a static equilibrium from a dynamic story has a certain unreal quality about it. This is not our problem; it is in the nature of the beast. The transparency of the difficulty in the *General Theory* can be put to advantage, for it reinforces the idea of equilibrium as an organizing device while preventing us from taking it too seriously, certainly from seeing it as the only coherent position of the system.

In the full short-period model, the mode of adjustment to a new equilibrium is discussed: it is the multiplier. This too has static and dynamic aspects: the 'logical theory of the multiplier', which is static, and the process analysis which spells out the approach to a new position of rest. Let us look again at monetary retrodiction in the light of the multiplier. If the change in investment is viewed as a single change (and this can always be done with a suitable choice of length of time), textbook accounts tell us that income will return to its original level after being elevated for a time. This is exactly what our equilibrium requires. Actually the process is more complicated (Chick, 1996), but the textbook accounts are a reasonable approximation. Far from being, as Leijonhufvud (1968) has described it, a 'deviation amplifying' device, the multiplier is the adjustment mechanism following a change in the level of investment. It is when it has played itself out that we have full short-period equilibrium.

The Ricardian long period and chapter 17
One of the most vexed areas of Keynesian exegesis is whether there is a long-period equilibrium in the *General Theory*. Here again a mismatch may be discerned between the concepts in readers' minds and the mind-set of Keynes. The main protagonists are those who take their inspiration from the classical economists,[2] especially Ricardo, for example Caravale, 1992, the contributors to Eatwell and Milgate, 1983, especially Garegnani, 1976. The Ricardian criterion is expressed thus by Sebastiani (1992b, p. 61): long-period 'positions' (a looser word than equilibrium but with similar connotations) are 'situations of a full adjustment to forces deemed fundamental, systematic and dominant'.

To oppose the significance of such 'positions' appears virtually impossible: the dual is trivial, random and weak forces; who can support their study in preference?! The rhetoric of this school is as brilliant as their notion of long run is incoherent. The long run has nothing to do with time but is always present, as a centre of gravitation toward which the economy is always tending (though no adjustment mechanism is proposed), and the 'fundamental, systematic and dominant' forces are 'deemed' so, not placed in that position by sustained, reasonable argument. The equality of rates of return on capital is 'deemed' the dominant force. Why not the urge of labour to obtain employment in order to live and reproduce, rather than the urge of 'capital' to reproduce itself? The choice is never defended.

Though the classical long period has nothing to do with time, there are affinities with Marshall's radically different classification. Marshall's long period considers what will happen when the capital stock is taken out of the pound of *ceteris paribus* and allowed to change. Capital accumulation takes even more time than production, and it is through change in the capital stock that returns are equalized. This aspect is briefly addressed in chapter 17. Keynes explores only one question in the context of the long period in this shared sense: will the result of sustained capital accumulation be full employment or not?

To analyse this, Keynes takes the concept of own-rates of interest from Sraffa (1932). He provides two definitions of own-rates: actual rates can be inferred from spot and forward rates where these exist and the 'cause' of rates of return has four elements, *q, c, l* and *a*: return, carrying cost, liquidity premium and expected appreciation of the asset. Keynes then argues that sustained capital accumulation progressively lowers the rate of return on capital, but the rate of return on money, dominated by *l*, may prevent the rate of interest from falling to the level which will give full employment. If accumulation stops before full employment is reached, the level of income will fall to the point where the level of intended saving is no greater than the level of investment.

The equi-profit condition is satisfied, but the neo-Ricardians are not. It is not clear why. Perhaps a neoclassical element has crept in[3] which asserts that there is always full employment in the long run, and Keynes gives the 'wrong answer'. Perhaps the problem is that Keynes's answer depends on the unique properties of money, which has no serious place in the Ricardian system.

There are other objections: Potestio (1986) maintains that the long period must be a position of no uncertainty, and thus chapter 17, especially its monetary theory, is inconsistent with the rest of the *General Theory*:

> [T]here are no possibilities for a unitary consideration of the *General Theory* ... [T]he two blocks of analysis corresponding to Chapters 1-15 on the one hand and to Chapter 17 on the other express radically different approaches: the method of expectations and eventually of short period equilibrium is incompatible with the method of stationary long period equilibrium (p. 386).

Similarly Hansson (1985) wonders whether it is 'really possible for liquidity preference to exist in such a tranquil situation [as the long period]' (p. 326); Potestio makes a similar point in a later article (1989), that chapter 17 cannot support the same monetary theory as the rest of the book.

I find their allegations of incompatibility difficult to entertain. I believe they are carrying over from the classical view of the long period baggage which Keynes had dropped without saying so. They argue that since the long period must entail tranquillity and perfect knowledge (by tradition), it therefore cannot be compatible with liquidity preference. Look at the matter from the other direction: since Keynes's long period had an important role for liquidity preference, and liquidity preference can only play a role in the presence of uncertainty, we can infer that uncertainty plays a role in Keynes's long period. Therefore Keynes's long period must be different from the Ricardian concept of the long period.

In fact, Keynes always maintained that the long run was *more* uncertain than the short, and that while it was not unreasonable to assume (in chapter 3) that short-period expectations are met, such an assumption was never suitable for long-period expectations. These expectations are fundamental to the rates of return which are at the centre of chapter 17. It seems to me unlikely that Keynes's long period would abandon the uncertainty which is fundamental to the whole enterprise of the *General Theory*.

Tonveronachi (1992) maintains that the two definitions of own-rates in chapter 17 (as inferred from spot and forward rates and in terms of q, c, l and a) are not consistent, and 'only the first definition is coherent with the concept of equilibrium proposed by Keynes, but that this latter [concept?] is not coherent with his notion of uncertainty, if interpreted as market equilibrium' (p. 25). The objection is that the four elements incorporate subjective elements. Here again the classical long period is misapplied to Keynes: in the *General Theory* (as in the real world) there can be no hope at all of a long period composed exclusively of objective and fully-known observables. Under uncertainty, individuals must take a view of the future: the subjectivity Tonveronachi deplores is precisely what particularly recommends the explanation of rates of return in chapter 17. Caravale (1992), in the same volume (Sebastiani 1992a), proposes altering the traditional (objective) concept of rates of return to incorporate expectations; this is precisely to the point.

Long-period employment
There is another concept of long-period equilibrium in the *General Theory*. In order, one supposes, to reinforce the idea of persistent unemployment, Keynes proposed a concept of 'long-period employment':

> If we suppose a state of expectation to continue for a sufficient length of time for the effect on employment to have worked itself out so completely that there is, broadly speaking, no piece of employment going on which would not have taken place if the new state of expectation had always existed, the steady level of employment thus attained may be called the long-period employment corresponding to that state of expectation. ... [E]very state of expectation has its definite corresponding level of long-period employment (CW, VII, p. 48).

This idea of the long period is as timeless as anything in the Ricardian tradition – a hypothetical situation designed not to mirror reality but to make a point. It is the only place where Keynes entertains the possibility that long-period expectations are met. The concept of long-period equilibrium symmetrical with short-period equilibrium, which would entail long-period expectations of the profitability of investment being confronted with actual outcomes, never makes an appearance, for the best of reasons. The time horizon of long-period expectations is too long for comparison with the outcome to have any meaning; the comparison could not guide behaviour, since the circumstances surrounding the investment decision would have changed markedly by the time the results are in.

Conclusion

The concepts of equilibrium on which we have been brought up, whether neoclassical or classical, 'ramify into every corner of our minds' and make it difficult to read the message of the *General Theory*. Fitzgibbons (1988) has most powerfully explained that Keynes had a different world-view, and that an uncertain future was fundamental to it. In the *General Theory*, time and uncertainty finally have their day in economic theory. There are valid concepts of equilibrium which are compatible with uncertainty, but they conform to the dominant concept of neither the neoclassical nor the classical school. And equilibrium is just a part of the *General Theory* story. Our struggle to escape has barely begun.

Endnotes

1. See also Kregel, 1992, though he confuses the determination of output and employment with their equilibrium values. In the *General Theory* the two can be different, though not in mainstream analysis. See Chick, 1996.
2. It is an extraordinary feature of Keynes that he conforms to and satisfies neither school of thought; in the history of economic theory he stands virtually alone. Some would probably argue, if they realized this was the case, that this fact alone was sufficient to discredit his views.
3. Ricardo's system was devised when Britain was an underdeveloped capitalist country. The distinguishing feature of underdevelopment is insufficient capital to provide full employment. Thus 'normal capacity' is compatible with underemployment. But in a developed capitalist economy, full employment of labour can be expected before normal capacity is reached.

References

Caravale, G. (1992), 'Keynes and the Concept of Equilibrium', in M. Sebastiani (ed.), *The Notion of Equilibrium in the Keynesian Theory*, London: Macmillan.

Chick, V. (1992), 'The Small Firm Under Uncertainty: A Puzzle of the *General Theory*' in B. Gerrard and J. Hillard (eds), *The Philosophy and Economics of J.M. Keynes*, Aldershot: Edward Elgar.

Chick, V. (1996), 'Equilibrium and Determination on Open Systems: The Case of the *General Theory*', *History of Economics Review*, 25, 184–9.

Chick, V. (1996), 'The Multiplier and Finance', in G.C. Harcourt and P.A. Riach (eds), *Maynard Keynes' General Theory*, London: Routledge, pp. 154–72.

Eatwell, J. and M. Milgate (1983), *Keynes's Economics and the Theory of Value and Distribution*, London: Duckworth.

Fitzgibbons, A. (1988), *Keynes's Vision: A New Political Economy*, Oxford: Clarendon Press.

Garegnani, P. (1976), 'On a Change in the Notion of Equilibrium in Recent Work on Value and Distribution', reprinted in Eatwell and Milgate 1983, pp. 129–45.

Gilbert, J.C. (1982), *Keynes's Impact on Monetary Economics*, London: Butterworth.

Hansson, B. (1985), 'Keynes's Notion of Equilibrium in the *General Theory*', *Journal of Post Keynesian Economics*, 7, 332–41.

Harrod, R.F. (1935), *Letter to Keynes*, 1 August, in CW, XIII, pp. 533–4.

Hicks, J.R. (1937), 'Mr Keynes and the Classics: A Suggested Interpretation', *Economica*, 5, 147–59.

Hicks, J.R. (1965), *Capital and Growth*, Oxford: Oxford University Press.

Kahn, R.F. (1989), *The Economics of the Short Period*, London: Macmillan.

Keynes, J.M. (1971–1980) *The Collected Writings of John Maynard Keynes* (eds D.E. Moggridge and Austin Robinson). 30 vols, London: Macmillan. (References above to CW and volume number. Dates of original publication are given in text; page references to the *General Theory* are to the original.)

Keynes, J.M. (1930), *A Treatise on Money*. CW, vols. V and VI.

Keynes, J.M. (1936), *The General Theory of Employment, Interest and Money,* CW, vol. VII.

Keynes, J.M. (1937), *'Ex post and ex ante'*, notes for 1937 lectures, CW, XIV pp. 179–83.

Keynes, J.M. (1973), *The General Theory and After: Preparation,* CW, vol. XIII.

Keynes, J.M. (1973), *The General Theory and After: Defence and Development,* CW, vol. XIV.

Kregel, J.A. (1976), 'Economic Methodology in the Face of Uncertainty: The Modelling Methods of Keynes and the Post-Keynesians', *Economic Journal*, 86, 209–25.

Kregel, J.A. (1983), 'Conceptions of Equilibrium, Conceptions of Time and Conceptions of Economic Interaction', in G. Caravale, (ed.), *The Crisis in Economic Theories*, Milan: Franco Angeli Editore.

Kregel, J.A. (1992), 'The Identity between Aggregate Supply and Demand Price Equilibrium and Labour Market Equilibrium at Less than Full Employment', in Sebastiani (1992a), pp. 109–19.

Leijonhufvud, A. (1968), *On Keynesian Economics and the Economics of Keynes*, Oxford: Oxford University Press.

Messori, M. (1991), 'Keynes' *General Theory* and the Endogenous Money Supply', *Economie Appliquée*, **44** (1),125–52.

Potestio, P. (1986), 'Equilibrium and Employment in t*he General Theory*', *Giornale degli Economisti e Annali di Economia*, Lulio-Agosto, 363–88.

Potestio, P. (1989), 'Alternative Aspects of Monetary Theory in the *General Theory*: Significance and Implications', *Recherches Economiques de Louvain*, 55 (1989) 257–72.

Robinson, J. (1978), 'A Lecture Delivered at Oxford by a Cambridge Economist', in J. Robinson, *Contributions to Modern Economics*, Oxford: Blackwell.

Sebastiani, M. (1992a), *The Notion of Equilibrium in the Keynesian Theory*, London: Macmillan, pp. 61–73.

Sebastiani, M. (1992b), 'Keynes and Long-Period Positions', in Sebastiani (1992a).

Sraffa, P. (1932), 'Dr Hayek on Money and Capital', *Economic Journal*, 42, 42–53.

Tamborini, R. (1995), 'Price Determination in Polypolistic Markets and Exchange Rate Changes', *Metroeconomica*, **46** (1), 63–89.

Tobin, J. (1958), 'Liquidity Preference as Behaviour Toward Risk', *Review of Economic Studies*, 25, 65–86.

Tonveronachi, M. (1992), 'The Notion of Equilibrium in the Keynesian Theory', in Sebastiani (1992a), pp. 18–31.

Vercelli, A. (1991), *Methodological Foundations of Macroeconomics: Keynes and Lucas*, Cambridge: Cambridge University Press.

5 The modern relevance of post-Keynesian economic policies

Philip Arestis and Murray Glickman[1]

Post-Keynesian economics attributes instabilities in the capitalist system to the behaviour of private investment and to a number of obstacles and constraints. Full employment is very difficult to achieve in market economies, making it the exception rather than the rule. Even if it is achieved, it is unlikely to be sustained without government intervention, focused on the management of aggregate demand to achieve the growth required for full capacity utilization. However this potential role for government does not imply the existence in the abstract of a set of general prescriptions which can be applied in all circumstances and regardless of the specific prior macroeconomic experience of a given economy. Policy choice depends on concrete situations and here historical background as well as sociological characteristics matter crucially. Full employment is not the only objective of post-Keynesian economic policy. Governments should also strive to promote a more equal distribution of market power, income and wealth. For, as Keynes (1936) remarked, 'The outstanding faults of the economic society in which we live are its failure to provide for full employment and its arbitrary and inequitable distribution of wealth and incomes' (p. 372).

In reality, a completely 'free' market system does not exist.[2] Government intervention and appropriate institutions have evolved with the specific aim of reducing the fluctuations that are inherent in a 'free' market system. In an analysis of conditions in a mature economy ranging across the oligopolistic and small business as well as the personal and foreign sectors, the present authors have recently argued (Arestis and Glickman, 1996) that the potential for achieving this goal via the use of conventional fiscal and monetary policies is limited in the extreme.

The clear implication is that some control of the capital accumulation process should be an important policy dimension of post-Keynesian economics. Other economic policies, such as incomes policy, are also relevant. This chapter attempts to demonstrate the potential of these *economic* policies while taking full account of a number of constraints and obstacles that may be present.

Incomes policies and socialization of investment

Incomes policies might have a reasonable chance of success if applied to all forms of incomes without freezing the distribution of income, and were accepted rather than imposed. They must be seen to be fair, involve over time progressive redistribution of income and not merely be a device for reducing labour's income share. They also need the support of the trade unions and other economic groups. Such policies imply that non-governmental agents would have a substantial role to play in the formation of overall economic strategy. There are problems with this particular policy prescription. Firstly, the application of incomes policies to *all* forms of incomes is precisely what leads to their failure. One fundamental difficulty in this context is the measurement of productivity in some sectors, with the service sector being the obvious example. A further problem might be more serious. The decrease in the saving schedule needed to achieve full employment implies that firms would be operating in the peak capacity range. But once firms are convinced that the output growth rate has been raised, they will surely wish to return to a lower rate of capacity utilization so as to maintain entry barriers. Restoring excess capacity, however, will involve a rise in the investment function, which would be difficult to fund, given problems with credit availability at this phase of the cycle. Furthermore, as growth increases, the incremental capital output ratio will tend to rise if capital goods are produced with more capital-intensive technology than aggregate output, since the increase in the proportion of capital goods in total output will raise the aggregate incremental capital output ratio directly. Firms will thus be caught between a decrease in the saving schedule and an increase in the investment schedule, caused by the necessity to maintain expenditures aimed at securing market dominance (Arestis and Driver, 1984).

Incomes policies may, therefore, be an inadequate instrument to persuade market leaders to raise their investment output ratios. They may prefer a short period at peak capacity rather than commit themselves to faster secular growth by releasing their surpluses. Initiating fast sustained growth could lose market share for the dominant firms, given the fuller utilization levels it would imply. Caution on the part of the market leaders would be reinforced by the prospect that future governments, uncommitted to maintaining profitability, might be in power during the critical payback period of the investments. The experiences in the UK of 1963, 1972 and the late 1980s testify to the reluctance of industry to risk responding to consumer-led booms either with sustained capital investment or price restraint. It is doubtful that such behaviour could be changed drastically purely by a putative incomes agreement.

The other economic policy envisaged is industrial policy. The form such policy might take would vary, depending on historical and social experiences along with institutional and sociological characteristics (witness the examples of South Korea, Japan, Germany, Sweden and so on). One suggestion which sits comfortably with the analysis pursued in this paper is socialization of investment, which was one of Keynes's (1936) policy prescriptions. This can be ascertained from his suggestion that 'a somewhat comprehensive socialisation of investment will prove the only means of securing an approximation to full-employment;

though this need not exclude all manner of compromises and of devices by which public authority will co-operate with private initiative' (p. 378). In Keynes (1980b) this notion was made more explicit when he called for two-thirds to three-quarters of total investment in the economy, representing 7.5 per cent to 20 per cent of net national income, to be influenced by public or semi-public bodies, whose activities would be guided by 'private exchange' and 'technically social' motives (pp. 322–23). Such a stable long-term programme 'should be capable of reducing the potential range of fluctuations to much narrower limits than formerly, when a smaller volume of investment was under public control and when even this part tended to follow, rather than correct, fluctuations of investment in the strictly private sector' (*op. cit.*, p. 322). In this way socialization of investment fills the gap left by private investors and encourages more private investment by reducing uncertainty through the creation of a more stable environment.

Socialization of investment constitutes a long-term policy and views the state as a direct player in investment activity. The precise mechanism for its implementation remains unspecified, although three contenders exist. The first emanates from Keynes's (1982) reference to the establishment of a National Investment Board (NIB) which would aim to achieve full employment by strategically regulating the aggregate flow of investment through pooling and diverting the funds accumulated in the hands of socialized public and semi-public bodies. The NIB would ensure 'an adequate demand for them, partly by making them available at a rate which would attract a sufficient demand and partly by stimulating the undertaking of particular investment propositions' (*op. cit.*, p. 137). A slight variant on this interpretation is the employee investment funds idea as applied in Sweden (Arestis, 1986).

The second interpretation also emanates from Keynes's writings and sees a separate 'capital budget' for government, distinguishing sharply between investment and consumption expenditures (see, for example, Kregel, 1985). Government should aim to produce surpluses in the ordinary budget which are then 'transferred to the capital Budget, thus gradually replacing dead-weight debt by productive or semi-productive debt', and at full employment cyclical fluctuations should not be compensated 'by means of the ordinary Budget'. This role should be undertaken by the capital budget (Keynes, 1980b, pp. 277–8). This interpretation of socialization of investment is concerned with the composition of government expenditures and not with any increase in the share of government expenditures out of total expenditure in the economy. At the same time, though, public capital expenditure should be sufficient to enable government to stabilize aggregate investment spending over the business cycle. Keynes (1936) is explicit on this point when he suggests that 'State action enters in as a balancing factor to provide that the growth of capital equipment shall be such as to approach saturation-point at a rate which does not put a disproportionate burden on the standard of life of the present generation' (p. 220). This proposal is radically different from the NIB interpretation. Unlike the latter it does not entail public ownership of any means of production. But in neither case comprehensive ownership was implied. Keynes (1936) was clear when he argued that 'no obvious case is made out for a system of State Socialism which would embrace most of the economic life of the community' (p. 378).

The third interpretation of socialization of investment is the idea of 'industrial economic regulation' which implies a long-term perspective and aims at economic regulation to foster industrial development through 'public investment in an extended infrastructure fuelling endogenous development via supportive services' (Cowling and Sugden, 1993, p. 84). The imperative for government to adopt such a role is based on the analysis expounded above and on three additional sets of systemic deficiencies (Cowling, 1990): multinationalism (multinational corporations dominate economies and impose their strategies upon them, so that the economies' development is threatened), centripetalism (the tendency for higher economic and other activities to gravitate to the centre and away from the periphery), and short-termism (due to the short-term pursuit of profits, a problem particularly acute in the case of multinational corporations). In seeking to tackle these deficiencies, government should adopt a 'developmental' role, in that it should actively promote an appropriately 'democratic market structure' in concert with the interest groups involved, especially employees. The example of co-operatives in which the workforce actively participates in their affairs is a point in case (Cowling and Sugden, 1993, p. 89). This role should include restructuring of the financial system to provide the main source of corporate finance and thus encourage and promote long-termism, possibly through a national bank (Kitson and Michie, 1996).

The precise form 'industrial economic regulation' might take depends on the structure of the economy in question. The Japanese and East Asian models, and the 'social corporatist' countries of Europe which have implemented successfully these types of policy, have developed different institutional frameworks in their attempts to restructure their economies. In this process the critical role of the financial sector in determining the ability to restructure the industrial sector cannot be exaggerated, as the experience with large banks in Germany, France, and Japan, among other countries, testifies. For the institutional structure of an economy affects the impact of a given policy and the same policy could have differential effects when applied to countries with a different institutional structure (for similar views, see, for example, Eichengreen, 1996). The problem with Keynes's socialization of investment is that it cannot really be effective, as it excludes from the socialization process the participation of interest groups, crucially trade union involvement and co-operation, which is, we would argue, the *sine qua non* of its success (although this is more serious in the second interpretation). In this sense the third interpretation constitutes progress on

Keynes's (1936) socialization of investment. Trade unions, however, would be far more likely to co-operate if they were to be involved in collective bargaining, which in turn, is predicated upon a firm commitment to full employment. Such social compromise is likely to endure if there is successful economic restructuring of the type described here. Unemployment has been lower in those countries (Austria, Finland, Norway and Sweden) where commitment to full employment has been part of a broad consensus between trade unions, industry and the state (Glyn and Rowthorn, 1988). Furthermore, those countries which practice collective bargaining, either centralized or decentralized but with co-ordinated industrial relations, have a superior pay/jobs tradeoff (Soskice, 1993; Rowthorn, 1992). Cross-section evidence suggests a positive relationship between collective bargaining and investment, while time-series analysis provides no evidence of unionization adversely affecting investment (Metcalf, 1993).

Under decentralized bargaining, 'outside' influence is reduced. Holmlund and Zetterberg (1991) found that, in comparison to Norway, Sweden, Finland and Germany, industrial wage setting in the US was considerably less dependent on outside economy-wide influences, and much more dependent on price and productivity conditions within industries. In fact, in the Scandinavian countries, 'insider' influences on wage levels were negligible. Evidence for the US, UK and Japan seems to suggest that decentralized wage bargaining increases the influence of intra-firm productivity and profit trends and allows some workers to rent-share where their employers operate in imperfect product markets. This implies that decentralization favours a small minority of workers at the expense of the majority, enhancing wage dispersion and harming industrial relations. Rowthorn (1992) supports this view and offers evidence which shows that centralized collective bargaining, as in the Nordic countries, is associated with low wage dispersion and better employment prospects.

Potential constraints and obstacles to economic policy
Post-Keynesian economic policy analysis recognizes that there are obstacles to interventionist policies of this type. Political and social pressures impose significant constraints on the achievement of these objectives. Kalecki (1943) was sceptical about permanent full employment because unemployment had an essential disciplinary role. Although governments could gear the economy to full employment the 'power of vested interests' with their dislike of government interference in the private sector would not allow it. Kaldor (1983) gave further support to these ideas; he contended that the changes in the power structure of society, which came about as a result of Keynesian economic policies, were responsible for the antagonism towards these ideas. As an example of pressures against certain economic policies Kaldor (1982, p. xxi) refers to the early post-war cheap money policies, to which the banks and financial institutions in the

City objected, calling for a more 'active' monetary policy on the usual grounds of 'sound money'.

A different type of constraint is emphasized in the contributions of Myrdal (1957), namely the theory of 'circular and cumulative causation'. This is based on the dynamic interplay between investment and productivity growth, which reinforces inequalities and regional disparities. 'Cumulative causation' in economic terms generates inequalities in non-economic terms, such as political power, cultural domination and so on. Those regions which are relatively rich dominate, not just in the economic power sense, but also in terms of their ability to exert political superiority. They are in a position to impose their policy preferences and culture on less powerful regions, so that the institutions of the latter are under severe threat. The policy implication of this model is intervention at a regional level, which can be promoted through assistance to companies to locate production in depressed areas and through financial centres in the form of regional banking.

Given that these policies rely heavily on social co-operation and social consensus, a further problem is achieving agreement between the state, industry and labour. The conspicuous success of some countries with economic policies that relied on consensus (Sweden, Norway, Australia and Austria) is encouraging.[3] Indeed, there exists overwhelming evidence which suggests that increased participation is one of the dominant determinants of productivity, and that firms which involve workers in decision-making experience superior profitability, sales, growth, and better performance overall than similar firms which do not pursue policies of this nature (Knight and Sugden, 1989). However, in those economies where consensus has been delayed by actual government policies, the UK being a good example, post-Keynesian alternatives have the additional and difficult task to recreate it. This suggests that industrial policies as well as operating to achieve macroeconomic objectives, must also encourage economic activity to develop at regional and local level involving genuine community participation (Cowling and Sugden, 1993).

There is still the serious constraint imposed on these policies by the operation of transnational corporations and international financial capital. The operations of transnationals in the short run could jeopardize expansion, and UK experience indicates that this possibility is very real. In the long run it is expected that these firms would undertake a greater volume of investment once the economy has achieved a sustained expansionary path. In the short run, however, control over the operations of transnational corporations would have to be established. Fiscal measures could be used to promote domestic rather than foreign investment, although the evidence here is that transnationals could easily overcome measures of this type. The experience of other countries is revealing. Japan, the US, France, Canada and most notably a number of developing countries, have all adopted policies towards transnationals. These have ranged from monitoring their activities and taking positive steps to discriminate in favour of domestic firms where there were fears of multinational dominance, to more tight and direct regulation on their activities. Sugden (1989) suggests that a *transnational unit* with sufficient muscle to enable it to be active enough to monitor the activities of transnationals is paramount. Most importantly it would scrutinize their investment activity, including both inward and outward investment, whenever it exceeds a pre-specified size. This monitoring should then become part of overall strategic planning (Cowling, 1987).

Similarly policy-makers can, and should, attempt to have an impact on the regulation of international financial capital and trade flows. Keynes (1980b, p. 52) envisaged strict capital controls to deal with situations in which the centres of international financial capital became untameable. He argued that capital controls, both inward and outward, should be permanent. Also permanent, in his view, should be the control of the entire financial system. Indeed Keynes (1980b) went as far as to propose extending the idea of planning to embrace the whole of the international economic system. Hicks (1985) reinforces these views by advocating concerted action by a number of the more 'important' countries, and Tinbergen (1989) concurs, proposing close co-operation between the European Union (EU) and Japan.

The prospect of success of adopting capital controls for countries like the UK would be enhanced if such measures were taken at the European level. The recent proposal (Arestis, 1993; Arestis and Sawyer, 1996) for a European Clearing Agency (ECA), in place of the European System of Central Banks, is extremely relevant in this context.[4] It is predicated on the achievement of high levels of economic activity and full employment, based on the construction of a suitable EU financial system, the core element of which is a fixed, but adjustable, exchange rate system. Another proposal which sits comfortably with the idea of ECA is that of taxes on foreign exchange transactions to contain speculative capital movements (see, for example, Eichengreen, Tobin and Wyplosz, 1995). In the absence of financial costs in the transfer of funds from one currency to another, even a minimal prospect of devaluation can precipitate a crisis by causing a large-scale shift out of the troubled currency. A transaction tax increases the required interest rate differential necessary to spark off speculation, and can help contain it. There is the obvious advantage of this tax being a source of government revenue, but the transaction tax should essentially contribute to an orderly realignment of currencies when necessary. However, the possibility always exists that such a tax could potentially be passed on by speculators, and that a tax on spot transactions could lead to foreign exchange transactions driven offshore. To be effective a transaction tax would need to cover a wider grouping of countries than just the EU, and might be successful only under the aegis of a revamped international monetary system.

These measures, especially those taken in collaboration with other countries or groups of countries, have assumed more significance in those countries where international capital has taken a new twist. For example in the UK, what has apparently happened is that there has been a new form of internationalization of the City of finance capital, coinciding with, or perhaps induced by, the internationalization of British industrial capital. These developments have been taking place over the last 10 years or so, since the abolition of exchange and credit controls initiated at the beginning of the 1980s. The interesting implication of these developments is that while the interests of finance capital and those of domestic industrial capital do not coincide, those of finance capital and international capital are so tightly linked that the power of the latter is stronger than otherwise (Radice, 1989). The problem of controlling the activities of international capital, both industrial and financial, in the new environment becomes even more awkward when attempted in isolation. Globalization may have undermined the economic and political basis for effective economic policies at the level of individual economies, but at the same time it has created the impetus for a genuine internationalist programme. The inevitable conclusion is that there may be no alternative to policies being explicitly and firmly 'internationalist' (Harcourt, 1994); we may label it 'global Keynesianism'.

Conclusion

The major policy implication of post Keynesian thinking is a combination of socialization of investment with a 'social contract' among the three key groups in any economic system: trade unions, industry and the state. In this environment wage pressures that damage profitability and accumulation can be avoided, especially if there is a commitment to full employment by governments. These policies should be accompanied by appropriate industrial policies which would promote active participation of the trade union movement. However, some social control of multinationals and international capital is essential to any post-Keynesian strategy.

The approach of this paper is in the spirit of economic analysis and economic policies advocated by Keynes (1936, 1980a, 1980b), Kalecki (1971) and other influential post-Keynesians. It is based on an agenda which takes co-operation to be more constructive than competition. The economic policy implications of this approach are as relevant today as they have always been, and they can be defended as being both 'the only practicable means of avoiding the destruction of existing economic forms in their entirety and as the condition of the successful functioning of individual initiative' (Keynes, 1936, p. 380).

Endnotes

1. We are grateful to Nicola Allison, Massimo De Angelis, Geoff Harcourt, Mike Marshall, Peter Mottershead and Malcolm Sawyer for helpful comments.

2. Despite attempts in certain countries to 'roll back the frontiers of the State' (the UK in the 1980s is a good example), the trend in the twentieth century has been for more government intervention. Sawyer (1989, p. 302) argues that this trend continued even in the 1980s: on a crude indicator such as public expenditure as a percentage of GDP, it is shown that for a range of developed capitalist countries this ratio has increased in each of the decades since the 1950s and for all countries considered, the ratio being at its highest in the 1980s. Intervention ranges from facilitating industrial development through subsidies and tax concessions, to direct involvement in the process of capital accumulation and public ownership of key industries.
3. The case of Sweden is very interesting in that although economic policies of the type discussed here were successful for a long period, they appeared recently to work less than satisfactorily. The problems of the Swedish model may not be entirely due to weaknesses of corporatism but to mistakes in the conduct of macroeconomic policy by the government in response to the globalization of the economy.
4. The ECA proposal is firmly rooted in Keynes's (1980a) *International Clearing Union* and, more so, in Davidson's (1992/93) *International Money Clearing Unit*. The latter is in the spirit of Keynes but without the requirement of an international central bank.

References

Arestis, P. (1986), 'Post-Keynesian Economic Policies: The Case of Sweden', *Journal of Economic Issues*, **20** (3), 709–23.

Arestis, P. (1993), 'An Independent European Central Bank: A Post-Keynesian Perspective', paper delivered at the 11th *Keynes Conference*, University of Kent, 19, November.

Arestis, P. and C. Driver (1984), 'The Policy Implications of Post-Keynesianism', *Journal of Economic Issues*, December, **18** (4), 1093–1105.

Arestis P. and M. Glickman (1996), 'The Modern Relevance of Post Keynesian Policies', *Ekonomska Misao i Praksa*, **5**, (3), 19–43.

Arestis, P. and M.C. Sawyer (1996), 'European Monetary Integration: A Post Keynesian Critique and Some Proposals', in P. Arestis (ed.), *Keynes, Money and the Open Economy: Essays in Honour of Paul Davidson*, vol. 1, Aldershot: Edward Elgar, pp. 144–64.

Cowling, K. (1987), 'An Industrial Strategy for Britain: The Nature and Role of Planning', *International Review of Applied Economics*, November, **1** (1), 1–22.

Cowling, K. (1990), 'The Strategic Approach to Economic and Industrial Policy', in K. Cowling and R. Sugden (eds), *A New Economic Policy for Britain*, Manchester: Manchester University Press, pp. 6–34.

Cowling, K. and R. Sugden (1993), 'Industrial Strategy: A Missing Link in British Economic Policy', *Oxford Review of Economic Policy*, **9** (3), 83–100.

Davidson, P. (1992–93), 'Reforming the World's Money', *Journal of Post Keynesian Economics*, **15** (2), 153–79.

Eichengreen, B. (1996), 'Explaining Britain's Economic Performance: A Critical Note', *Economic Journal*, **106** (434), 213–18.

Eichengreen, B., J. Tobin and G. Wyplosz (1995), 'Two Cases for Sand in the Wheels of International Finance', *Economic Journal*, **105** (432), 162–72.

Glyn, A. and R.E. Rowthorn (1988), 'West European Unemployment: Corporatism and Structural Change', *American Economic Review*, Papers and Proceedings, **78** (2), 194–9.

Harcourt, G.C. (1994), 'A "Modest Proposal" for Taming Speculators and Putting the World on Course to Prosperity', *Economic and Political Weekly*, XXIX, 38, 2490–92. Reprinted in G.C. Harcourt (ed.), *Capitalism, Socialism and Post-Keynesianism: Selected Essays of G.C. Harcourt*, Aldershot: Edward Elgar, 1995.

Hicks, J.R. (1985), 'Keynes and the World Economy', in F. Vicarelli (ed.), *Keynes's Relevance Today*, London: Macmillan, pp. 21–7.

Holmlund, B. and J. Zetterberg (1991), 'Insider Effects in Wage Dermination: Evidence from Five Countries', *European Economic Review*, **35** (5), 1009–34.

Kaldor, N. (1982), *The Scourge of Monetarism*, Oxford: Oxford University Press.

Kaldor, N. (1983), 'Keynesian Economics After Fifty Years', in D. Worswick, and J. Trevithick (eds), *Keynes and the Modern World*, Cambridge: Cambridge University Press, pp. 1–48.

Kalecki, M. (1943), 'Political Aspects of Full Employment', *Political Quarterly*, October–December, 322–31.

Kalecki, M. (1971), *Selected Essays on the Dynamics of the Capitalist Economy, 1939–70*, Cambridge: Cambridge University Press.

Keynes, J.M. (1936), *The General Theory of Employment, Interest and Money*, London: Macmillan.

Keynes, J.M. (1980a), *Activities, 1940–1944: Shaping the Post-War World: The Clearing Union, The Collected Writings of John Maynard Keynes*, vol. XXV, London: Macmillan.

Keynes, J.M. (1980b), *Activities, 1940–1946: Shaping the Post-War World: Employment and Commodities, The Collected Writings of John Maynard Keynes*, vol. XXVII, London: Macmillan.

Keynes, J.M. (1982), *Activities, 1931-1939: World Crises and Policies in Britain and America, The Collected Writings of John Maynard Keynes*, vol. XXI, London: Macmillan.

Kitson, M. and J. Michie (1996), 'Britain's Industrial Performance since 1960: Underinvestment and Relative Decline', *Economic Journal*, **106** (434), 196–212.

Knight, B. and R. Sugden (1989), 'Economic Democracy and a Company Act for the Twenty-First Century', in *Beyond the Review: Perspectives in Labour's Economy and Industrial Strategy*, Industrial Strategy Group: University of Edinburgh.

Kregel, J.A. (1985), 'Budget Deficits, Stabilisation Policy and Liquidity Preference: Keynes's Post-War Proposals', in F. Vicarelli (ed.), *Keynes's Relevance Today*, London: Macmillan, pp. 28–50.

Metcalf, D. (1993), 'Industrial Relations and Economic Performance', *British Journal of Industrial Relations*, **31** (2), 255–83.

Myrdal, G. (1957), *Economic Theory and the Underdeveloped Regions*, London: Duckworth.

Radice, H. (1989), 'British Capitalism in a Changing Global Economy', in A. MacEwan and N.T. Tabb (eds), *Instability and Change in the World Economy*, New York: Monthly Review, pp. 64–81.

Rowthorn, R.E. (1992), 'Centralisation, Employment and Wage Dispersion', *Economic Journal*, **102**, 506–23.

Sawyer, M.C. (1989), *The Challenge of Radical Political Economy: An Introduction to the Alternatives to Neo-Classical Economics*, Hertfordshire: Harvester Wheatsheaf.

Soskice, D. (1993), 'Wage Determination: The Changing Role of Institutions in Advanced Industrial Countries', *Oxford Review of Economic Policy*, **6** (4), 36–61.

Sugden, R. (1989), 'The International Economy: Britain at the Mercy of Transnationals?', in *Beyond the Review: Perspectives in Labour's Economy and Industrial Strategy*, Industrial Strategy Group: University of Edinburgh.

Tinbergen, J. (1989), 'How to Reduce Unemployment', *Review of Political Economy*, **1** (1), 1–6.

6   Keynesian positions with the intertemporal new-Keynesian framework

Martin Zagler

Contrary to common belief, empirical analysis seems to suggest that countries able to stabilize gross domestic product (GDP) are the ones that also achieve high rates of economic growth. Moreover, it seems that the trade-off is larger for countries with pronounced stability oriented policies. This chapter discusses the new-Keynesian explanation for this phenomenon. Assuming nominal rigidities, an increase in money supply raises real money balances. This in turn increases aggregate demand and, given that the economy is below potential output, the level of real output. With increased running profit expectations for potential market entrants, both permanent and transitory monetary policy has a positive effect on research and development activities, which foster productivity and growth in the long run.

The chapter discusses the argument indicated above along seven lines. The first is empirical, and shows that new-Keynesian economics is a theory of the business cycle, rather than business slumps, or depressions. The second line argues that indeed the theory is more of a counter-attack against new classical economics and real business cycle theory than a research programme of its own. The third line of argument suggests that emphasis is stressed upon results, whereas most of the assumptions are taken from standard mainstream models, with the main deviation, as suggested in section five, being market failures. The fourth line of argument rests on rationality versus market failures. The main policy instrument is monetary policy, as shown in section six, since new-Keynesians' belief in the stability of the LM-curve, rather than IS. Section seven concludes the chapter by indicating that new-Keynesian arguments are linear rather than circular, which is relevant both from the theoretical and the policy perspective.

Stability versus economic growth

Empirical analysis seems to suggest that countries able to stabilize GDP are the ones that also achieve high rates of economic growth. Moreover, it seems that the trade-off is larger for countries with pronounced stability-oriented policies. When looking at long-run growth rates of GDP of the OECD (Organization for Economic Co-operation and Development) countries and the fluctuations around the trend, as shown in Figure 6.1. a negative correlation is suggested by the data, that is, countries with high growth rates exhibit high volatility in real

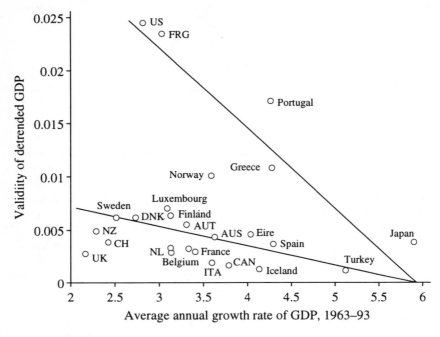

Source: OECD.

Figure 6.1   The trade-off between growth and volatility

GDP. When separating the OECD sample in 'institutional', or stability-oriented countries, and 'market economy', or growth-oriented countries,[1] the picture changes. Among conservative countries, such as the US, Germany or Japan, it appears that Japan, with the least volatility, exhibits the highest rate of economic growth. Similarly, the stability-oriented countries (for example Sweden, Austria, France, Spain) form a positive trade-off between stability and growth, but with much less volatility, while the intercept with the horizontal axis lies at around 6 per cent growth for both conservative and progressive countries. The question now arises why stability-oriented countries also achieve higher rates of economic growth. One is tempted to assume that there is a transmission mechanism between short-run policy and long-run performance. At this stage, it is interesting to observe that stylized facts, such as volatility and growth, are developed within a short-run business cycle framework. Whilst Keynesian theory started out to explain a depression that has lasted for several years, the basis of new-Keynesian analysis is annual data. In other words, new-Keynesian economics is a theory of the business cycle, and not of depressions.

The theory behind new-Keynesian economics

New classical economics has targeted post-war Keynesians by repeatedly asking two questions. The first question addresses the problem of time inconsistency of the Keynesian IS-LM framework. It is the equivalent to the monetarist critique of the short-run Keynesian model, and it suggests that even if resources are allocated towards the present, they would lack in the future, and potentially more than have been used up today. The Keynesian models up to then were models of the very short run, with huge explanatory problems when it comes to discussing long-run implications.

The second question relates to the Lucas critique, which states that any model set-up that is not based upon individual reasoning may be inconsistent on the aggregate level. This of course does not imply full rationality on behalf of individual agents. Yet rationality assumptions, in particular utility and profit maximization or rational expectations, seem theoretically sensible, as conclusions under these assumptions are not based upon *ex post* false anticipations, but upon the fundamental argument of the model. Moreover, if one assumes that agents know the environment they are acting in much better than the non-involved observer, it is very likely that rational behaviour describes economic behaviour better than many other assumptions.

For a long time Keynesians have not found a reasonable response to this question, and government intervention has been widely refuted on theoretical grounds. It was not until the new-Keynesian ideas started to come around, supported by the empirical threat of persistent unemployment, that government action became fashionable again within the profession. The breached literature uses the standard notion of rational, forward-looking agents in long-run models, introducing one or two assumptions, which seem very plausible, and obtains results that relate closely to a Keynesian analysis. The extensions consist of two factors: a monopolistic competition market structure, which ensures price-setting suppliers, and which does not seem implausible at all, and some kind of price rigidity, such as small menu costs, to obtain results that call for intervention. (see Mankiw, 1985; Blanchard and Kiyotaki, 1987)

There has been much critique within the profession against the concept of price rigidities. The first argument against price rigidities on the macro-level comes from the observation that not all firms adjust prices at the same time, but those that do adjust prices rationally over-adjust them, so that in the aggregate prices are flexible under the assumption of identical shocks (see Caplin and Spulber, 1987).

A second line of arguments focused on long-run perspectives, arguing that the cost of changing prices is the smaller, the longer the planning horizon, both for permanent and transitory shocks. Hence policy is ineffective in the long run. Zagler (1996) argues that policy is effective in the long run, as price rigidities reveal a transmission mechanism for monetary policy to foster Research and Development (R&D).

Results versus assumptions

Rationality of agents implies that households are utility maximizers. For simplicity, assume that there is a representative agent, who maximizes an intertemporal, time separable utility function in a wide array of different consumption goods and in real money balances, subject to an intertemporal budget constraint. This of course implies that households have access to credit markets independent of wealth. Due to homogeneity assumptions, we can separate the household problem into two parts, where households first select a consumption basket among the variety of consumption goods available at the moment and then choose the quantity of consumption they intend to purchase, or equivalently, the amount of wealth they want to transfer into the next period, both in the form of money holdings and savings.

Suppose that point-in-time utility is of the CES or Dixit-Stiglitz type, then demand $x_{i,t}$ for a given variety of product at a given point of time takes the form

$$x_{i,t} = \left(\frac{p_{i,t}}{p_t}\right)^{-\varepsilon} c_t,$$

where $p_{i,t}$ is the price of that product, c_t is aggregate demand, and ε is the elasticity of substitution between two distinct products. The aggregate price index is defined as

$$p_t = \left[\int_0^{n_t} p_{i,t}^{1-\varepsilon} di\right]^{\frac{1}{1-\varepsilon}},$$

where n_t is the number of available products at time t. While the assumption of households actually choosing between an (infinite) number of products seems quite ridiculous, the result that demand declines whenever the relative price $p_{i,t}/p_t$ of a given product increases, and aggregate demand falls is quite sensible and fits empirical data.

In the rational agent model, the Keynes–Ramsey-Rule best suggests the intertemporal trade-off that is taking place. First derived by the mathematician Frank Ramsey after a suggestion of John Maynard Keynes, the rule suggests that households should accumulate whenever saving is more rewarding than consuming, or when the real rate of interest exceeds the individual rate of time preference δ. In the monetary economy that this chapter tries to establish, the Keynes–Ramsey-Rule takes the form,

$$\frac{\dot{c}_t}{c_t} = \frac{1}{1-\alpha(1-\sigma)}[r_t - \delta] + \frac{(1-\alpha)(1-\sigma)}{1-\alpha(1-\sigma)}\left[\frac{\dot{m}_t}{m_t}\right],$$

where m_t is real money balances, $(1 - \alpha)/\alpha$ is the (constant) share of real money balances in consumption, and σ is the (constant) intertemporal elasticity of substitution. It suggests that consumption should grow (should be higher tomorrow than today) if the interest rate exceeds the rate of time preference. While this rule seems simple and intuitive, for example with a high substitution elasticity consumption should be delayed to a larger extend, it does imply a rather profound knowledge of all future income in order to adjust initial consumption correctly. For that matter, it seems questionable whether rationality, in particular when it comes to future events, is better adopted in explaining consumption behaviour than early Keynesian models. Yet empirical analysis does find evidence. (for example Hall, 1978).

In the days of the shareholder society, it seems much more likely that firms behave rationally in that they maximize profits. When labour markets are well functioning to prevent exploitation of the labour force and bubbles at stock markets cannot be influenced by market participants, maximizing profits is equivalent to maximizing the stock market value of the firm. Suppose that firms uniquely supply a single product on the goods market, then the price they choose is given by mark-up over wage costs w_t, or

$$\frac{p_{i,t}}{p_t} = \frac{\varepsilon}{\varepsilon-1} w_t.$$

In order for firms to accrue monopoly rents as indicated above, they have to invent a new variety. Assuming that the invention process takes a given quantity of labour resources l_t, and fails with a rate $1 - p$, the number of products grows at the aggregate level at the rate

$$\dot{n}_t = p\, l_t\, n_t,$$

where aggregation of a large number of firms has eliminated individual uncertainty. The quantity of labour employed in R & D (and ultimately success) evidently depends upon profit expectations, which themselves depend upon the elasticity of demand, the size of the competition (both negatively), and aggregate demand (positively).

Rationality versus market failures

Discussion so far has focused on rationality in the form of optimizing behaviour and in the form of expectations formation, and on market failures due to monopolistic competition, the presence of money and access of researchers to previous results in the form of existing blueprints. It is sometimes perceived that rationality by itself implies market clearing at potential output, which indeed it does not. The model presented so far falls behind potential output due to market failures which cannot be eliminated under rational expectations.

It can therefore be assumed that it is a world of imperfections rather than non-rationality which calls for policy intervention. Moreover, as will be evident from section seven, rational expectations do not prevent policy effectiveness. Quite the contrary, the closer expectations are to full rationality, the larger will be the benefits of policy.

Money

The reason for holding money in this model is a pure transaction costs argument, as the pecuniary yield of money is always dominated by interest-bearing asset holdings. Given the fact that there is a large variety of products, people incur high costs in finding trading partners in a pure exchange economy. Hence they hold real money balances, the larger their consumption demand, in order to easier execute transactions. Instead of explicitly formulating this process, money is incorporated into the utility function, as suggested earlier. Evidently the marginal utility of holding on to another unit of money (the money service yield) relative to the marginal utility of an extra unit of consumption must be equal to the relative price, which is the nominal rate of interest i_t, or with Cobb–Douglas preferences,

$$\frac{(1-\alpha)/m_t}{\alpha/c_t} = i_t.$$

While the Keynes–Ramsey-Rule as stated so far may have suggested that money has a direct effect on economic growth, the above relation has a revealing implication. Assuming constant interest rates, money demand grows at the same rate as aggregate consumption, hence the Keynes–Ramsey-Rule simplifies to

$$\frac{\dot{c}_t}{c_t} = \frac{1}{\sigma}\big[r_t - \delta\big].$$

Ignoring the second term in section three therefore does not reduce generality of the discussion. But this implies that money does not have a direct effect on economic growth, or that monetary policy is irrelevant for the long-run evolution of the economy.

Monetary policy will evidently not even exhibit indirect effects whenever prices are fully flexible and perfectly adjust to increases in nominal money supply, as agents do not care about nominal money holdings, but about holding purchasing power.

Some sort of price rigidity is therefore required to assure a monetary transmission mechanism. Alan Blinder (1994) suggests a dozen theories and tests their empirical relevance. He finds that among the theories tested co-ordination failures, cost-based pricing with lags, nominal or implicit contracts and adjustment costs are considered to be the main reason for price stickiness. Whether it is just costly to raise prices, or whether more complicated mechanisms are at work does not matter for the argument that monetary policy is able to raise real money balances. Once real money balances rise, aggregate consumption must increase in order to fulfil the money service yield equation.

Keynesian theory acknowledges at least three reasons for money holdings, a transactions, a speculative and a precautionary motive. This chapter is reductionary as it focuses solely on the first motivation and ignores the others. Yet it is quite straightforward to introduce those as well to yield very similar results as the ones presented below.

The IS-LM framework revisited
Rearranging the money service yield above, one finds a stable relation between liquidity demand m_t, aggregate consumption c_t and nominal interest rates. Except for consumption instead of real output, and together with fixed money supply, this very much resembles the standard notion of the LM-curve.

The stability of the LM-curve depends crucially upon the exclusion of a speculative motive for money holdings, as this would open a channel for the very short-run oriented behaviour of financial markets to influence the real economy, something that has been excluded in the framework presented here.

On the other hand, there appears no evident counterpart in the form of an IS-curve. The only relation between aggregate consumption and interest rates, the Keynes–Ramsey-Rule, is formulated dynamically and appears highly volatile, as expected permanent income may vary heavily across agents. A very central point of the IS-curve is carried over, however. Various authors, such as Matsuyama (1995) and Keuschnigg (1996), have suggested that there is a dynamic investment multiplier incorporated in the monopolistic competition framework. In that context, a favourable demand shock, increasing profit expectations, fosters private investment (impact effect) and in turn increase productivity in R & D, thereby further increasing investment (multiplier effect). Here the number of products can be viewed as investment in human capital.

Circularity versus linearity

The multiplier process, as suggested earlier, is a circular argument. The idea that once investment has started additional investment opportunities arise which, once carried out foster investment again until eventually this process dies out, is clearly a circular argument. Most disequilibrium models, such as the Keynesian framework, are circular in nature. By contrast, the central argument in favour of monetary policy which one may draw from the discussion in this chapter is clearly linear.

Starting out from nominal rigidities like the new-Keynesian models sketched in section two, section five argued that an increase in money supply raises real money balances. This in turn increases aggregate demand and, given that the economy is below potential output, as suggested in section four, the level of real output. With increased running profit expectations for potential market entrants, as indicated in section three, both permanent and transitory monetary policy has a positive effect on research and development activities, which foster productivity and growth in the long run, as has been empirically postulated in the first part of the chapter.

Endnote
1. I am using the principal ruling political party as a separating device, where conservatives are assumed to be growth oriented and progressive parties to be stability oriented. This device is certainly very problematic, therefore the results obtained should be treated with care.

References

Blanchard, O.J., and N. Kiyotaki (1987), 'Monopolistic Competition and the Effects of Aggregate Demand', *American Economic Review*, **77** (4), 647–66.

Blinder, A.S. (1994), 'On Sticky Prices: Academic Theories meet the Real World', in N.G. Mankiw, *Monetary Policy*, NBER, Chicago: University of Chicago Press, pp. 117–54.

Caplin, A.S. and D.F. Spulber (1987), 'Menu Costs and the Neutrality of Money', *Quarterly Journal of Economics*, 102, 703–25.

Hall, R. (1978), 'Intertemporal Substitution in Consumption', *Journal of Political Economy*, 96, 971–87.

Lucas, R.E. (1976), 'Econometric Policy Evaluation: A Critique', *Carnegie Rochester Conference Series on Public Policy*, 1, 19–46.

Keuschnigg, C. (1996), 'Business Formation and Aggregate Investment', *mimeo*, Saarbruecken.

Mankiw, N. G. (1985), 'Small Menu Costs and Large Business Cycles: A Macroeconomic Model of Monopoly', *Quarterly Journal of Economics*, 100, 529–39.

Matsuyama, K. (1995), 'Complementarities and Cumulative Processes in Models of Monopolistic Competition', *Journal of Economic Literature*, 33, 701–29.

Snowdon, B., H. Vane and P. Wynarczyk (1994), *A Modern Guide to Macroeconomics*, Aldershot: Edward Elgar.

Zagler, M. (1996), 'Long-Run Monetary Non-Neutrality in a Model of Endogenous Growth', Vienna University of Economics and B.A. Working Paper No. 37.

7   The interwar economic thought and Keynes
Ivo Ban

Great ideas and works do not appear very often. That is exactly the reason that they last long and serve as a basis for other ideas and practice. Such is the case with Keynes's *General Theory* which has both been praised and contested frequently during the last 60 years. Throughout this period, despite numerous new ideas and models which have attempted to look for the 'right' solutions, the shadow of Keynes has always been present.

Basic social changes take place when the existing state of affairs is not satisfactory, and when the available 'tools in the box' fail to respond to the challenges of the time to establish a new social equilibrium. The same rule is also valid for economic theory and economic practice.

Despite a significant advance in economic science in general, towards the end of the nineteenth and the beginning of the twentieth century, an ever greater gap occurred between microeconomics and macroeconomics. Economic problems persisted for which classical or neoclassical theory could not provide a complete answer. The weakness of the existing theory was revealed particularly in the 1930s during the Great Depression, which so badly shook the entire industrial world.

It was in such a crisis time that Keynes's *The General Theory of Employment, Interest, and Money* (1936) appeared. He injected new ideas into his theory and policy proposals, so as never to happen again what happened in 1929–33. Keynes's prescription was effective as far as the early 1970s, but old-new diseases appeared in new conditions and with additional characteristics of 'stagflation', for which Keynes's model was not effective enough. That was the reason for new elements and further contemporary formation of already known ideas into monetarist theory, supply–side economics, and rational expectations theory (Galbraith, 1995, pp. 197–208). Business cycles and political turmoils are often accompanied by radical currents in the economy, which would like to change the existing systems radically and quickly. But, fortunately enough, they appear suddenly and disappear quickly without more serious consequences (Samuelson and Nordhaus, 1995, pp. 381–2).

If we analyse systematically the events and the development of economic thought, we can conclude that all the theories[1] were right for their own time, but because outworn, to a greater or lesser extent, by passage of time, and thus weakened they were not able to cope effectively with emerging new problems.

With the breakdown of the communist system in central and eastern Europe, and in ex-USSR, economic theory faces another challenge – finding ways out of going through, from a non-market economy to a market economy, with as little pain as possible. Time will show what solutions are offered. At the moment, it is evident that highly unstable and chaotic conditions prevail which will not be cured by themselves.

Emergence of the *General Theory*

The traditional, or 'classical theory',[2] as Keynes called it, studied trade cycles and fluctuations even before the Great Depression, but it was not the central theme of the dominant economic thought. The causes of economic fluctuations were sought mostly outside the economic system, because everyone believed in the validity of Say's paradigm of self-correcting economic mechanism (Napoleoni, 1982, p. 69). A theory of depression did not exist, which is understandable because classical tradition, to which almost all the economists belonged, excluded depression (Galbraith 1995, pp.143–4).

Economists believed that there were no serious economic ills in the system, that depression comes and goes away, and that there was no need for a strong remedy and therapy. The tendency to full employment is the essential characteristic of the existing economic system; after disturbance from equilibrium state, recovery is inevitable and certain within a short period and without long-term consequences (Chick, 1984, pp. 285–6).

However, as mentioned earlier, only difficult economic conditions could provoke a basic economic discussion and changes in the views and opinions of economists, because those who were predestined to think were on the other side – on the side of the few and relatively privileged.

Through the nineteenth and the early twentieth century, economic thought was dominated by the problems of prices, wages, interest rates and profit. Special attention was paid to the role of money and to banking. Economic thought was essentially concentrated upon the explanation of prices, that is of values and the incomes obtained on this basis. Attention was directed towards the buyer instead of to the seller; emphasis was given to consumers' benefit instead of cost; focus was on demand rather on supply; and prices were seen as the result of the fact that supply and demand are mutually conditioned and dependent, and not the result of the cost of production.

Despite such a relative harmony, and economists' belief (in classical and neoclassical theory) that the traditional, firm and stable rule about economic life being prone to equilibrium – regardless of temporary signs of disharmony – was still valid, reality showed the signs of disharmony, contrariety and tension.

Low wages, unequal distribution of income and economic power,[3] financial depression, unemployment, the strengthening of trade unions and an air of hopelessness put the existing economic system more and more under pressure. Such a reality was theoretically incompatible with classical views.

The critics, and opposition to views and opinions which had defended that system, appeared in all industrial countries in such conditions.

As classical theory proved to be powerless in face of the economic problems, new theories appeared which were 'closer' to actual practice. They were a forerunner to and/or contemporary with J.M. Keynes (for example Wicksell, Lindahl, Myrdal, Ohlin in Sweden; Kalecki in the UK; Foster and Catchings in the US).

Classical economists were convinced that income distribution was unchangeable. They argued that government intervention for the alleviation of poverty would be counterproductive, as the final result would be a decrease of total national income.

However, Ricardian and generally classical limitations regarding government interference with economic flows did not prevent Otto von Bismarck in Germany from having recourse to governmental measures as early as the 1880s. Evidently this was done in face of the existing ever sharper social tensions and with the objective of alleviation of the existing state of affairs and the 'heaviest cruelties of capitalism'. In spite of a great resistance, the Reichstag, nevertheless, passed the necessary laws, in the mid-1880s, which provided help in the case of accident, illness, incapability and old age (Galbraith, 1995, p.155).

The example of state intervention in Germany has been especially emphasized, because it was the first official case of state interference in income distribution despite the rigid views of classical orthodoxy.

However Germany was not alone in creating a welfare state.[4] Its example was followed by Austria, Hungary, and then Britain, and, in the 1930s, by the US. Government social measures (of different or similar proportions) were applied in all industrial states. Thus the 'correcting' role of government in the existing economic system was inaugurated with greater or lesser opposition and without strong theoretical support.

The country which was the cradle of classical belief, Great Britain, especially surprised the world by promoting a welfare state. Without great enthusiasm, these changes in the system were accepted, which actually meant a considerable alleviation of its rigidity. Representatives of the classical theory also influenced the softening of the view towards changes (for example Pigou), with views supporting income redistribution, following necessarily from the application of measures to increase welfare.

It is evident, then, that the rigid frameworks of the classical theory weakened under the pressure of real life, and that the changes extended to the economic systems of all industrial countries. Orthodox liberalism suffered defeat, and new ideas broke the earlier rigid opinions. The Great Depression intensified and speeded up all this. Its forceful attack came after the stock market crash in October

1929, and its main characteristics were: a vertiginous fall in prices resulting in financial disaster for industrial and agricultural firms; unemployment; and misery, especially for the more vulnerable groups of the population.

In such circumstance, Keynes presented his controversial *The General Theory of Employment, Interest and Money* in 1936, embodying the ideas he had nurtured since 1929.

A new hope

Difficult economic circumstances of the Depression years had traumatized not only the economies but the economic profession as well. Economics was neither unanimous nor effective in its approach for improving the state of economy. A sense of guilt and powerlessness had prevailed (Leijonhufvud, 1983, p. 30). Therefore the *General Theory* came as a new hope and as the basis for rejection of old models.

The main task of this monumental work was directed towards the treatment of 'difficult questions of theory', whereas the practical application of this theory was of secondary importance. The general approach, characteristic of the work, had to serve universally and encourage the 'critical reappraisal of basic postulates' (Keynes, 1987, p. 13). Keynes was aware in advance that he wrote 'the book ... which will change considerably...the way in which the world thinks about economic problems' (Harrod, 1951, p. 447).

Keynes also tried to find, in his *General Theory*, solutions to the economic policy which would solve economic problems by the application of general theoretical principles from which several theoretical discoveries were derived (Leijonhufvud, 1983, p. 23).

The significance of Keynes's work becomes clear if it is considered in context of the devastating effect of the Great Depression of the 1930s. The collapse of a number of firms, millions of unemployed without any hope of finding work, poverty of the population on a large scale, struggle for survival especially of those most endangered – the unemployed, homeless, old and sick people, and young people – with energy and knowledge but with little prospect of using them and proving themselves.

In such darkness, Keynes carried a torch that lighted the way of hope and escape from the existing system, which had to be reorganized by the involvement of the state.

> [The foregoing theory] indicates the vital importance of establishing certain central controls in matters which are now left in the main to individual initiative, there are wide fields of activity which are unaffected. The State will have to exercise a guiding influence on the propensity to consume partly through its scheme of taxation, partly by fixing the rate of interest, and partly in other ways. Furthermore, it seems unlikely that the influence of banking policy on the rate of interest will be sufficient by itself to determine an optimum rate of investment. I conceive, therefore, that a somewhat

comprehensive socialisation of investment will prove the only means of securing an approximation to full employment; ... (Keynes, 1987, p. 213).

The views exposed in his earlier works,[5] or his lectures show that the ideas expressed in the *General Theory* were the result of Keynes's conviction and commitment. In 1926, when the post-war boom was at its peak, he pointed out 'great inequalities in richness' in one of his lectures in Germany under the title *The End of Laissez-faire* and proposed the remedy that

> the cure lies outside the operations of individuals; it may even be to the interest of individuals to aggravate the disease. I believe that the cure for these things is partly to be sought in the deliberate control of the currency and credit by a central institution, and partly in the collection and dissemination on a great scale of data relating to the business situation...These measures would involve Society in exercising directive intelligence through some appropriate organ of action over many of the inner intricacies of private business, yet it would leave private initiative and enterprise unhindered (Keynes, 1994, p. 26).

The basic idea of Keynes was the escape from classical fallacies in order to remove the contradictions and the drawbacks of our economic society (Keynes, 1987, p. 210). He claimed that the market economy did not necessarily find an equilibrium at full employment, that is that it could be caught in an equilibrium trap at less than full employment, at such a balance of aggregate supply and aggregate demand – in which production is much smaller than the potential output and when, logically, there would be a great number of involuntary unemployed people. He emphasized that a lack of demand was possible, which meant a rejection of Say's law. Therefore, the government has the duty to enhance the weak demand by intervening through available measures. A fiscal policy including that of public debt and public spending can counter efficiently the disequilibrium. A deliberate budget deficit is an efficient instrument in overcoming such a sub-optimal situation which is harmful from the employment point of view.[6]

If fiscal policy is used 'as a thoughtful means of obtaining an even distribution of income' then its contribution to 'increasing the propensity to consume, is, of course, even greater' (Keynes, 1987, p. 69). That is to say, in crisis conditions when:

1. it is not possible to wait for these self-correcting forces to correct disequilibrium (to secure an equilibrium at full employment level),
2. it is not reasonable to expect that lowering of wages reduces unemployment, and
3. it is illusory to expect that lower interest rates will result in an increase of investment spending,

then the only remaining solution is government intervention so as to raise the aggregate demand. At a disequilibrium between aggregate supply and aggregate demand, the rules of balanced public spending must be relaxed to stimulate demand so as to reduce unemployment (see for a detailed analysis Galbraith, 1995, pp. 164, 171–4 and Tobin, 1983, pp. 19–22).

The essentials of Keynes's revolution in economic theory and economic policy are: the concept of an equilibrium at less than full employment level, rejection of Say's law and advocacy of deficit public spending in order to increase the level of effective demand.

The next 60 years

Keynes's theory made its way with some difficulty. The existing economic circumstances of the time, especially in the industrial countries very much helped his theory of employment to come into the limelight. Despite all this the classical orthodoxy was stubborn in its belief that a way out of the situation was only possible within the framework of its ideology.

But World War II in principle confirmed Keynes's theory and pushed aside classical thinking, because it was a time of unavoidable government intervention. In the UK (and in some cases even abroad) younger economists, who accepted Keynes's theory and economic policy, gained influential positions in the government so the road to implementation of his ideas was open. One of the essential facts derived from the war, in an economic sense, was a completely new vision of the role of government and the possible effects of its intervention (Galbraith, 1995, pp. 197–80).

As far as the 1970s, that is for 25 years after the war, there was no strong force in the economy of the industrial countries that would necessarily drive economics to face new challenges of life. The economy was in a state of 'balanced growth' and not, as the classicists expected, in a 'stationary state'. Those gloomy expectations of the classical economists have not been proved true, because most governments followed Keynes's policies and managed to reduce through governmental measures excessive rise and falls to moderate oscillations around a rising trend of production and prices. Employment also maintained a steady growth, but at a somewhat slower rate than the rise in per capita incomes and production (Napoleoni, 1992, p. 110). In the years immediately after the war, attention was mostly focused on the post-war reconstruction and recovery, and on the development of newly decolonized countries. It was then that a modern theory of growth, directly linked to Keynes's ideas, was founded in the famous Harrod–Domar model. However, two novelties: Leontief's output–input analysis, and Tinbergen's econometric models took root and became characteristic of this period.

One economic problem – which was constantly present in some form or other but did not attract great attention – that appeared at the end of the 1960s and early 1970s was a new type of inflation – the cost inflation, which meant a sudden rise in wages and prices.[7]

Keynesian economics did not have a 'right' and 'ready' answer as it did not pay appropriate attention to that problem. It was neither preoccupied with economic nor with political repercussions of inflation. The problem of inflation was 'left over' to microeconomics and classical market ideology (Galbraith, 1995, pp. 197–8).

In these circumstances, the monetarism of Milton Friedman appeared which forced the Keynesian paradigm into defence and retreat. The basic idea of monetarist theory was that all macroeconomic problems derived from a badly run monetary policy (Modigliani, 1991, p.16) from which one could conclude that the solution must only be sought in the monetary sphere.

This concept of monetary policy was based on the classical model – the model of the classical competitive market and disbelief in the authority of government. However it was also connected with Keynesianism in the belief that, at least in principle, monetary and fiscal policies affect money and real income. But, monetarists were stubborn to claim that only money was important. Keynesians, on the other hand, had a broader outlook and emphasized that 'money is important, but fiscal policy is also important'.

As inflation was progressing in the 1970s, and a proper solution could not have been found in higher taxes, lower public expenses, the control of wages and prices, the politicians in the US (Jimmy Carter) and in the UK (Margaret Thatcher) had recourse to measures of monetary policy, and the Keynesian approach had to give way to monetarism.

Several years were needed to stabilize prices. It is claimed that it was finally achieved in the 1980s. But it was at the expense of great sacrifices: the withering away of small firms, the inflow of foreign capital influencing the rise in value of the US dollar and thereby a fall in US exports and rise of imports, the deficit in balance of payments, the slowing down of economic growth, and rise of unemployment and so on. Some progress was visible. But the claim by the monetarists that monetary policy is a cheap anti-inflation strategy, proved to be unconvincing.

'Supply-side economics' was a great step forward for a tired US economy in the 1980s. There were two basic ideas in this concept. Firstly, an emphasis on motivation and supply, unlike the Keynesian emphasis on demand, and secondly, a considerable decrease in taxation. This model, which nevertheless cast some shadow over the Keynesian approach, was founded on classical principles, but it did not last long, as soon after the departure of its staunchest advocate, President Reagan, it was dropped.

Speaking about the supply-side economics one can conclude that opinions are diverse regarding its efficiency and theoretical foundation. However, practice did show that during this period: the budget deficit increased; inflation decreased but at a great price – recession, unemployment; national savings reached a low level; and, a fall of production was noted. This was all contrary to what the advocates of that idea were forecasting (Samuelson and Nordhaus, 1995, pp. 559–63; Thurow, 1987, pp. 93–104).

Although it had its roots even in the 1960s (for example Muth) and the traces could be found back in Keynes's *General Theory*, the rational expectations theory or new classical economics did emerge during the last 20 years (R. Lucas and others). It was founded on the classical approach and presuppositions that individuals base their expectations on the best available information, and that prices and wages are flexible, that is that they adapt very quickly to the balance of supply and demand (Thurow, 1983, pp. 106–24). The advocates of this theory consider that a great part of unemployment is voluntary.

Sixty years have passed since economics was permanently enriched by the Keynes's *General Theory*.

Economic theory 60 years after the *General Theory* and the present state of the economy of the world remains in a state of uncertainty. Many fresh ideas, opinions, and theories have developed. They all intertwine among themselves. All seem to be new shoots grafted on to the old branches, already dried up, which try to feed – with their sap – the tree that bears them. But times and circumstances change, bringing small or big changes, which are necessarily reflected in economic theory, because economic thought cannot, by any means, be separated from its economic context.

However, despite an intellectual confusion among the economists (Thurow, 1983, pp. 7–11) and despite, metaphorically speaking, numerous stronger or weaker lights which enlighten the ways of economics, the light of J.M. Keynes can easily be discerned. Time is the 'culprit' that its intensity has somewhat weakened, but nevertheless, Keynes's light still shows direction; there would be more wanderings and failures without it.

In modern market economics for the economy of the developing countries, of the countries in transition, and the developed countries, there is enough room for the application and combining of various models, including Keynes's.

Endnotes
1. It refers only to the theories which left deeper traces in the development of the economic thought.
2. Keynes decided to call the then existing approach 'classical theory', which he explained in note 1 in the first chapter of the *General Theory* (cf. Keynes, 1987, p. 13, 23).
3. Marshall, admittedly, also spoke about 'evils of inequality' without explanations and reserves. He proved theoretically that *laissez-faire* does not bring the maximum of welfare to the society as a whole (see Schumpeter, 1975, vol. II, p. 637).
4. The leading representative of German cameralism, J.H.G. Justi (1717–71) is considered to be one of the creators of the welfare state, and so it is logical that the idea of the welfare state, and its application, occurred in Germany first (see Schumpeter, 1975, pp. 142–4).
5. For example in his (1933), *Essays in Persuasion*, Keynes points out the necessity to reconcile 'utility and generosity' (Keynes, 1994, p. 26).

6. Keynes applied the new approach of deficit financing only when he entered the Treasury in the 1940s, and that was an 'intellectual revolution', as they called it then (Kahn, 1972, p. 107).
7. The oil shock of 1973 encouraged inflation a great deal in the industrial countries, when the members of OPEC increased the price of oil several times; from under US$3 a barrel in 1973 to almost US$11 in 1974 and above US$30 in 1982.

References

Chick, Victoria (1984), *Macroeconomics After Keynes – A Reconsideration of the General Theory*, Cambridge, Mass.: The MIT Press.

Galbraith, John K. (1995), *Ekonomija u perspektivi – kritička povijest*, Zagreb: Mate.

Harrod, Roy F. (1951), *The Life of John Maynard Keynes*, New York: Harcourt Brace.

Kahn, Richard (1972), *Selected Essays on Employment and Growth*, London: Cambridge University Press.

Keynes, John Maynard (1987), *Opća teorija zaposlenosti, kamate i novca*, Zagreb: Cekade.

Keynes, John Maynard (1994), 'Kraj laissez-fairca' in J.M. Keynes, *Izabrana djela*, Zagreb: Privredni vjesnik i Matica hrvatska, pp. 295–309.

Leijonhufvud, Axel (1983), *O kejnezijanskoj ekonomici i ekonomici J.M. Keynesa*, Zagreb: Cekade.

Modigliani, Franco (1991), *Rasprava o stabilizacijskoj politici*, Zagreb: Cekade.

Napoleoni, Claudio (1992), *Ekonomska misao dvadessetog stoljeća*, Zagreb: Cekade.

Samuelson, Paul A. and William D. Nordhaus (1995), *Economics*, 15th edn., New York: McGraw-Hill.

Schumpeter, Joseph A. (1975), *Povijest ekonomske analize*, Zagreb: Informator.

Thurow, L.C. (1983), *Dangerous Currents in the State of Economics*, New York: Vintage Books Random House.

Tobin, J. (1983), *Akumulacija imovine i ekonomska aktivnost*, Zagreb: Cekade.

PART II

GLOBAL GOVERNANCE
AND THE STATE

8   Keynes and global governance
Gerald M. Meier

Keynes wrote during the interwar period of international economic disintegration – a period that he recognized as far different from 'the extraordinary episode in the economic progress of man that.... came to an end in August 1914!' (Keynes, 1919, pp. 6–7). Beginning with *The Economic Consequences of the Peace*, Keynes sought to persuade the international community to re-establish elements of international economic harmony. Fifty years after Keynes's death, the forces of global integration have become ascendant. But now many of the issues of global governance that confronted Keynes still remain to be solved? In a decentralized world economy, how is international economic order to be established? How to establish norms and correct international economic conduct?

This chapter explores the problem of global governance by examining Keynes's views during the interwar period before Bretton Woods, his role at Bretton Woods, and finally, the future of global governance from the perspective of the past 50 years.

Problem of global governance
Economists now applaud the process of globalization because it integrates economies, promotes competition, and yields a more efficient allocation of resources on an international scale. To a national policy maker, however, internationalization is troubling: it heightens the vulnerability of a nation to external developments. Domestic autonomy in policy making is subordinated to international policy considerations. National politics is therefore likely to oppose international economics. And when the domestic economic objectives of different nations clash, international tension and conflict arise, often resulting in a zero sum game among nations.

These conflicts give rise to competitive governmental policies over markets, the terms of trade, the terms of foreign direct investment, over which country is to adjust to balance of payments problems, over domestic stabilization policies and conflicts over the common resources of the world and the environment.

In sum, international trade and financial conflicts can be grouped in three categories:

81

- those that arise because a nation seeks to acquire a larger share of the gains from trade or foreign investment;
- those that arise when a country tries to avoid being damaged by developments in another country; and
- those that arise because a country wants to maintain its domestic autonomy in policy making when confronted with an international event.

These various conflicts arise because the globalization process itself creates gains or losses to different nations and to different groups within a nation. As long as the forces of internationalization create dynamic change in world production and in the distribution of the world product, the distribution of benefits and detriments will be a vexing problem.

The driving technological, economic and political forces behind the internationalization process will not wane; but as internationalization proceeds, we shall have to seek policy solutions for future conflicts. The challenge is to improve these policy solutions and provide more effective structures of global governance. This is difficult because the outlines of decision-making processes in the world community remain vague, supranational institutions are few and their power to pursue international public policy making is limited.

There is no well-defined international normative process to keep pace with other features of the internationalization process. We therefore must search for a normative order that will accommodate conflicts, make better policy choices, and control change. Is it possible to establish more effective international public management, so that there will be an economic order with less discord? What rules, norms or standards can be invoked to control the behaviour of nations in the world economy?

Answers to these questions cannot come from a set of institutions that are already in place for economic management with a transitional reach. The world economy is a decentralized system that involves decisions by households and firms within each nation, national governments, regional organizations, multinational corporations, international agencies. There is no central decision mechanism, and – in a literal sense – there can be no 'management' of the international economy. We cannot yet appeal to an international public sector that might engage as extensively in international economic management as is done by national economic management. There is no international central bank. There is no international fiscal policy. There is no international anti-trust legislation. There is no international industrial policy. There is no international regulation of the natural environment.

What then are the institutions and procedures for making decisions that might govern international order? Before considering answers for the future, we may gain some insights by reviewing Keynes's views on the problem of global governance.

Interwar views

From Keynes's writings during the interwar period, we can glean his thoughts on the governance of international economic affairs.[1]

His first work – *Indian Currency and Finance* (1913) – was concerned with international monetary arrangements, a concern that was to remain until his death. His desire to eliminate gold – 'a relic of a time when governments were less trustworthy' (p. 51) – was to persist until he gained its demise at Bretton Woods.

Keynes's next classic – *The Economic Consequences of the Peace* (1919) – argued for the precedence of economics over politics in re-establishing the benefits of an orderly international economy, rationally designed. In the pre-war economy, the interference of frontiers and tariffs had been reduced to a minimum and there had been an easy flow of capital and trade (p. 13). The earlier global system, based on free trade with the export of capital, which had supported a growing population with an increasing standard of living, depended on a shared morality. As Skidelsky (1983, pp. 384–5) notes, 'Keynes was staking the claim of the economist to be Prince. All other forms of rule were bankrupt. The economist's vision of welfare, conjoined to a new standard of technical excellence, were the last barriers to chaos, madness and retrogression.' Moreover 'The war had been fought in the name of nation, state, emperor. These, Keynes argued, were false gods, from whom he sought to divert allegiance towards economic tasks. It was a message calculated to appeal to the nation of Cobden and Bright.... It helped form the outlook of a new generation. The nineteen-twenties saw a new breed of economist-politician, who talked about the gold standard and the balance of trade as fluently as pre-war politicians had talked about the Two-Power standard and the balance of power....The idea that the creation of opulence was the main task of rulers was born in 1919 though it came of age only after the Second World War. The Keynes of the *General Theory*...cannot be separated from the Keynes of the *Economic Consequences*....' (Skidelsky, 1983, p. 399).

Clearly evident in these early works was Keynes's critique of gold, his emphasis on the proper management of international credits, and the foundations for his proposal of the 'bancor' system as the basis for international monetary reconstruction after World War II (Johnson, 1978, pp. 111–18).

His writings in *The Nation* during the 1920s were in response to Britain's unemployment and argued against anti-deflation policies and against a return to gold at the pre-war pound:dollar rate. Mistakenly, however, in a neo-Malthusian fashion Keynes asserted that unemployment was in part a problem of population. He was also critical of foreign investment: an excessive amount of savings went abroad that could have been usefully invested at home, 'and must be if our national equipment is to grow as fast as the population.'[2]

The *Tract on Monetary Reform* (1923) was the start of Keynes's macro-theory, advocating monetary management to control the business cycle. His attack on the gold standard persisted: periodic devaluations should be allowed according to the needs of the domestic economy. Domestic price stability should be preferred to external exchange stability. There should be management of the dollar and pound, with other countries basing their currencies on the dollar or pound. Moreover, he asserted the 'right of the State to control vested interest.'[3]

In objecting to a restoration of the gold standard, Keynes observed that the British should not generalize their own national practices – or what they imagined their national practices to have been – into an objective code of good behaviour that other nations would follow more or less automatically. Keynes recognized that other nations might define their interest in terms other than a British code of behaviour, and that it would not be in Britain's national interests to try to restore a system that it could no longer control.[4] If Britain no longer had the power to manage an international system, national self-sufficiency became the only viable option.

The End of Laissez Faire (1926) was a strong plea for public policy to restore the peace and prosperity of the pre-war epoch. 'It is not a correct deduction from the principles of economics that enlightened self-interest always operates in the public interest....We must aim,' he said, 'at separating those services which are technically social from those which are technically individual.' The most important items on the Agenda of government are 'those functions which fall outside the sphere of the individual, to those decisions which are made by no one if the State does not make them.' Keynes then advocates 'deliberate control of the currency and of credit by a central institution...a coordinated act of intelligent judgement' concerning the aggregate volume of savings and their distribution between home and foreign investment, and a population policy. Although Skidelsky (1994, p. 228) recognizes that *The End of Laissez Faire* is a flawed production, he concludes that 'it remains the most impressive short attempt on record to define a social and economic philosophy fit for the time of troubles framed by the two world wars.'

In his *Treatise on Money* (1930), Keynes returned to his dominant theme that the monetary system exercised the 'central controls of our economic life' and that the monetary authority should regulate the stock of money so as to keep savings equal to investment. The overriding objective is to preserve both internal equilibrium and external equilibrium: internal equilibrium should not be subordinated to external change. Again, there was the criticism of the gold standard, and the persistent questioning of whether there should be an international standard of value (p. 332). The practice of foreign investment was also again criticized: it would worsen the terms of trade or else cause bank rate to be raised with resultant unemployment. Significantly for his future international monetary proposals, Keynes proposed an increase in international liquidity with reserves in foreign exchange and fiduciary reserves in a supernational bank (Keynes, 1930, vol. 2, pp. 395 ff). He expressed 'great hopes in a Supernational Bank for the future' (p. 311) with deposits of 'supernational bank-money' (p. 399). The objective of the supernational bank was to avoid inflations and deflations of an international character. Chapter 38 of the *Treatise* discusses 'Problems of Supernational Management'. There is also the proposal of an international commodity standard (p. 391).

At the World Economic Conference in 1933, Keynes proposed an international authority issuing gold-convertible notes to increase international liquidity, a fixed parity with gold, but exchange rate fluctuations of plus/minus 2.5 per cent on either side of parity. The *de facto* parity should also be alterable if necessary from time to time. The Conference, however, took no action.

Although he sought international governance of the monetary system, Keynes advocated nationalistic measures in trade policy. His article on 'National Self Sufficiency' (1933a) recognized the logic of the free trader, but argued that in the context of 1932–3 protection could benefit Britain. In 1930–31, Keynes had argued for the short-term advantages in protection over the alternative of devaluation. Writing again on 'National Self Sufficiency' (1933b), Keynes stated that contrary to his long time belief in free trade, 'the orientation of my mind is changed' and that he now sympathizes with those who would minimize, rather than with those who would maximize, economic entanglement among nations....[L]et goods be homespun whenever it is reasonably and conveniently possible, and, above all, let finance be primarily national.' (p. 758)...[E]conomic internationalism embracing the free movement of capital and of loanable funds as well as of traded goods may condemn my own country for a generation to come to a much lower degree of material prosperity than could be attained under a different system' (p. 763). But protectionism was only warranted by the depression context of the early 1930s, and there were dangers in economic nationalism – namely, 'silliness, haste, and intolerance of criticism.'

As a member of the Macmillan Committee (1930), Keynes had recognized the international character of the depression – 'the downward slope of an international credit cycle.' The troubles were not primarily domestic: 'the international problem is at least equally important' (Skidelsky, 1994, p. 355–6). When, however, he wrote *The General Theory of Employment, Interest and Money* (1936), he restricted his analysis to a model of the closed economy. There was no concern for or intimation of anything that he was to propose five years later when he began to write on the post-war currency problem. Not the *General Theory* but *How to Pay for the War* (1940) – with its concern for Britain's external financial position and the shape of the post-war world – was the predecessor for Keynes's 1941 memoranda on 'Post-War Currency Policy' and 'Proposals for an International Clearing Union.'

To summarize: Keynes never wrote directly about politics but he was deeply concerned about public affairs throughout the interwar period. In his economic writings, political activities, and policy advising, his guidelines were those of reason and the scientific approach to policy issues. To Keynes, a policy failure was the result of mistaken theory. The economist was a Platonic Guardian who could shape economic policy for the intelligent management of short-run problems (Skidelsky, 1994, p. 224). A world of economic change called for the end of *laissez-faire* and a positive agenda for government. But while Keynes gave much attention to domestic policies for economic prosperity, his attention to international problems was only secondary. As for international liberalization, he was at best ambivalent. He strongly opposed the confines of the gold standard, but he did recommend protection in the Great Depression, and he criticized foreign investment. Although he concentrated on savings and investment, he did so only in the context of a closed economy. National autonomy in policy making should 'enable a Central Bank to protect the credit structure of its own country from the repercussions of purely temporary disturbances abroad' (Keynes 1930, vol. 2, p. 326). In focusing on such international problems as reparations, international currency arrangements, war finance, and post-war reconstruction, Keynes could have elicited principles of international governance. But before Bretton Woods, he rarely did so. Instead, to the extent that the national interests of Britain were his first priority, his attention to international governance was diminished.

Bretton Woods

Keynes's views on global governance came to be most clearly expressed in connection with the establishment of the Bretton Woods institutions. His first proposal for an International Clearing Union was prefaced with the following summary of the mistakes of history:

So far from currency *laissez-faire* having promoted the international division of labour, which is the avowed goal of *laissez-faire*, it has been a fruitful source of all those clumsy hindrances to trade which suffering communities have devised in their perplexity as being better than nothing in protecting them from the intolerable burdens flowing from currency disorders. Until quite recently, nearly all departures from international *laissez-faire* have tackled the symptoms instead of the cause.

International currency *laissez-faire* was breaking down rapidly before the war. During the war it had disappeared completely. This complete break with the past offers us an opportunity. Things are possible today which would have been impossible if they involved the prior disestablishment of a settled system.

Moreover in the interval between the wars the world explored in rapid succession almost, as it were, in an intensive laboratory experiment all the alternative false approaches to the solution:

1. The idea that a freely fluctuating exchange would discover for itself a position of equilibrium;
2. Liberal credit and loan arrangements between the creditor and the debtor countries flowing from the mere fact of an unbalanced creditor–debtor position, on the false analogy of superficially similar nineteenth-century transactions between old-established and newly developing countries where the loans were self-liquidating because they themselves created new sources of payment;
3. The theory that the unlimited free flow of gold would automatically bring about adjustments of price levels and activity in the recipient country which would reverse the pressure;
4. The use of deflation, and still worse of competitive deflations, to force an adjustment of wage and price levels which would force or attract trade into new channels;
5. The use of deliberate exchange depreciation, and still worse of competitive exchange depreciations, to attain the same object;
6. The erection of tariffs, preferences, subsidies *et hoc genus omne* to restore the balance of international commerce by restriction and discrimination.[5]

With these lessons in mind, and looking to the future, Keynes's objectives were to avoid the recurrence of a depression in the US that would spread to other countries, to allow nations to pursue full employment policies without concern for the external value of their currency, and to deal with an anticipated surplus in the US balance of payments without nations having to resort to restrictive and discriminatory measures of trade policy.

His overall view of global governance was that international organizations should allow nations to achieve internal balance and external balance without sacrificing full employment and the gains from trade. This required nations to accept the unprecedented actions of surrendering sovereignty over their exchange rates and creating international liquidity by a collective decision. The mistakes of the interwar period were to be avoided by creating a post-war economic system ruled by law.

To this end, Keynes's International Clearing Union would have established considerable official international liquidity based on international bank money (called bancor), a margin of flexible exchange rates subject to institutional approval, and obligations of remedial policies of adjustment to be undertaken by creditor as well as debtor countries.

To achieve the objectives of the International Clearing Union, Keynes enunciated some principles of international economic diplomacy that are highly relevant for global governance. If 'an international economic system... is to prove durable':

1. There should be the least possible interference with internal national policies, and the plan should not wander from the international *terrain.*
2. The technique of the plan must be capable of application, irrespective of the type and principle of government and economic policy existing in the prospective member states.
3. The management of the Institution must be genuinely international without preponderant power of veto or enforcement to any country or group; and the rights and privileges of the smaller countries must be safeguarded.
4. Some qualification of the right to act at pleasure is required by any agreement or treaty between nations. But in order that such arrangements may be fully voluntary so long as they last and terminable when they have become irksome, provision must be made for voiding the obligation at due notice. If many member states were to take advantage of this, the plan would have broken down. But if they are free to escape from its provisions if necessary they may be the more willing to go on accepting them.
5. The plan must operate not only to the general advantage but also to the individual advantage of each of the participants, and must not require a special economic or financial sacrifice from certain countries. No participant must be asked to do or offer anything which is not to his own true long-term interest . . . .

> More generally, we need a means of reassurance to a troubled world, by which any country whose own affairs are conducted with due prudence is relieved of anxiety for causes which are not of its own making, concerning its ability to meet its international liabilities; and which will, therefore, make unnecessary those methods of restriction and discrimination which countries have adopted hitherto, not on their merits, but as measures of self-protection from disruptive outside forces.[6]

Keynes placed his specific proposal for an International Clearing Union in a much wider political and economic context. In the original Preface to his Proposals, for instance, Keynes had argued that international economic cooperation should proceed along four main lines: (1) the mechanism of currency and exchange; (2) commercial policy; (3) production, distribution and pricing of primary products; and (4) international investment. But Keynes never related Bretton Woods to his own plan for primary products, and he left it to the Americans to devise an international investment organization.

After Bretton Woods, Keynes argued against the perpetuation of organized trade discrimination by Britain. Believing that the US would not resort again to isolationism, he advocated a multilateral system.

There was also the anticipation that after the Bretton Woods conference another international organization would be established to deal with trade policies. In 1945, there was the Havana Charter with a proposal for the International Trade Organization, but it was never ratified by the US Congress.

The IMF (International Monetary Fund) and IBRD (International Bank for Reconstruction and Development) thus stood in isolation – there was not the co-ordinated institutional recognition of the interdependence of trade, investment and finance. Only a partial step toward global governance was taken.

Future in perspective
Let us now consider the future of global governance from the perspective of Keynes – 50 years on and beyond.

Keynesian analysis has concentrated on the domestic public sector. Although there is no fully developed international public sector, there are elements of such a sector: for instance, the IMF, World Bank group, GATT (General Agreement on Tariffs and Trade) and WTO (World Trade Organization), and specialized agencies of the UN. In combination with the operation of international market forces, these institutions establish a variety of international governance mechanisms. A number of extra-market mechanisms also influence international economic conduct: international codes of conduct as represented by the IMF and WTO, international treaties (Treaty of Rome, NAFTA (North American Free Trade Agreement)), negotiation or bargaining (OPEC (Organization of Petroleum Exporting Countries), Paris Club), arbitration, adjudication, and policy co-ordination among countries to reach a collective decision that resolves conflict (creation of SDRs (Special Drawing Rights), Louvre agreement on exchange rates).

Given an international policy problem, what mechanism or mechanisms of governance are most appropriate? Most of these problems do not lend themselves to mathematics-intensive policy analysis or to 'optimization science'. For the problems normally involve multiple principals and agents, an ill-defined objective function, variables that are not amenable to subjective probability analysis, and outcomes that cannot be converted to a single utility index. Especially significant is the distinction between 'instrumental rationality' and 'constitutive rationality'. The former is the basis of a rational choice model in which an objective is predetermined, dominant weight is given to the attainment of efficiency relative to other values, and one seeks the most effective policy instrument to achieve the objective. In contrast, 'constitutive rationality' requires a 'constitution', that is, decisions about how decisions are to be made. Many of the issues calling for global governance require a determination of the way in which decisions will be made and the boundary of the decisions. Most of the tensions and conflicts that arise from changes in the world economy need for their resolution a governance mechanism that will ameliorate the conflict, provide some social control of the allocation of benefits and costs, and exercise some means of monitoring orderly change.

Although at the level of transnational governance, policy analysis cannot be as rigorous as at the national level, we may at least establish some criteria by which to evaluate the different mechanisms of international governance.

Evaluating a particular policy, a benefit-cost analysis would consider the fulfilment of the objective of the international policy, its external benefits, economic costs to the governing agency and the affected parties, detrimental externalities, and the transition or adjustment costs to the final state.

There are also other objectives to be evaluated beyond the fulfilment of the policy's immediate objective, namely, efficiency, equity, and the appropriateness of the process or procedure for reaching the policy decision.

Finally, there are criteria of 'policy technology': the information needed, speed of implementation, specificity in results, simplicity in operation, reversibility or corrective mechanisms, and the jurisdictional domain (correspondence between the reach of the policy and the operational area of the activity being controlled).

Various governance mechanisms will meet these criteria to different degrees. The market, for instance, would receive high marks for such criteria as efficiency, process, information, implementation and simplicity. But the state might devise governance mechanisms that would merit higher marks for equity, specificity, reversibility and jurisdictional domain.

Among the various governance mechanisms, centralized decision making and codes of conduct are the most difficult to establish. To reach agreement among diverse countries, any code will have to contain loopholes and escape clauses that will render the code ineffective, or it will have to be written to satisfy the demands of the lowest common denominator. Otherwise, the code is likely to impose undesirable rigidity, provoke unnecessary controversy, and overstress control or the negative aspects instead of facilitating the creation of opportunities, providing incentives, and promoting desired behaviour. Even the GATT and WTO are not really legalistic, but a form of what has more aptly been called 'diplomats' jurisprudence'.

Nor did the Articles of Agreement of the IMF attempt to specify the meaning of the key condition of 'fundamental disequilibrium', but left it to future consultation. The ambiguity in the operations of these international organizations demonstrates that their effectiveness depends on consensus, and that nations must agree on the constitutive rationality of rules. Absent global government or adherence to a definitive international code of conduct, the international economic conduct of firms and states needs to be shaped by other forms of global governance.

The need for an international reach in policy making is simply a corollary of the principle that the level at which a decision is taken should be high enough to cover the area in which the impact is non-negligible. In order that the decisions regarding necessary policy instruments be optimal, there must not be 'external' effects, that is, the influences exerted on the well-being of groups outside the jurisdiction of those who make the decision should be weak. The area in which the impact of the instrument will be felt determines what decision level will be optimal. For many issues that we have discussed, the nation state is an inappropriate decision-making unit. Decisions taken at the national level are often far too low to be optimal.[7] Governance must reach beyond national jurisdiction.

The Bretton Woods Conference and the Havana Charter recognized some of these underlying issues of governance. But they did not deal with other issues that still remain unsettled. And with intensified globalization, unforeseen problems have come to the fore.

During the first 25 years of its operation, the IMF performed effectively, essentially in conformity with Keynes's views. But during the second 25 years of its operation, the Fund has had to be modified in conformity with changes in the world economy that were unanticipated by Keynes.

At Bretton Woods there were 44 nations; today 180 nations are members of the IMF. Many of these are less developed. Although Keynes was chairman of the World Bank commission, he gave little attention to problems of economic development. Indeed, on arrival at Bretton Woods, he sent the following dispatch to the British Treasury:

> Twenty-one countries have been invited which clearly have nothing to contribute and will merely encumber the ground, namely, Colombia, Costa Rica, Dominica, Ecuador, Salvador, Guatemala, Haiti, Honduras, Liberia, Nicaragua, Panama, Paraguay, Philippines, Venezuela, Peru, Uruguay, Ethiopia, Iceland, Iran, Iraq, and Luxembourg – the most monstrous monkey-house assembled for years. To these might perhaps be added: Egypt, Chile and (in present circumstances) Yugoslavia.[8]

Bretton Woods was dominated by the US and the UK, who wanted to avoid a recurrence of the pre-war Great Depression and the international currency disintegration of the interwar years. The Anglo-American collaboration originally viewed European reconstruction as the fundamental problem of the time. When the Mexican delegation pressed for equal treatment in the Bank, they had to settle for 'equitable' treatment. Nor was any special reference made in the IMF's articles to 'economically underdeveloped countries' or 'economically backward countries' as the Indian delegation had sought. Instead, the Fund emphasized the principle of uniformity – the rights and obligations are the same for all countries, regardless of their stage of development.

After Bretton Woods, however, came a wave of decolonization and the 'revolution of rising expectations'. Since the mid-1970s, less developed countries (LDCs) have become the major users of IMF resources. And today the transition economies join the LDCs as the main clients of the Bank and Fund. Although during the 50 years since Bretton Woods, the World Bank and IMF have added functions directed to developing countries. The central question is: have these institutions evolved sufficiently to be effective in meeting the present – and future – problems of the LDCs and transition economies?

While Keynes concentrated on the savings-investment problem in a closed economy, it is now the international savings-investment problem that is important for development internationally. Keynes's concern with over-saving has given way to the present concern with under-saving.

There still is, however, the persistent Keynesian questions of whether there is sufficient international official liquidity and what should be the responsibilities of the surplus country. And while Keynes worried about unemployment in advanced economies, the major problem now is that of surplus labour in the less developed economies. Fifty years ago, one could not have imagined the success stories of East Asia, but we now confront the challenge that in the next 20 years the world's labourforce will increase by 40 per cent, and 95 per cent of this increase will be in developing countries that will account for less than 15 per cent of the world's capital investments.[9] The Bretton Woods institutions will have to respond to this challenge of transferring savings from rich countries to poor countries with surplus labour.

Despite the increase in international liquidity provided by the IMF and the loans from the World Bank, the international public sector has not yet solved the international saving-investment problem. Bretton Woods was unwilling to follow Keynes and create more international official liquidity and also to put pressure on chronic surplus countries. Instead, the international financial intermediation task of transferring savings from rich countries to investment in the poor countries and transition economies was met first through the US balance of payments until 1971, and then through the World Bank group, IMF, and Eurocurrency loans from commercial banks. Not only do problems of debt servicing and conditionality remain, but so too does the severe fundamental problem of providing a greater net resource transfer to the LDCs and the transition economies. These challenges mean that if the domestic public sector in the LDC or transition economy is to be diminished through policies of stabilization, liberalization and privatization, the international public sector will actually have to be strengthened. The IMF, World Bank and WTO will have to support the economy's structural transformation through demand management and supply management based on project and programme loans, budgetary support, and balance of payments support.

Prospects for debt flows are limited. The worldwide competition for private capital combined with a decline in official development assistance intensifies the demand for increased flows from the World Bank group. At the same time, resources of the World Bank are not increasing sufficiently in real terms. Replenishments of the International Development Association (IDA), soft loan window of the Bank, are still insufficient to meet the growing needs of eligible countries. A capital increase for the International Finance Corporation (equity lending agency of the bank) is also required.

After Bretton Woods, the hegemony of the US was to disappear along with the dollar shortage. Inflation – not depression – became the central post-war problem. International capital movements grew markedly. Regional blocs arose. The new protectionism was practised by many countries. And the transition economies sought to liberalize and integrate into the world economy.

With the US's unilateral action in 1971 of removing two foundations of the IMF, namely, the par-value system of exchange rates and the gold convertibility of the dollar, the Fund's management of exchange rates was weakened by the establishment of floating exchange rates, albeit with interventions by central banks and monetary authorities.

The IMF has also been marginalized through actions of the G-7 and the rise of regional associations. But while the Fund is now less significant for G-7 countries, its functions have become of extreme importance to developing countries and transition economies – its main clients. Much of the success from adopting appropriate policies within developing countries and transition economies now depends on the conditionality exercised by the Fund, together with policy advice offered by the World Bank.

In the future the Fund may become even more influential if it devises mechanisms to meet the serious international problem of incomplete risk markets. With floating exchange rates and the globalization of financial markets, the risks from volatile price changes have increased. The risks have increased especially for developing countries that experience volatility in international commodity prices and the repercussions of wide movements in exchange rates and interest rates. Although the solution is not to fix prices, some institutional changes – led by the IMF – should be devised that would allow world capital markets to spread risk and permit it to be borne more efficiently.

Most important, in the changing world economy, the World Bank, IMF and WTO must recognize the interdependence of trade, investment, and finance and co-ordinate their operational activities accordingly. The WTO should complement the programmes of the Bank and Fund more than did GATT. Joint consultations among the three institutions are needed to consider how trade policy affects the balance of payments or other monetary issues, and, in turn, how monetary affairs, including exchange rates, can affect trade policy. An integrated approach is especially relevant for governing the developing countries. Although the time has not yet come for a merger of the IMF and World Bank, they too will have to collaborate more closely on common problems of governance.

It may be asked why not simply leave the 'rules of the game' with respect to international trade and an international monetary regime to the operation of international market forces? Governments have revealed that this will not be allowed. Governments intervene to affect the direction, composition, and terms of trade. And they intervene to affect the foreign exchange rate. An international public sector is therefore necessary, not only to remedy international market failure, but also to mitigate competitive policy making by national governments. If the IMF was initially concerned with the avoidance of competitive devaluations, international economic agents now have to be concerned with international competitive monetary policies, competitive subsidization policies, competitive trade policies and competitive foreign investment policies. The forces of globalization and liberalization create conflicts in international monetary and trade affairs that call for surveillance over international economic conduct and efforts at international peace-keeping. Improvement in global governance is as important as improvement in domestic governance especially with respect to trade policy, international monetary affairs, international development and multinational enterprises.

Of these problem areas, Keynes was mainly concerned with international monetary affairs. Still unresolved are some of the fundamental issues of international monetary reform that exercised Keynes throughout the interwar period and at Bretton Woods. As long ago as 1972, the Executive Directors of the IMF published a study on *Reform of the International Monetary System.* This report identified five main problem areas of the international monetary system that may call for new arrangements through international discussion and negotiation:

1. the exchange rate mechanism, including both the indications of when changes in par-values are necessary and the respective responsibilities of the deficit and surplus countries for making par-value changes;
2. the re-establishment of convertibility and the arrangements for the settlement of imbalances among countries;
3. the position in the system of the various reserve assets and in particular the status and function to be given to foreign exchange reserves, gold, and SDRs;
4. the problem of disequilibrating capital movements and what might be done to lessen the intense market pressures that accompany them; and
5. the possibility of new provisions in the Fund arrangements for the special needs of developing countries.

Twenty-five years later, this is still a succinct summary of the agenda for international monetary reform.

The dimensions of an international monetary system involve foreign exchange rates, nature of official reserves and degree of convertibility. The functions involve provision of liquidity, adjustment mechanisms and confidence. The dimensions and functions may be established by any of a number of organizing principles: automaticity (as in the pure gold standard with spontaneous governance by the market and complete domestic autonomy), supranationality (as with the IMF and its extra-market code of conduct), hegemony (as when the US was the hegemonic power and the dollar ruled), or negotiation (as in the Plaza and Louvre agreements or establishment of the SDR-based on international agreement). Application of these principles affects national sovereignty, the degree of domestic autonomy in policy making and especially the burden of the adjustment mechanism.

Exchange rates   We may recognize some strong reasons for believing that freely floating exchange rates is the best exchange rate regime. The impersonal and non-politicized market price system may be favoured by economists. But the exchange rate is a special type of price affecting all tradables, and governments reveal their preference for intervention to manage their exchange rates. Going against the market, governments resort to competitive depreciations and the use of the exchange rate as an instrument of trade policy. To counter these actions, a clear and predictable code of conduct with some sanctions would be desirable.

Since the beginning of managed floating in the early 1970s, however, the IMF has been marginalized, and the best it can do is attempt some surveillance of exchange rates. Although the IMF may profess surveillance as an absolute priority,[10] the present monetary regime still makes the practice difficult. The Fund is limited in its ability to control volatile exchange rates, disequilibrating capital movements and governmental interventions. The provision of data to the Fund and consultations help, but without a strong code of conduct the Fund's governance of member actions remains weak.

For those seeking a stronger system of governance, the concepts of 'objective indicators' and 'target zones' have recurrent appeal. Countries appear unwilling, however, to agree on the magnitudes of 'objective indicators' or to undertake the degree of international policy co-ordination required to maintain exchange rates within target zones. The leading proposal of target zones, by John Williamson of the Institute for International Economics, would commit the G7 countries to using monetary and fiscal policy, as well as intervention, to keep their exchange rates within bands of plus or minus 10 per cent around an 'internationally agreed' estimate of the 'fundamental equilibrium exchange rate,' which would be automatically adjusted to allow for differential rates of inflation (in effect, a system of crawling pegs surrounded by bands). Monetary policy would be designed in part to avoid real exchange rate disequilibrium while fiscal policy would be assigned to stabilizing domestic demand. The IMF would be responsible for servicing the international policy co-ordination process.[11]

Of this proposal, however, *The Economist* states:

As Benjamin Cohen, of the University of California at Santa Barbara puts it, 'International monetary cooperation, like passionate love, is a good thing, but difficult to sustain.' Experience shows that policy coordination between the three big economies, America, Japan and Germany, is not willing to subordinate national economic policy to an international target. It is hard enough to get agreement on interest-rate changes; on fiscal policy it is near impossible. And yet it was fiscal policy that was largely to blame for the two greatest exchange-rate upsets in recent years – in America in the 1980s and Germany after unification.

Another snag is that nobody is sure what might be the 'right' level for the dollar, or any other currency. There is no reason why governments should be better judges than the markets. Moreover, even if the governments of the big three economies could agree on policies to keep currencies within their bands, target zones would still be vulnerable to speculative attack as rates approached their limits. In a world of highly mobile capital, there may be no comfortable middle ground between floating exchange rates and permanently fixed rates. Pegged but adjustable exchange rates tend to be unstable.[12]

Far short of the ideal of macroeconomic governance of the exchange rate regime, the feasible arrangements that nations will tolerate in the near future are probably limited to more intensive surveillance by the IMF and the imposition of the Fund's conditionality over a country's exchange rate and macro policies when it draws on its upper credit tranches in the Fund.

Liquidity   The amount of liquidity created by the IMF also affects the governance of balance of payments policy. The greater the amount of official international liquidity and the more receptive is the lender of last resort, the less is the discipline exercised by the balance of payments. Just as there is a question of what is the 'right' exchange rate, however, so too is there a question of what is the 'right' amount of liquidity and how should it be created and for whom? With the internationalization of financial markets and the large flows of private capital, one may argue that there is no shortage of liquidity. If creditworthy, countries can engage in sovereign borrowing from international capital markets. The issue, however, is the adequacy of a country's 'owned reserves', without recourse to debt.

The IMF still believes that official reserves should be provided by an international institution. An international decision to increase quotas in the IMF and possibly a new allocation of SDRs could be more efficient and equitable than resort to independent accumulation of 'borrowed reserves' from private capital markets. And, of course, if the IMF were ever to evolve into a World Central Bank, it would have to influence or control international liquidity creation.

The management of the IMF estimated that the global demand for reserves would expand by several hundred billion SDRs during the sixth allocation period of quotas (1992–6). Moreover, at the end of 1992, 20 per cent of the developing countries, and nearly 40 per cent of the transition countries, held non-gold international reserves equivalent to less than eight weeks of imports. An allocation of owned reserves is deemed especially necessary for the growth of the LDCs and transition economies.

Even though in the last two decades the share of SDRs in world reserves has averaged only some 5.3 per cent, its share has actually diminished in recent years. If the SDR is ever to become 'the principal reserve asset' of the international monetary system as specified in the IMF's Articles of Agreement, an increase in SDRs will be necessary. Although some would favour a special SDR allocation to the developing countries, such special and differential treatment has been denied previously, and it remains unlikely to happen as the IMF reasserts its principle of uniformity in governance. Opposition to an increase in SDRs is also likely to come from industrial countries that enjoy low costs of holding other reserves and see little benefit from SDR allocations that do not give a rate of return above that of other reserve assets.

Adjustment   The relation of international governance to balance of payments adjustment policies is subsumed under the feasible degree of governance over exchange rates, macro-policy co-ordination, and provision of official liquidity. Underlying this issue, however, is the stumbling block of imposing symmetric adjustment responsibilities on the deficit country and surplus countries. And how can the burden of adjustment be minimized?

While deregulation of national capital markets and the liberalization of international banking and capital markets have been beneficial, they have also imposed costs of greater financial instability and fragility. Systemic risk across markets has become more internationalized. Policy issues related to exchange rates, liquidity, and adjustment are being increasingly shaped by the rapid expansion of global financial markets.

This expansion raises policy questions of global supervision and regulation. Together with the Bank of International Settlements (BIS), the IMF must become more involved with harmonizing different national regulatory authorities and avoiding financial crises that create major international adjustment problems. The Mexican peso crisis in 1994 illustrates the need for the IMF to help countries deal with temporary balance of payments difficulties that stem from capital flows. To help governments cope with speculative attacks on their foreign exchange markets, the IMF may have to establish an intervention fund.

Although the IMF has been the prime agent in governing adjustment policies, greater collaboration with the World Bank and the WTO is desirable. A study of the Fund's historical evolution and the key issues in the future concludes as follows:

'The world faces an institutional choice between an order in which these aspects of surveillance (over management of global liquidity, adjustment policies, confidence, and trade policy) are fragmented and treated in separation, with a smaller IMF or, preferably, one in which the elements of surveillance are more effectively coordinated, with a stronger IMF. The case for greater coordination between international institutions rests on the substantial extent of the linkages that exist between different global economic problems. Issues such as interest rate levels, macro-economic orientation, debtor problems, and capital flows cannot be treated adequately in isolation from each other.'[13]

International co-operation   Over the past 50 years, the Keynesian preoccupation with macroeconomic policy has stimulated interest in the possibilities for international co-operation – ranging from the exchange of information and consultation to the co-ordination of policy decisions among nations. Or they might even agree on presumptive rules that limit national discretion and constrain the use of international policy instruments.[14]

Periodically 'top level' negotiations among nation states may reach understandings or formal agreements that establish the 'rules of the game' for a given area of international economic conduct. An international regime environment is thus created. Such a regime has at least two dimensions or attributes. One dimension refers to the incidence of agreements among national governments and the principles, norms, rules, and decision-making procedures around which their expectations converge. Another dimension indicates the numbers and strengths of international or supranational institutions and the forums, processes, and decision-making procedures that may be associated with them.

Some types of international regimes also have another dimension denoting the extent of rules versus discretion. Strong governance in an international monetary regime, for example, would emphasize rules of conduct over the discretionary action by national governments. The collapse of the Bretton Woods regime in the early 1970s with a move to flexible exchange rates diminished international co-operation and allowed more national discretion with respect to exchange rates. Through economic summits with the G7, consultations within the OECD, meetings of the Bank for International Settlements and greater surveillance by the IMF, there could in the future be a weak movement towards more international co-operation and governance of the international monetary regime.

Few would deny the desirability of greater global or transnational governance. A summary case for more governance over international economic transactions can be made as follows. 'Spontaneous' governance through international markets is not sufficient because some markets are missing, incomplete or subject to market failure.[15] Especially significant are externalities that spill over from one country to another. Not valued by any market, these externalities have to be internalized by mechanisms of governance. When the cross-border spillovers are detrimental, other nations need to be protected from damage. When the externalities are beneficial, a greater supply needs to be encouraged. The forces of globalization are now increasing cross-border spillovers that call for more international management.

The market also underestimates international public goods (the environment, monetary stability). Moreover, competitive policy making by nations needs to be avoided. Instead of allowing 'beggar-my-neighbour' policies, mechanisms of governance should seek policy optimization in the sense of making all countries better off (avoidance of trade wars, avoidance of competitive depreciation). Intergovernmental co-operation and co-ordination are required.

Governance beyond the nation is also necessary to give jurisdictional reach over economic conduct that is international in scope. The activities of multinationals cannot be covered by simply national regulations; nor can the allocation of the world's resources that are shared among nations (ocean mining, space) be solved by only national legislation.

The feasibility of transnational governance, however, is limited for a number of reasons. National governments are unwilling to give up sovereignty or their domestic autonomy in policy making. Prisoner's dilemma type of situations also apply. Each country has an incentive to act rationally at the other's expense, but the result is collective irrationality as both lose if both act according to only self-interest. In their self-interest, countries pursue a protectionist trade policy although it would be in their collective interest to follow free trade. But free trade is not a natural order; it must be enforced by governance mechanisms that lead each country to act in its self-interest and collective interest.

Governance that promotes a common goal or common interest among nations can be viewed as an international public good: all countries benefit, irrespective of whether they have contributed to its costs or not.[16] But the free rider problem results in an undersupply of international public goods. Each country, knowing that others may not contribute, lacks the incentive to contribute to something that benefits others, including itself. If countries want to be free riders and not contribute, of if they fear that, even if they do contribute, no other country does, then the outcome will be that no country contributes.

In game-theoretic analysis of strategic interactions among individual decision makers, the 'supply of co-operation' often falls short of what would be mutually beneficial because collective action is a public good. Individual agents, making decentralized and rational decisions, may fail to achieve their mutual interest. These general results for individuals are all the more likely to occur when national governments are the individual decision-making agents.[17]

A corollary is that 'public bads' are oversupplied. A single country tends to have no incentive to remove or reduce them, without assurance that others will also share the costs (situations of competitive depreciation, protection, monetary instability, global pollution, overexploitation of exhaustible resources to which no property rights are attached). Again, nationally rational actions will result in a suboptimal collectively irrational outcome.

It might be thought that if there are well-established property rights and low transactions costs, then there can be efficient negotiations among decision makers, as postulated in the Coase theorem.[18] But negotiations among national governments over the issues we have been considering are limited because property rights may not be well defined, the nation state does not act as a unitary agent (different bureaucratic interests and various domestic constituencies), information may be asymmetric, and outcomes are unpredictable.[19]

Finally, the intellectual underpinning for mechanisms of global governance is ambiguous and subject to differing interpretations. Competing models of international economic behaviour have different implications for the degrees and kinds of governance.[20] When no professional consensus exists about the single best model, international co-operation becomes all the more remote.

The problem of rival models is especially severe for matters of global governance when the type of rationality involved is constitutive rationality. Insofar as the task of designing a structure of global governance is akin to writing a constitution, it is more difficult than simply selecting policy instruments.

In addition to 'model uncertainty,' the feasibility of international cooperation is also handicapped by other types of uncertainty about the objectives and intentions of national governments, their ability to perform on agreements, and about their ability to monitor the compliance of other governments.[21]

Given the barriers to global governance, how can they be overcome? In the future, as in the past, agreement on some form of governance is most likely to emerge under conditions of crisis management. Governments may then share a common aversion and co-operate to avoid a particular outcome.[22] Aside from the need to take action in a crisis, nations may also submit to more governance, the more often are the attempts to institute such governance (as in repeated games). Progress is also more likely, the fewer the number of nations involved, such as in regional arrangements.[23] As Olson emphasizes,[24] cooperative solutions are easier to attain in smaller than larger groups for three reasons: the fraction of a collective benefit enjoyed by any individual agent tends to decline as the size of the groups increases; larger groups are less likely to exhibit the small-group strategic interactions that facilitate the supply of collective goods; and organization costs tend to increase with an increase in group size.

Clearly, global governance is only rudimentary. There is still a long way to go before legal and political institutions catch up with the potential of economic globalization. There must be wider understanding of the potential benefits from global governance. Ultimately, political leadership must promote this understanding and provide the incentives for commitment to global cooperation.

In the meanwhile, if globalization continues in the *de facto* sense, there will be less need for mechanisms of global governance in the *de jure* sense provided that global markets deepen, become more complete and more perfect. For the future, however, as in the past, the central issue for both private and public management will be how states and markets confront the challenge of increasing the 'size of the pie' (through efficiency and growth) and distributing it (with equity or fairness). In helping to meet this challenge, mechanisms of global governance need to remedy failures in international markets and avoid failures of the international public sector.

At the inaugural meeting of the IMF, Keynes warned 'There is scarcely any enduringly successful experience yet of an international body which has fulfilled the hopes of its progenitors. Either an institution has become diverted to be the instrument of a limited group, or it has been a puppet of sawdust through which the breath of life does not blow.' In actuality, although the Bretton Woods institutions have evolved and adapted to some changes in the world economy, the IMF and World Bank are no longer institutions of global management. They are relevant for the developing and transitional economies, but not the industrial world. The Bretton Woods institutions are operating far within the initial vision that Keynes had at Bretton Woods. At the same time, international problems are now more complex than those that confronted Keynes. And new global problems have made some students call for new international organizations. Fred Bergsten, for instance, expects the birth of four new organizations during the next 50 years: a Global Environmental Organization, another to supervise international capital markets, one to deal with issues arising from international investment, and one to deal with migration. So, too, does Paul Streeten propose the creation of an International Investment Trust, a World Central Bank, an International Debt Facility, an Industrial Investment Board, a Technical Agency, a Health Agency, and an Environment Protection Agency.[25]

New supranational institutions will, however, be extremely difficult to establish. Nor is this the time for a second Bretton Woods Conference. Not only would such a Conference with 180 delegations be infeasible: it is not necessary insofar as the Bretton Woods institutions already possess the procedural powers to evolve in a substantive manner.

Fifty years ago, when moving the acceptance of the Final Act at Bretton Woods, Keynes concluded: 'Mr. President, we have reached this evening a decisive point. But it is only a beginning. We have to go from here as missionaries, inspired by zeal and faith. We have sold all this to ourselves. But the world at large still needs to be persuaded.' This is still true.

Instead of simply zeal and faith, however, we now need greater understanding of how to reduce the conflict between cross-border economic integration and national political sovereignty, avoid international policy competition and promote international cooperation in the changing world economy. After considering problems of governance similar to those tackled by Keynes, a recent multi-volume study of 'Integrating National Economics' by the Brookings Institution concludes:

> As the twentieth century comes to a close, three roads to the economic future lie before economic policymakers. They can rely on the historical policies of reducing at-the-border trade barriers, the agenda of shallow integration. They can seek to harmonize and reconcile national differences, the agenda of deeper integration. Or they can reverse previous liberalization and reassert national autonomy. Which road today's leaders choose will shape the world in which their children and grandchildren live.[26]

Another Keynes who could persuade with reason and vision could be such a leader.

Endnotes

1. This section is heavily indebted to Keynes's *Collected Writings* (1980); Johnson (1978), Moggridge (1992), Skidelsky, Robert (1992), *John Maynard Keynes – The Economist as Saviour*, New York: Allen Lane.
2. Skidelsky (1992), *ibid*, p. 184.
3. Skidelsky (1992), *ibid*, p. 160.
4. R.J.A. Skidelsky, 'Retreat from Leadership', in B.M. Rowland (ed.) (1976), *Balance of Power or Hegemony*, New York: New York University Press, pp. 170–71.
5. D.E. Moggridge (ed.) (1980), *The Collected Writings of John Maynard Keynes*, London: Macmillan, vol. XXV, pp. 22–3.
6. *The Keynes Plan*, Cmd. 6437, April 1943.
7. J. Tinbergen, 'Building a World Order', in J.N. Bhagwati (ed.) (1972), *Economics and World Order from the 1970s to the 1990s*, New York: Macmillan, pp. 145–57.
8. D.E. Moggridge (ed.) (1980), *The Collected Writings of John Maynard Keynes*, London: Macmillan, vol. XXVI, *Activities 1941–1946* , p. 42.
9. L. Summers (1991), 'Research Challenges for Development Economists', *Finance and Development*, September, p. 5.
10. M. Camdessus (1995), 'Presentation of the Fiftieth Annual Report', IMF *Summary Proceedings*, Annual Meeting, Washington, DC: IMF, p. 33.
11. For details, see J. Williamson and M. Miller (1987), 'Targets and Indicators: A Blueprint for International Coordination of Economic Policy', Washington, DC: Institute for International Economics, September; O.E. Williamson and C.R. Henning, 'Managing the Monetary System' in P.B. Kenen (ed.) (1994), *Managing the World Economy*, Washington, DC: Institute for International Economics, ch. 2.
12. *The Economist*, October 7, 1995, p. 34.
13. H. James (1996), *International Monetary Cooperation since Bretton Woods*, New York: Oxford University Press, pp. 617–20.
14. This section follows the analysis of R.C. Bryant, 'International Cooperation in the Making of National Macroeconomic Policies: Where Do We Stand?' in P.B. Kenen (ed.) (1995), *Understanding Interdependence*, Princeton: Princeton University Press, ch. 11.
15. For the distinction between 'spontaneous' governance and 'intentional' governance structures, see O.E. Williamson (1991), 'Economic Institutions: Spontaneous and Intentional Governance', *Journal of Law Economics and Organization*, pp. 159–87.
16. P.P. Streeten (1995), *Thinking About Development*, Cambridge: Cambridge University Press, pp. 90–5; C.P. Kindleberger (1986), 'International Public Goods Without International Government,' *American Economic Review*, March.
17. Bryant, *op. cit.*, p. 408.

18. For elaboration, see R.N. Cooper (1995), 'The Coase Theorem and International Economic Relations,' *Japan and the World Economy,* 7, 29–44.
19. Another recent approach to international organization stems from the new institutional economics that focuses on contracting. See B.V. Yarbrough and R.M. Yarbrough (1994), 'International Contracting and Territorial Control: The Boundary Question,' *Journal of International and Theoretical Economics,* **150** (1), 239–64.
20. Bryant, *op. cit.,* pp. 427–34.
21. Bryant, *op. cit.,* pp. 427–30. For a critique of international cooperation – and the belief that it should not even be attempted, for example see M. Feldstein (1988), 'Distinguished Lecture on Economics in Government: Thinking about International Economic Coordination,' *Journal of Economic Perspectives,* **2** (2), 3–13.
22. A.A. Stein (1990), *Why Nations Cooperate,* Ithaca: Cornell University Press, ch. 2.
23. B.V. Yarbrough and R.M. Yarbrough (1994), 'Regionalism and Layered Governance: The Choice of Trade Institutions,' *Journal of International Affairs,* **48** (1), 95–117.
24. M. Olson (1971), *The Logic of Collective Action: Public Goods and the Theory of Groups,* 2nd edn., Cambridge, Mass.: Harvard University Press.
25. P.P. Streeten (1995), 'Global Prospects in an Interdependent World,' in Soumitra Sharma (ed.), *Macroeconomic Management,* London: Macmillan, pp. 22–39.
26. R.Z. Lawrence, et al. (1996), *A Vision for the World Economy,* Washington, DC: Brookings Institution, p. 104.

References

Johnson, E.S. and H.G. (1978), *The Shadow of Keynes,* Oxford: Blackwell.

Keynes, J.M. (1913), *Indian Currency and Finance,* London: Macmillan and Co.

Keynes, J.M. (1919), *The Economic Consequences of the Peace,* London: Macmillan and Co.

Keynes, J.M. (1923), *A Tract on Monetary Reform,* London: Macmillan and Co.

Keynes, J.M. (1926), *The End of Laissez Faire,* London: Macmillan and Co.

Keynes, J.M. (1930), *Treatise on Money,* London: Macmillan and Co.

Keynes, J.M. (1933a), 'National Self Sufficiency', *The New Statesman.*

Keynes, J.M. (1933b), 'National Self Sufficiency', *Yale Review.*

Keynes, J.M. (1936), *The General Theory of Employment, Interest and Money,* London: Macmillan and Co.

Keynes, J.M. (1940), *How to Pay for the War,* London: Macmillan and Co.

Keynes, J.M. (1980), *Collected Writings,* London: Macmillan.

Moggridge, D.E. (1992), *John Maynard Keynes: An Economist's Biography,* London and New York: Routledge.

Skidelsky, R. (1983), *John Maynard Keynes: vol. 1, Hopes Betrayed, 1883–1920,* New York: Allen Lane.

Skidelsky, R. (1994), *John Maynard Keynes, vol. 2, The Economist as Savior, 1920–1937,* New York: Allen Lane.

9 How relevant is Keynesianism today for understanding problems of development?
Sir Hans W. Singer[1]

The Keynesian and Washington consensus

It is now 50 years since Keynes's death and 60 years since he published his pioneering work *The General Theory of Employment, Interest and Money*. When the *General Theory* was published, the great problems were unemployment, deflation, collapse of commodity prices, international beggar-my-neighbour policies and so on but of all these unemployment was identified as the basic cause of all the other troubles. So Keynes and Keynesianism were governed by the intention of 'never again' – never again to permit a recurrence of mass unemployment. For 25 years after World War II, under the Keynesian Consensus, the world in fact enjoyed a 'golden age' of full employment, rapid growth, greater welfare and equality – and for a long time also low inflation. The developing countries also were doing well, partly as the result of full employment in the industrial countries, partly as a result of high commodity prices, and partly as a result of applying Keynesian doctrines of high effective demand and promotion of public investment in their own active domestic macroeconomic policies. It looked as if the Keynesian Consensus had fully established itself as a permanent solution.

It was not to be. The era of the Keynesian Consensus terminated in the early 1970s. Rising inflationary pressures had already begun to undermine the sustainability of the golden age even before the death blows of the collapse of the Bretton Woods exchange rate system in 1971, and the quadrupling of oil prices in 1973. The object of 'never again' shifted from the fight against unemployment to the fight against inflation. The era of the Keynesian Consensus was superseded by the era of the Washington Consensus.[2] This also claimed to be a lasting and permanent solution to the problems of its day, but once again after another 25-year cycle this claim is beginning to be shaken by experience and events. As the Keynesian Consensus was terminated by the inflationary pressures (partly at least engendered by the inherent logic of the Keynesian Consensus itself), so the Washington Consensus is now being shaken to its foundations by the re-emergence of the spectre of unemployment and the evident dangers of social exclusion and rising inequalities, and the doubtful effects of structural adjustment and stabilization programmes. The pendulum is swinging back. This is indicated by increasing attempts in recent years to add a 'human face' to the original tough

'Washington Consensus' but this comes more naturally when it is part of the objective itself rather than an 'add-on'. The Washington Consensus is not what it used to be – unemployment is its nemesis, as inflation was the nemesis of the Keynesian Consensus.

Of the two objectives, full employment and control of inflation,[3] the employment objective clearly has the advantage. It deals with the real economy and real people rather than the financial phenomena of prices. It is inherently egalitarian insofar as moving people from unemployment into employment is one of the major ways of dealing with poverty. It can claim to have a 'human face', at least more plausibly than observance of the fundamentals of the Washington Consensus. Indeed the main defence of the emphasis on inflation control under the Washington Consensus is the claim that its indirect and ultimate effect is precisely to make possible, at a later stage, the pursuit of Keynesian full employment policies. The Keynesian answer would be that the hoped-for long run may never arrive because the initial effects create their own downward dynamic and that in any case there is no need for such a sacrificial short-term J-curve approach where the worse today leads to a better future ('in the long run we are all dead'). Keynes himself also argued that once a condition of full employment has been reached and maintained (the 'Special Case'), market forces could be reinstated and relied on for effective supply incentives. But as far as sequence is concerned, this is the reverse of the Washington Consensus where inflation control and proper observance of the fundamentals are presented as a precondition for full employment, whereas Keynes presented full employment as a precondition for bringing the free market fundamentals back into their own. Keynes was as concerned to avoid inflation as the advocates of the Washington Consensus, only he believed that an acceptably low Non Inflation Accelerating Rate of Unemployment (NIARU) could be achieved by proper macroeconomic policies.

In the European industrial countries the growth in effective demand and investment are clearly below the 'warranted' full employment level, that is labour supply plus the rate of productivity growth. On the official count unemployment in Western Europe amounts to 18 million people (equivalent with their family members to the total population of the UK or France or Italy). Beyond that – just as the Keynesians explained – there is a vastly larger number of people suffering from underemployment and disguised unemployment, that is not working at the full level of their productive capacity or working short time, or not offering themselves in the labour market because of the absence of jobs. Currently the EU is embarking on its Inter-Governmental Conference (IGC) in which the unemployment issue has emerged paramount on the agenda. The present label for what the Keynesians called open plus disguised unemployment is social exclusion. So the question today is not whether Keynes's thinking is *still* valid and relevant today, but rather whether it is *again* valid and relevant today.

International Keynesianism and the developing countries

However my subject is the relevance of Keynesianism in the field of development, meaning the development of the poorer or Third World countries rather than the industrial countries. Here the current relevance of Keynes and Keynesianism is even more glaringly obvious – in this case referring especially to the later Keynes who was the guiding spirit in establishing the new international economic order at Bretton Woods in 1944 rather than the Keynes who wrote the *General Theory* in 1936. One needs only mention a single dominant fact to establish this. It is estimated that at present there is something like a US$500 billion per year resource outflow from the developing countries, offsetting many times over the reverse flow of aid. This US$500 billion outflow is made up of four major items:

- *Terms of trade losses*: compared with say 30 years ago, the terms of trade of the primary commodities and simple low-tech manufactures on which most developing countries still depend have sharply deteriorated in relation to their imports of high-tech manufactures. This factor alone amounts to a tax of 20–25 per cent on the export earnings of developing countries. During the decade of the 1980s the decline in real commodity prices cost the developing countries no less than US$540 million.[4] The precise extent of the terms of trade losses depends of course on the initial point from which the deterioration is measured, but the 30-year period has as its base the commodity prices of the 1960s which were much lower than those of the immediate post-war period.
- *Debt servicing*: these debts have their origin in the early 1970s arising from the way in which the big financial surpluses of the OPEC countries were recycled by the commercial banking system and reacted to by the industrial countries. Debt servicing amounts to another 20–25 per cent tax on export earnings. The debt pressure and terms of trade losses are mutually interrelated (in a way which Keynes had already described 15 years before the *General Theory* in connection with the reparations imposed on Germany after World War I).
- *Repatriation of profits and transfer pricing*: this source of outflows by foreign investors and especially multinational corporations operating in developing countries is volatile and in any case difficult to estimate, but it may well be of a similar order of magnitude in terms of trade losses and debt servicing.
- *Capital flight from developing countries*: also volatile and difficult to control or even to trace, this is facilitated by the globalization and

liberalization of financial services and currency transactions. Assets held in developed countries are subject to less risk of inflation, devaluation, and political instability.

What is the point of listing here these four major drains which together deprive the developing countries of half or more of their potential export earnings? The point is that under the arrangements which Keynes proposed in his preparatory memoranda for Bretton Woods and which were partially implemented during the golden age of the Keynesian Consensus in the 1950s and 1960s, these catastrophic drains would not have occurred. Terms of trade losses would have been avoided or reduced by stabilization of primary commodity prices through international buffer stocks and international commodity agreements. Keynes was a fervent supporter of such stabilization. He even proposed initially a world currency based on a bundle of 30 primary commodities, thus automatically stabilizing their average price (while not ruling out fluctuations of individual commodities against this average). This would also have contributed to global macroeconomic stability: in slack times when commodity prices were low international buffer stocks would have been accumulated, thus injecting additional liquidity into the world economy, and vice versa in case of inflationary demand pressures and high commodity prices. In the system proposed by Keynes there was in addition to the IMF and World Bank an essential third pillar: an International Trade Organization (ITO) with commodity price stabilization as its major function. In fact the ITO was duly negotiated and established in Havana in 1947 but never came into existence, failing to obtain ratification by the US Congress. Neither GATT nor the newly established WTO has any of the commodity functions envisaged for the ITO.

Similarly, debt servicing would not have arisen, or would be much less under the Keynesian Consensus. Keynes had proposed an international tax on balance of payments surplus countries (for 'exporting unemployment') and liquidity support for balance of payments deficit countries from an 'International Clearing Union' – his original term for the IMF, but visualized as much larger and operating with less conditionality (to save deficit countries from having to deflate).

The transfer of profits out of developing countries and repatriation of investment by multinational corporations would also have been prevented if Keynes's original ideas had been followed. He advocated control of capital movements and regulation of foreign investment (as practised by South Korea during its successful rise to the status of an industrial power). In his own words: he wanted 'homespun economies'. He was deeply suspicious of financial markets and the 'casino economies' which dominated them. 'The proper job of finance is to see that nothing is done on purely financial grounds.' Control of outflows turned out to be very difficult, in view of transfer pricing and increased globalization of capital markets. This mattered less when aid was coming in quantities overshadowing private capital movements, but the decline of aid has reduced the capacity of developing countries to obtain favourable conditions from the multinationals. Some of the volatile investment practising, uncontrolled outflows through transfer pricing and so on would have been kept out by selective entry controls in the first place.

As far as capital flight is concerned, this also would have been eliminated or reduced by controls on capital movements. In any case, if the economies of developing countries had been put on the expansionary path of full employment growth suggested by Keynesianism (as expressed by the Harrod–Domar formula to which we later turn), the incentive for capital flight would have been much less.

So much for the question of relevance of international Keynesianism to our current development problems. We now turn to two specific contributions of national Keynesianism to our understanding of development policy, that is the concept of disguised unemployment and the Harrod–Domar model of sustained growth.

Disguised unemployment

The concept of disguised unemployment or underemployment is associated more directly not so much with Keynes himself than with one of his closest disciples and followers, Joan Robinson.[5] Keynes himself had thought of the labour supply only in two broad categories: one part fully employed and another part fully unemployed. The purpose of his macroeconomic proposals was to increase the first part and reduce the second part. Joan Robinson pointed out that there is in fact a more complicated spectrum in the labour market. Apart from those fully employed and fully unemployed, there are those who are employed at low productivity, partly employed with reduced working hours, self-employed making a precarious living because of the absence of an employer willing to take them on and so on. A lack of effective demand for labour may show as much or more in these intermediate categories of disguised unemployment as in the official unemployment figures. The concept of underemployment fitted in well with the concepts of underdevelopment or underdeveloped countries (the original name for what we now call more diplomatically, but less accurately, the developing countries).

Joan Robinson's concepts, like those of Keynes, were initially applied to the UK and industrial countries in general, as indicated by her favourite identification of disguised unemployment with 'selling matches in the Strand'. This is certainly of direct relevance at the present time. Quite recently, John Eatwell has undertaken a detailed study of disguised unemployment in the G7 countries.[6] According to his results, relating to 1990, disguised unemployment – mainly in the form of low-productivity employment in the services, construction, and agriculture sectors – was larger than open published unemployment. According to his figures, in 1990 average open unemployment in the G7 countries (simple average of the seven countries) was 6.7 per cent. But true unemployment including disguised unemployment was 14.9 per cent. In other words disguised unemployment was 8.2 per cent compared with open unemployment of 6.7 per cent. Between 1973 and 1992 the percentage of part-time employment increased from 16 per cent to 23 per cent in the UK, from 14 per cent to 21 per cent in Japan, from 16 per cent to 18 per cent in the US, from 10 per cent to 16 per cent in Germany and from 6 per cent to 13 per cent in France. Underemployment can be visible (shorter working hours than desired) or invisible (low-productivity work: the 'working poor').

However, it soon became apparent that the most important application of the concept of disguised unemployment is in developing countries where it amounts to 20 per cent, according to ILO estimates in its more visible form alone. Here full and open unemployment is not usually practicable – except by support through the kinship system – because there is no social insurance and a fully unemployed person could simply not survive. Moreover, in the agricultural sector, which provides the main reservoir of labour in developing countries, work is in any case shared among all the household members and in the same way in slack seasons unemployment is shared among the household members. Furthermore the available data show that labour productivity in agriculture and also in services is much lower than in manufacturing. It was thus a small step from there for the early development economists to draw the conclusion that the low-productivity agricultural sector constituted a labour reserve and the transfer out of this sector into higher productivity sectors, particularly manufacturing, was the royal road to development. In fact, a rudimentary model of this kind had already been sketched by Adam Smith in *The Wealth of Nations*. The economist most strongly associated with this strategy of using the disguised agricultural employment as an opportunity for economic growth through transfer was Arthur Lewis, with his emphasis on 'unlimited supplies of labour'.[7] Joan Robinson herself in 1937 was also well aware of this application to developing countries, for in addition to mentioning 'selling matches in the Strand' she also mentions 'cutting brushwood in the jungles'. Rural unemployment has been well described as 'a first cousin of Keynesian unemployment equilibrium'.[8]

The strategy of using disguised unemployment in agriculture as a means of growth by transfer to higher-productivity industry has been criticized as leading to lopsided development through neglect of agriculture, notably by T.W. Schultz.[9] This criticism may be legitimate in relation to the emphasis on industrialization and the 'urban bias' inherent in treating agriculture mainly as a reservoir for feeding the labour demands of industrialization. But it is not legitimate when applied to the concept of disguised unemployment as such. It is quite open to policy makers to decide to deal with the problem by reducing the degree of disguised unemployment in agriculture itself, that is by raising the productivity and output of farming. Which is the better strategy – or rather the best combination of the two strategies – is a matter of analysing which combination yields the highest net benefits in terms of economic growth. In support of Arthur Lewis, it can be stated that a reduction of the proportion of population in agriculture and an increase in the share of industrial production in GDP has been an invariable feature of economic growth. In support of T.W. Schultz, the example of the Green Revolution in India and Pakistan, or the high agricultural productivity in Korea and Taiwan, can be quoted as demonstrating the potential of a more agriculture-led growth. Another element in favour of the Schultz position was introduced by the Harris–Todaro model. This pointed out that because of the different levels of earnings in agriculture and formal industrial employment the volume of transfer from rural to urban areas would be excessive and hence a significant proportion of the transfer would amount to a transfer from low-productivity employment in agriculture to urban unemployment, or at best to equally low-productivity employment in the urban informal sector, that is disguised unemployment. The implication of the Harris–Todaro model is that Keynesian policies of increasing effective demand may thus *increase* rather than diminish unemployment! But the balance was tilted back again towards the Lewis position when the ILO Employment Mission to Kenya pointed out that the developmental productivity of employment in the urban informal sector was larger than had previously been assumed.[10]

The simultaneous existence of open unemployment, disguised unemployment and underemployment in various forms is a recognition that unemployment is not a homogeneous phenomenon. Keynes dealt with open unemployment – the most pressing problem of his day – as a homogeneous case and suggested a single remedy, that is an increase in effective demand. Yet even within this category of open unemployment there is no homogeneity. For example, the case of the long-term or elderly unemployed may be different from that of the short-term or young unemployed, and accordingly different remedies may be appropriate for these different categories. It is plausible that an increase in effective demand will not be sufficient to persuade employers to take on the long-term unemployed who in their perception are no longer used to the discipline of work and have lost necessary skills and work habits. In their case, supply side measures such as training or perhaps direct employment subsidies may be necessary, while an increase in effective demand mops up the short-term or younger unemployed.[11] There is no reason to think that Keynes as an active policy maker would have denied that measures related to effective demand would need supplementation on the supply-side in such specific cases. In fact, a combination of both types of measure is necessary as essential complements of each other: without a strengthening of effective demand the increased employment would still go to the short-term unemployed, while without supply-side measures even the increase in effective demand will not be sufficient to persuade employers to take on the long-term unemployed. In that sense, the discussion of supply-side measures ('flexible labour markets') *versus* demand-side measures is beside the point.

With surplus labour, capital becomes the scarce factor. This leads directly to the emphasis on capital accumulation (investment) as the source of economic growth in the Harrod–Domar growth model. These two avenues of influence of Keynesianism on development thinking are thus clearly and directly connected.

The Harrod–Domar formula
Like disguised unemployment, this other influential contribution of Keynesianism to development studies was due less to Keynes himself than to one of his close disciples, in this case Roy Harrod. Keynes himself, until he later (1942) became involved in the preparation of the post-war international economic order, was interested in the practical problems of reducing unemployment in the UK, and not what would happen once full employment had been achieved and how it could be sustained. 'In the long run we are all dead.' When Keynes exceptionally and outside his main work gave some attention to long-term problems, as in his essay on 'The economics of our grandchildren', he did this not in terms of a dynamic model of continued growth of GNP. On the contrary, he thought of the long-run equilibrium as one of reaching a plateau of reasonable satisfaction of basic needs when further accumulation and growth would be pointless and the fruits of further technical progress would be taken in the form of increased leisure, development of non-economic artistic and cultural activities and improved quality of life. In this respect Keynes was the forerunner of development economists like Dudley Seers, Paul Streeten and others, who also questioned the objective of growth of GNP as the beginning and end of economic development.

Harrod's model (later supplemented by Evsey Domar) does not belong to this school of thought. It explores the preconditions for self-sustaining dynamic economic growth over time, implicitly accepting this as equivalent to development. It directly derives from Keynes in so far as like Keynes it uses the concept of the multiplier and puts capital accumulation or physical investment at the centre of the analysis as the element most suitable for manipulation in order to produce the warranted growth rate which leads to full employment. The basis of Harrod–Domar is so simple as to amount almost to a tautology. The rate of growth is determined by the share of investment in output (in equilibrium equal to the share of saving) divided by the capital output ratio. If the rate of investment is 12 per cent and the capital output ratio is 3 (that is three units of capital needed to produce one unit of output in all subsequent years) the rate of growth will be 4 per cent. If the rate of population increase is 1 per cent per annum, then the rate of per capita income growth will be 3 per cent. Simple, but all the same illuminating and also controversial.

The formula is illuminating because capital accumulation or physical investment is clearly an important element in economic growth, just as disguised unemployment identified industrialization and structural transformation from agriculture as important elements in development. Without first creating a capital base, countries cannot take advantage of trade and growth of markets and effective demand. A high and steady rate of investment has been an outstanding feature of the high-performing East Asian economies. A recent authoritative study of these economies finds that 'these countries top the international league tables not just with respect to the long-term growth of their GDP but also to their national savings and investment rates'.[12] More questionable was the limitation of the concept of investment to physical capital. Development economists have come to place more and more emphasis on the importance of human capital (which Keynes, concentrating on short-term problems and the UK, took more or less for granted, as he did the capacity to supply higher rates of capital investment). In the formal sense this is not a valid criticism of the Harrod–Domar formula itself, which remains tautologically true. An increase in human capital – say better education, higher skills, or better health – will improve the capital output ratio and by lowering it increase the rate of sustainable growth. Mathematically it makes no difference whether human capital is taken care of by adding it to investment in the enumerator or by lowering the capital output ratio in the denominator.

However, while it may make no difference mathematically, it is true to say that by expressing everything in relation to physical capital accumulation the formula may lead to a neglect of other factors important for growth. The role of technical innovation for instance, as emphasized by Schumpeter, is not easily accommodated in the Harrod–Domar formula. Does it find expression in additional capital formation – this seems to be at odds with Schumpeter's emphasis on 'creative destruction' – or in improving the capital output ratio? Also, in the Harrod–Domar formula the rate of investment and the capital output ratio are presented as two separate and presumably independent factors. Keynes himself, in line with neoclassical growth theory, seemed to believe that continued capital accumulation would be associated with falling marginal efficiency of investment. Subsequent development economists, like Kaldor, have presented development models where growth feeds upon itself with constant or increasing returns, that is an incremental capital output ratio (ICOR) equal to or lower than the average capital output ratio, the foundation of the 'new growth theory'. Myrdal's cumulative causation may also lead to similar results, but in a downward as well as an upward direction. With these new insights the Harrod–Domar model may be seen to be in the nature of a razor's edge (as Harrod himself had already made clear) where a steady rate of growth is achieved almost

by rare accident and the normal case would be either inflation or
in fact a combination of both in the form of stagflation. Devi;
warranted rate of growth would be self-amplifying. There are n
in recent history to support such a knife-edge model.

The Harrod–Domar formula does not distinguish to what extent the crucial
rate of investment, and the crucial increase in the rate of investment needed for
full employment growth, are to be achieved by public or private investment. But
Keynesians, while advocating a mixed economy, tended to stress the catalytic
role of public investment and the complementary relation between the two.
Reliance on private investment might also involve the acceptance of income
inequalities and of a high rate of profits (a major source of savings and
investment). Many Keynesians, and Keynes himself in his later life, wanted
greater equality in the form of a welfare state: hence they were leaning towards
public investment and strategic *public* investment planning, project appraisal
and cost-benefit analysis. This had an influence on the early development
economists who were much concerned with techniques of development planning.
The early Indian 'five-year plans' and the Mahalanobis model on which these
plans were based served as a centre-piece of analysis and debate.

The emphasis on physical capital accumulation also provided an intellectual
basis for aid to developing countries. Aid was supposed to go into capital
formation rather than consumption. Moreover aid was supposed to be a transfer
from capital-abundant donor countries with low marginal returns to capital (that
is a high capital output ratio) to poorer countries with little capital and hence a
favourable capital output ratio. The success of the Marshall plan – the most
formidable aid project of the time – also seemed to support an emphasis on capital
investment. However, this last point could be questioned: it was pointed out that
the success of the Marshall plan might be due to the ready availability of
human capital in the recipient countries and also to the fact that rehabilitation
and reconstruction is easier and has a lower capital output ratio than building
up capital from scratch. Also it could be pointed out that the development
institutions were in place, which leads us to the criticism of the Harrod–Domar
formula that it does not explicitly include institutional factors in the growth
formula. Political stability, solid financial institutions, social harmony, the rule
of law and so on are clearly factors in economic growth, but do not explicitly
figure in the Harrod–Domar formula, although Harrod and Domar would have
readily accepted them as important determinants of both the rates of investment
and the incremental capital/output ratio (ICOR).

In the extreme case when there is no supply response due to structural
deficiencies (lack of infrastructure, entrepreneurship or market institutions), the
ICOR in the Harrod–Domar model becomes zero. Increases in investment will
simply result in inflationary pressures unless the investment itself is specifically
directed towards removing the bottlenecks causing an infinite ICOR. However,

in Keynesian thinking, the inflationary pressures can be contained or suppressed if the expansion of effective demand is accompanied by relevant macroeconomic controls.

Conclusion

Thus in answer to the question raised by our title, we may point to disguised unemployment and the Harrod–Domar formula as two examples of Keynesianism which have had a deep and lasting effect on development thinking and development policy. Neglect of employment effects (including disguised unemployment), of maintenance of effective demand, of a full employment sustainable growth path and of the promotion of capital accumulation (both physical and human) have had harmful effects in the stabilization and structural adjustment programmes imposed on developing countries. There are signs that this is being increasingly recognized and that the pendulum is swinging back from the excesses of the neo-liberal counter-revolution and towards an updated Keynesian Consensus.

The neoclassical counter-revolution, proclaimed as supplying an alternative (and superior) development paradigm to that derived from the original Keynesian revolution, is not really an alternative but a supplement. Once full employment has been achieved and sustained much of the neoclassical teaching about the importance of the market as a welfare-maximizing allocative force becomes valid and relevant. But the Keynesian principle of providing full employment effective demand comes first. The Keynesian dog should be wagging the neoclassical tail. Today, under the Washington Consensus, the tail is wagging the dog, with unhappy results for development economics and, more important, for the developing countries.

Endnotes

1. I am grateful to Syed Nawab Haider Naqvi, Brian Reddaway, Adelino Torres and Adrian Wood for comments on an earlier draft.
2. The term 'Washington Consensus' is usually attributed to John Williamson but the author can also claim a modest part in its genesis. The Washington Consensus is a conglomerate of trade liberalization, privatization, deregulation, and observance of the fiscal and monetary 'fundamentals'.
3. Reflecting its Keynesian foundations, the Articles of Agreement of the IMF set it the task of 'promotion and maintenance of high levels of employment' (Article I). There is no mention of control of inflation – this may come as a surprise to many today!
4. South Centre, *International Commodity Problems and Policies – the Key Issues for Developing Countries*, The South Centre, Geneva, 1996, Annexe Table 4.
5. Robinson, J.V., 'Disguised unemployment' in *Essays in the Theory of Employment* (London: Macmillan), 1937.
6. John Eatwell, *Disguised Unemployment: the G7 Experience*, UNCTAD Discussion Paper No. 106, November 1995.
7. Lewis, W.A., 'Economic Development with Unlimited Supplies of Labour', *The Manchester School*, May 1954.

8. Syed Nawab Haider Naqvi, *Development Economics: A New Paradigm*, Sage Publications, New Delhi, 1993.
9. T. W. Schultz, *Transforming Traditional Agriculture*, Yale University Press, New Haven, 1964. Ironically Arthur Lewis and T.W. Schultz received a *joint* Nobel Prize in Economics.
10. ILO, *Employment, Incomes and Equality – A Strategy for Increasing Productive Employment in Kenya*, International Labour Office, Geneva, 1972.
11. See Brian Reddaway 'How Useful are Keynesian Ideas in 1996?', *Royal Economic Society Newsletter*, issue 93, April 1996. The same point also emerged in a study of long-term unemployment in the UK undertaken during 1936–38, shortly after the publication of the *General Theory, Men Without Work: A Report to the Pilgrim Trust*, Cambridge University Press, 1937.
12. Ajit Singh, 'The causes of fast economic growth in East Asia' in *UNCTAD Review*, 1995, p. 118.

10 Is a revival of Keynes's ideas likely?
(Some comments on chapters by Gerald M. Meier and Sir Hans W. Singer)

Kunibert Raffer

People commenting on scholarly works of others are expected to disagree respectfully. My task is to do so with regard to the two excellent chapters on global Keynesianism by Sir Hans and Professor Meier. I shall focus on two connected issues, namely whether an imminent demise of anti-Keynesian policies is likely, and what kind of global governance should be envisaged. As will be noticed I disagree more, respectfully, with Professor Meier.

An imminent demise of anti-Keynesian policies?
Sir Hans presented a compelling analysis, stating that while inflation was the nemesis of the Keynesian Consensus after a 25-year-cycle, unemployment has now become the nemesis of the Washington Consensus, again after 25 years. I fully agree that effective demand is inadequate at present, and that likely increases will not suffice to solve the problem of long-term unemployment. Other measures, such as (re)training – already recommended in *Men without Work* in 1937 (H.W. Singer was one of the authors not mentioned in his paper), are necessary. Keynes's perception of a long-run equilibrium with increased leisure – reduced working hours, in modern lingo – is another important way to reduce unemployment. Such reductions have occurred continuously, absorbing a substantial part of the effects of technical advance. Comparing the hours of a typical working week in 1949 and nowadays illustrates clearly that the so-called 'golden years' are also due to a continuous and unspectacular process of reducing working hours.

Regretfully I am less optimistic with regard to the demise of present orthodoxy. Quite on the contrary, anti-Keynesian policies are increasingly gaining the upper hand at present. This evolution was predicted by Kalecki (1971, p.138) already in 1943 when his paper, also quoted by Malcom Sawyer in this volume, was originally published: 'The assumption that Government will maintain full employment in a capitalist economy if it only knows how to do it is fallacious.' Powerful pressure by big business and rentiers – presumably disagreeing that their disappearance is a great advantage (Keynes, 1967, p. 376) – would prevent governments from doing so. This lobby, Kalecki (1971, p. 144) argues, 'would probably find more than one economist to declare that the situation is manifestly unsound. The pressure of all these forces, and in particular of big business would most probably induce the Government to the orthodox policy of cutting down the budget deficit.' In line with Kalecki's reasoning, a historically long period of full employment brought about by consequent Keynesian politics was experienced in industrialized countries (ICs), which was finally stopped by an anti-Keynesian revolution justified by the necessity to fight inflation. But the anti-Keynesian wave goes much further. At present an institutional framework is being constructed, which might make Keynesian policies virtually impossible in the future.

The arguments of the 1930s would not do after the *General Theory*. Budget cuts, reducing the role of governments and the dismantling of social standards are now justified by globalization or – in the case of the European Union (EU) – the Maastricht convergence criteria. Instead of policies of competitive deflation and exchange rate depreciation as in the 1930s 'to force adjustments of wage and price ... levels' (Meier), wages have come under direct attack. In the name of a hard currency devaluation is declared anathema by the EU. Real, even nominal wage reductions are justified by international competition, while factors influencing export prices much more are not mentioned. Elsenhans (1996) shows how the repeated appreciations of the Mark resulting from Germany's current account surplus – or export success – have had much stronger effects on German labour costs than changes in wages. In the spring of 1995 for instance appreciation immediately compensated prior effects of cutting costs. A Keynesian policy of reducing external surpluses could help, but one concentrates on labour costs instead. Additional payments, such as for overtime or work during the weekend, are described as hindering necessary flexibility. Some OECD countries have liberalized laws protecting employees, increasing the maximum number of hours a person may legally work per day or are considering such steps. Even South Korea has recently enacted anti-employee legislation to enhance international competitiveness – the only country, by the way, where the workforce defended their interest with great determination.

Globalization and regionalization are not solely responsible for labour market problems, although they contribute noticeably. Present high unemployment results from two factors: technological advances destroying many jobs, and productivity gains from economic internationalization, regional or global, which have increased these losses.

Internationalization is always mentioned as an evolution forcing governments to adopt 'sound' policies. It is conveniently forgotten that internationalization and integration are the result of deliberate policies and treaties by the same governments that use them as an excuse for policies in favour of the rich, including politicians themselves. The new international framework, which is being created, reduces any government's room for manoeuvre of future anticyclical Keynesian policies, which will become much more difficult if not impossible.

Productivity increases resulting from technological advances and internationalization dampen the demand for labour. Easier possibilities to shift production – real or perceived – increase the bargaining power of employers, allowing them to depress real and increasingly nominal wages. Doing so employers eventually reduce their own market outlets. Both lower wages and job insecurity reduce effective demand, as people spend less than they would otherwise have done. These negative effects of private actions are further compounded by legislation dismantling employees' rights and fiscal policies.

Fiscal cuts are justified by the Maastricht criteria in Europe. The validity of this argument is quickly shown by the fact that Belgium and Luxembourg have had the same currency for decades, although one country has fulfilled these criteria and the other has not. Germany does not meet these criteria at the moment, without the Mark devaluating perceptibly – which should cast some doubt on whether these criteria are necessary for a hard currency. The catchword 'Maastricht' has become a generally accepted justification to commit the errors of the 1930s all over again plus a few new ones. The criteria of national debts of no more than 60 per cent of GDP and of budget deficits of 3 per cent of GDP or less mean that practically all EU members have to cut government spending severely.

In the negotiations on the new common European currency, Germany – running itself a larger than allowed deficit – proposed automatic fines for member countries whenever the budget deficit exceeded 3 per cent of GDP, unless output dropped by 2 per cent in 12 months, a devastating economic shrinkage. At the Dublin summit this automaticity was not accepted, but the compromise reached still means – for the first time in history – an institutional penalty on Keynesian policies. Once this fine is agreed any member government is able to claim that it has to obey international constraints beyond its political influence, when its electorate should demand counter-cyclical policies. Comparing the Maastricht criteria with present data shows that Keynesian policies have been excluded by internationally concerted action for the foreseeable future. The limit of 60 per cent of debt to output is likely to be the main obstacle to Keynesian demand stimulation in the foreseeable future.

While fiscal austerity is defended on the grounds of the Eurocurrency and of putting public finances on a sound base again, large tax cuts in favour of the rich are granted. They aggravate fiscal deficits and contribute towards impeding Keynesian policies. Redistribution from above to groups with lower marginal propensities to consume reduces effective demand. As the marginal propensity to consume is generally weaker in richer societies the problem of closing the gap between actual investment and investment necessary for full employment (Keynes, 1967, p. 31) is enlarged.

Present policies were predicted by Kalecki (1971, pp. 142f). Arguing that business leaders could oppose Keynesian policies but not any kind of government intervention to alleviate slumps, he predicted the stimulation of private investment, for instance by reducing income taxes and subsidizing private investments directly. Observing 'That such a scheme would be attractive to 'business' is not surprising', he also showed why this was not an adequate method for preventing mass unemployment. Briefly, he explained the present situation.

When effective demand is not growing sufficiently, lay-offs must be good news to shareholders: increased profits – in modern lingo: increased shareholder values – have to result mainly from cutting costs. Limited investment possibilities in real production accompanied by soaring profits increase the amount of money available for globalized financial markets. As storing money in the basement is not considered acceptable, firms with money are forced to invest somewhere. This feeds financial speculation and the instability brought about by large masses of volatile funds moving around the globe. IC (industrialized countries) governments are unwilling to consider stabilizing the global financial system, for instance by introducing the so-called Tobin tax on international currency transactions, which would make interest-rate-based short-term speculation prohibitively expensive. It would recreate a room for manoeuvring for national economic policy, heeding Keynes's (1967, p. 160) advice of a government transfer tax on transactions 'to mitigate the predominance of speculation over enterprise'. It deserves mentioning that Senator Bob Dole introduced a bill in the Senate (Second Session, 104th Congress) which prohibits UN officials and UN agencies to do research on Tobin's proposal, even to think about it aloud. It appears to have suppressed discussion about the Tobin tax quite successfully.

Present austerity policies and redistribution are accompanied by a strong dissociation of politics from the interests of the electorate at large to favour small groups. In the US the percentage of those voting has fallen to a very low level. Those particularly suffering from policies are either unable or unwilling to register. European regional integration has a very strong anti-democratic bias, allowing politicians to accommodate the interests of small, rich lobbies much better than democratic structures would. The European Parliament has neither the right to make laws nor even to propose them. Real legislative powers remain firmly in the hands of the administration, unelected bureaucrats and ministers, which reduces the influence people in any European country can wield substantially. National parliaments are overruled by administratively made legal norms. One article in the Maastricht Treaty would have sufficed to confer full legislative power to the European Parliament. Even national veto rights exercised by elected parliamentarians could have been incorporated easily.

But we witness the spectacle that EU governments busily rolling back democracy in their own countries request aid recipients sternly to strengthen democracy in the South. Freely elected parliaments with full parliamentary powers is one important demand – which some donors themselves are eagerly undoing at the moment. As mentioned above, this reduces both the possibilities of any member country to embark on Keynesian policies and the power of any electorate to demand it. A sceptic might be tempted to apply Kalecki's approach to politics. It could be argued that wealthier people get more self-assured and prepared to challenge the decisions of politicians. Many projects, particularly in infrastructure such as highways or extensions of airports, illustrate this clearly. Crises and fear of unemployment tend to make people more malleable – allowing politicians to govern them more easily.

Unfortunately a demise of the Washington Consensus in favour of a new wave of Keynesianism is not likely at all. On the contrary, important decisions – going even beyond Kalecki's lucid projection – were implemented that will reduce the possibilities of Keynesian policies in the future.

Keynesian or anti-Keynesian global governance

While agreeing with Professor Meier that more international governance would be useful, I have to disagree with his concrete proposals. Advocating close co-operation between the Bretton Woods Institutions (BWIs) and the newly formed World Trade Organization (WTO) he proposes 'an integrated approach ... for governing the developing countries'. In plain English this can only mean a neo-colonial rule, as already proposed by List (1920, p. 211) some 150 years ago. List advocated joint exploitation of the South by the North as 'promising much richer and more certain fruits than the mutual enmity of war and trade regulations'. The present strong intrusion into Southern economies by the BWIs can already be interpreted as governing Southern Countries (SCs).

One must doubt whether these institutions would be able to provide good international governance, and whether they should serve as the channels for transferring savings to the South. The fact apart, that rich countries too have surplus labour at the moment, the past record of the BWIs certainly does not suggest to give them more power, if one uses the normal standards of efficiency as the measuring rod.

Before discussing that point it must be underlined that for the present the IMF did neither perform effectively nor 'in conformity with Keynes's views'. It was not meant to. The BWIs are the result of US requests, not of Keynes's vision. Meier himself makes this clear shortly before, when he writes about the international currency, or adjustment obligations by creditor countries. He also quotes Keynes's principles for a durable international economic system, which include that no special economic or financial sacrifice must be required. The BWIs have clearly done the very opposite of Keynes's advice, for instance by applying pressure exclusively on debtor countries. Their record proves that they have never operated according to Keynes's principles. Nor do they plan to do so.

Compared with Keynes's vision the new order established after World War II was distorted and incomplete. It was distorted because the original intention of pressure on balance of payments surplus countries rather than deficit countries, or at least symmetrical pressure on both, was turned into its opposite. It was incomplete as the International Trade Organization (ITO) did not come into being (Singer, 1993, pp. 8f; Raffer and Singer, 1996, p. 59), which would have incorporated commodity price stabilization to preclude depressing effects from trade. The GATT became, according to Singer (1989, p. 6) 'a weak version, almost a caricature, of the intended ITO', without 'not only the chapters on commodity agreements, but also those on employment, development and restrictive business practices.' (*ibid.*, pp. 6f) Thus the 'third pillar' of Keynes's system remained missing, a gap which – as Sir Hans has repeatedly stated – made the Bretton Woods system vulnerable, helping to bring about its final demise.

The twin institutions survived. While the IBRD had the task of financing projects as a *raison d'être*, the demise of Bretton Woods left the Fund without functions. Its few remaining facilities could easily have been handed over to another institution, for instance the IBRD. Institutional persistence, though, won the day against economic efficiency.

Considering the record of the BWIs the proposal that they should govern the South appears highly problematic. According to *Finance & Development*, the official BWI quarterly, the IMF started Structural Adjustment (SA) policies in Africa already after 1973 (Kanesa-Thasan, 1981). During this early phase, when the Fund was apparently glad to find clients, conditionality was considered lenient 'in relation to the required adjustment effort' (*ibid.*, p. 20). Adjustment programmes were initially planned for one year, apparently because of convenient accounting. In 1979 conditionality became stricter. Eighty-eight arrangements were approved by the IMF between January 1979 and December 1981, to support adjustment policies, particularly measures to reach a sustainable balance of payments position (Crockett, 1982). All countries asking for rescheduling in 1981 'had adopted an adjustment program' with the Fund when negotiating with their creditors (Nowzad, 1982, p. 13). Officially the IBRD started its involvement in programme lending in 1980, but it exerted influence in connection with projects before. The Bank always used its leverage to support the IMF's policy against resistance by SCs. The BWIs, particularly the IMF, did not arrive on the scene until after August 1982 to solve a problem created by others, but they had been part of the process creating it. Their adjustment did not prevent the debt crisis. The first failed adjustment programmes existed before the crisis and exacerbated it.

The date 1982 disguises the long, dismal record of debt management and the ineffectiveness of the policies enforced by the BWIs in restoring the sustainable economic viability of debtor countries. Already in the 1960s the Pearson (*et al.* 1969, p. 153 ff) Report, prepared on request of the president of the IBRD, identified structural origins of the debt problem and strongly recommended debt relief. Although this Report warned of 'many serious difficulties' that could result from 'very large scale lending', the BWIs encouraged SCs to borrow in international financial markets during the 1970s when money was easily available. The behaviour of commercial banks in the uncontrolled and unregulated Euromarket, showering money on SCs without obeying even the most basic principles of prudent banking, surely qualifies Meier's statement that deregulation and the liberalization of international banking were beneficial. So does the recent example of Mexico: some $50 billion of public money were needed to bail out private investors. As Mexico followed the IMF's 'advice' closely, one must question whether the IMF is really able to help countries to deal with the problems created by the Fund's own recommendations, such as unconditional liberalization of capital movements. Sceptics might think of a fox guarding the chicken run.

The BWIs were the last to recognize the debt crisis. After August 1982 BWI publications thought the money market functioned well, seeing no signs of liquidity bottlenecks, nor of restrictions regarding the capital base of private banks limiting lending to SCs, which was supposed to continue on a large scale (for examples versus Raffer, 1994). For quite some time the BWIs had claimed that the debt crisis was a temporary illiquidity problem not a problem of insolvency. More recently the IBRD's (1992b, pp. 10 ff) *World Debt Tables 1992/3* lectured: 'In a solvency crisis, early recognition of solvency as the root cause and the need for a final settlement are important for minimizing the damage ... protracted renegotiations and uncertainty damaged economic activity in debtor countries for several years'. Ahmed and Summers (1992, p. 4) quantify the costs of delaying the recognition of the now generally acknowledged solvency crisis as 'one decade' lost in development. The role of the BWIs in these renegotiations is conveniently forgotten. They present themselves again as the wardens of good economic policies.

Gravest and unbelievable shortcomings can even be found in official documents, such as the so-called Wapenhans Report. Suffice it to mention that the Wapenhans Report (IBRD, 1992a, Annex A, p. 8) felt it necessary to point out expressly that 'the perception that the literary quality of the SAR [Staff Appraisal Report] is in itself a criterion of performance', is wrong. The personnel of an institution calling itself 'bank' had to be reminded of the need to 'drive' this point 'home' (*ibid.*).

The IMF is more secretive, but since the Structrual Adjustment Facilities are administered by both institutions jointly, it is logically impossible that the

Fund's performance differs crucially from the IBRD's. But outspoken criticism exists only from outside the institution, such as in the case of the so-called Budhoo affair (Raffer and Singer, 1996, pp. 179f). It must be pointed out that the Fund has failed to show any proof of success so far, after more than 20 years of SA. Asking what might happen to a salesperson with the same record – assuming that he could stay employed that long – may be a useful help in judging the IMF's performance.

The most important systemic shortcoming of the BWIs is the present incentive system, which is exactly the opposite of an efficient arrangement. The BWIs decide on debtors' economic policies, supervise projects and programmes closely, without accepting the financial risks connected with their decisions. They are even allowed to gain financially from their own errors at their clients' expense. A loan has to be repaid fully, even if failures caused by their staffs created damages. A sufficient amount of failures by multilateral institutions will render BWI-administered SA necessary, just as failed SA programmes are likely to call for new SA programmes, as long as unconditional repayment to BWIs is upheld. This might be described somewhat cynically as 'IFI flops securing IFI jobs' (Raffer, 1993, p. 158).

Their absurd incentive structure, irreconcilably inimical to the very idea of the market mechanism and to any principle of sound management, produces a systemic bias towards accommodating other goals. The Wapenhans Report (IBRD, 1992a) showed this clearly in the case of the IBRD. Institutions exempt from the most basic principle of civilized legal and economic systems, namely that those guilty of damages must pay compensation, cannot be expected to administer effectively. This conclusion is corroborated by the fact that multilateral debts have themselves become a problem. If their projects and programmes had been reasonably successful, economic returns would make BWI loans more or less self-liquidating. Sound economic principles do therefore not allow the conclusion that the BWIs should govern the South. Their record as reliable bailiffs of creditors, on the other hand, may recommend them as agents of a new form of Listian colonialism.

There is also no reason why the WTO should 'govern' the South. First, it remains to be seen how impartial it will be and whether it can be expected to promote development. In contrast to Keynes's ideas it fosters liberalization and the roll-back of government interventions, at least in those sectors where this is in the interest of powerful countries. The WTO sees its own role as promoting deregulation and reducing the government's room for economic manoeuvring, seeing external liberalization as 'a *driving force for domestic liberalization*' or stating that domestic efforts to liberalize 'are best served by a strong external framework' (WTO, 1996, p. 31, emphasis in original). This contrasts vividly from the role of government envisaged by Keynes, not to mention his idea of buffer stocks. The new framework shaped by the WTO is anti-Keynesian, perceptibly reducing the options of national governments for anticyclical policies.

Liberalization is not always equally requested, though. ICs can go on protecting their textile and clothing sector for another decade. Introduced as a 'temporary' measure to allow orderly adjustment decades ago, restrictions on trade in this sector were taken in clear violation of the GATT and explicitly against the effects of the world market. The Decision by the GATT Contracting Parties of 19 November 1960 on the Avoidance of Market Disruption explicitly defined 'market disruption' as a situation where 'price differentials do not arise from governmental intervention in the fixing or formation of prices or from dumping practices.' In spite of this clear anti-market orientation the WTO allows continuing protection against Southern imports. The first phase of 'liberalization' covered – with the exception of one product imported by Canada – only items that had not been subject to restrictions. A sector that could only become competitive in ICs by protection when England destroyed the Indian textile industry is kept alive and 'competitive' by protection, a shining example of actually existing free trade. Like in the case of all 'temporary' Multi-Fibre Arrangements it remains to be seen whether protection of textiles and clothing will actually be phased out as stipulated. This example contrasts with the quick and ruthless adjustment forced on SCs by the BWIs with which the WTO has to co-operate to achieve greater coherence in global economic policy making.

The fact that the WTO stole the acronym of the World Tourist Organization, clearly violating its own Article 15 of the TRIPs Agreement, which explicitly protects letters and combinations of letters, does not show great concern for the rights of less powerful players or the rule of law. Article 3.7 of the Understanding on Rules and Procedures Covering the Settlement of Disputes, to give another example, states: 'Before bringing a case, a Member shall exercise its judgement as to whether action under these procedures would be fruitful. The aim of the dispute settlement mechanism is to secure a positive solution to the dispute.' In plain English this means derogating the rule of law in favour of the law of the jungle.

One has to agree with Professor Meier that more international management, and a strengthening of the international public sector are needed. But global governance must differ from his proposal. Keynes warned against institutions that have 'become diverted to be the instrument of a limited group', as Professor Meier himself writes. Rather than institutions tolerating one law for the rich and another for the poor, an institutional framework of global governance is needed that is committed to the rule of law on the basis of equal treatment. Establishing that will be difficult. Limited space does not allow to do more than sketching the main lines of possible alternatives briefly. These are a strengthening and reforming of the UN system, as proposed by the UNDP (1994) and Jan Tinbergen (in UNDP, 1994, p. 88), the creation of an Economic Security

Council, a World Anti-Monopoly Authority and a World Central Bank. This Authority could revive and adapt the norms on restrictive business practices of the ITO. The Central Bank should pick up Keynes's original idea of a global bank rejected at Bretton Woods. An institution modelled after Keynes's ideas of an International Trade Organization to preclude depressing effects from trade – which would contrast most clearly from the present WTO – would be needed to create a framework without the incompleteness of the former Bretton Woods system. The role of trade must be reconsidered to allow SCs to follow Keynes's ideas and the example of South Korea, as pointed out by Sir Hans, controlling trade and regulating foreign investment. The Tobin tax would provide a counter-incentive against short-term capital movements, enlarging the room for manoeuvring of national economic policy.

The following mechanisms proposed by Raffer and Singer (1996, pp. 195ff) could improve the quality of development co-operation:

- self-monitoring by aid recipients, following the successful example of the Marshall plan;
- financial accountability of multilateral financial institutions and donors in general for damages in the same way private consulting firms are liable to their clients;
- international insolvency procedures internationalizing US Bankruptcy Act Chapter 9 regulating the insolvency of municipalities to deal with the present debt crisis and to help avert future ones. As municipalities have governmental powers these procedures could be applied immediately to sovereign debtors.

Disagreeing with Professor Meier on what kind of international governance is desirable, I have to admit that his vision is more likely to prevail. At present a revival of policies in line with Keynes's ideas looks unlikely. The anti-Keynesian wave is in full swing, going even beyond Kalecki's scenario by creating an institutional framework against Keynesian policies in the future.

References

Ahmed, M. and L. Summer (1992), 'Zehn Jahre Schuldenkrise – eine Bilanz', *Finanzierung & Entwicklung* **29** (3), 2.

Crockett, Andrew (1982), 'Issues in the use of Fund resources', *Finance & Development* **19** (2), 10.

Elsenhans, Hartmut (1996), 'Les fausses modélisations de la globalisation', Paper prepared for the Colloquium *'Insertion dans l'économie mondial et anomie'*, Centre de Recherche sur le Développement, University of Neuchâtel, Switzerland, 9–11 January 1997 (mimeo).

IBRD (1992a), *Effective Implementation: Key to Development Impact, Report of the World Bank's Portfolio Management Task Force* (Wapenhan's Report), Washington DC: IBRD.

IBRD (1992b), *World Debt Tables 1992–1993*, vol. 1, Washington DC: IBRD.

Kalecki, Michał (1971), *Selected Essays on the Dynamics of the Capitalist Economy 1933–1970*, Cambridge: Cambridge University Press.

Kanesa-Thasan, S. (1981), 'The Fund and adjustment policies in Africa', *Finance & Development*, 18 (3), 20.

Keynes, John Maynard (1967), *The General Theory of Employment, Interest and Money*, Macmillan: London.

List, Friedrich (1920), *Das nationale System der politischen Ökonomie*, Jena: Fischer (originally published in 1841).

Murshed S.M. and K. Raffer (eds) (1993), *Trade, Transfers and Development, Problems and Prospects for the Twenty-First Century*, Aldershot: Edward Elgar.

Nowzad, Bahram (1982), 'Debt in developing countries: some issues for the 1980s', *Finance & Development* **19** (1), 13.

Pearson, Lester B., Sir Edward Boyle, Roberto de Olivera Campos, C. Douglas Dillon, Wilfred Guth, W. Arthur Lewis, Robert E. Marjohin, and Saburo Okita. (1969), *Partners in Development: Report of the Commission on International Development*, New York: Praeger

Raffer, Kunibert (1993), 'International Financial Institutions and Accountability: The Need for Drastic Change', in Murshed and Raffer (eds), p. 151.

Raffer, Kunibert (1994), '"Structural adjustment", liberalisation, and poverty' *Journal für Entwicklungspolitik*, 10 (4), 431.

Raffer, Kunibert and H.W. Singer (1996), *The Foreign Aid Business: Economic Assistance and Development Co-operation*, Cheltenham: Edward Elgar.

Singer, H.W. (1937), *Men Without Work*, Cambridge: Cambridge University Press.

Singer, H.W. (1989), 'Lessons of Post-War Development Experience 1945–1988', *IDS Discussion Paper* no. 260.

Singer, H.W. (1993), 'Prospects for Development', in Murshed and Raffer (eds), pp. 7ff.

UNDP (1994), *Human Development Report*, Oxford Oxford University Press.

WTO (1996), *Annual Report 1996*, vol. I, Geneva: WTO.

11   The state and the economy 50 ye
Keynes

Đuro Benić

The state's role in the economy is a much discussed subject in the history of economic thought. While Adam Smith advocated the philosophy of minimization of the state's interference in the economy, which served as the basis of economic liberalism and classical economic theory for more than a century, Keynes was the prophet of state interventionism. This chapter deals with Keynes's interpretation of the role of the state (government) in economic policy. Keynes pointed out many possibilities, open, in general, for a government to regulate economic life in a country. Accordingly, since the 'Keynesian Revolution' the government has greatly been responsible for the overall functioning and the effectiveness of the economic system. It is true that since the late 1960s, different opinions and discords have existed concerning the measures which a government should adopt, but all economists do agree that the government is responsible for the overall effectiveness of the economy. Here an effort has, however, been made to put forward a simple thesis that Keynes wrote for his time and day and that times have changed since then. In the 1990s the more neo-liberal world and thinking of the 1970s and the 1980s may also be in a process of change and to no one's surprise the world may possibly shift back to some extent towards a more Keynesian position.

Keynes's vision of government's role

The inevitability of governmental intervention in the economy is usually implied by the expression 'Keynesian economy' and it consequently implies some rules in the conduct of economic policy. However Keynes's most important work, *The General Theory of Employment, Interest and Money*, devotes very little space to the implementation of that theory in the running of economic policy. The reason is probably that policy ought to be determined for specific circumstances; while theory covers a broad range of circumstances (Chick, 1983, p. 316).[1] Keynes was aware of this and he always believed that ideas could and should be adapted to a specific practice (Kahn, 1972, p. 103). However the fact is that the appearance of John Maynard Keynes and his macroeconomic theory meant a break with the classical paradigm of the inevitability to equilibrate under conditions of full employment, and that it opened wide opportunities for the government to run a macroeconomic policy of stabilization.

The post-war period was marked in the majority of economies by strong governmental legal regulation, a strengthening of the public sector and operations in the open market, which meant a strong role for the government in regulating economic flows. The monetarist approach has tried to prove, since the 1970s, the advisability of decreasing governmental intervention in the economy through the narrowing of its legal interference, privatization of the public sector and elimination of the budget deficit. The fact should be borne in mind that the abandonment of illusions about 'Keynesianism' was caused by the fact that Keynesian policies were used for a world for which they had never been intended (Chick, *op. cit.*, p. 317). Just because of that, it is necessary to remember for a moment the problem Keynes tried to resolve, and consequently the role of the government in his interpretation.

Keynes was writing at a time when there was a vacuum in economic thought, that is to say when it was impossible to explain and to resolve the economic problems which cropped up after World War I. The central problem he tried to explain and resolve was unemployment, which was high for more than a decade without any sign of decline. Granting priority to reducing unemployment, and not to other macroeconomic aims, such as stability of prices and economic growth, defined the role of the government, and a new direction of economic policy. Namely, that government should participate actively in the struggle against unemployment, since the monetary policy, under conditions of high unemployment, is completely ineffective in increasing employment. Thus the alternative, according to Keynes, is an expansionist fiscal policy, or more exactly, government spending on public works, financed by budget deficits, that is to say by creation of new money. How did Keynes come to this solution? This can be examined here briefly in two ways.

Firstly, according to the quantity theory of money, the demand for money consists of transactional demand and precautionary demand. Keynes adds a third element to this – the speculative demand of money conditioned essentially by interest rates. Thus the demand for money is divided into active demand, indispensable for transactions and/or precaution and inactive demand intended for speculations. While active demand depends on the level of national income of the economy, the inactive demand depends on interest rates. At low interest rates, expectations will be linked to the rise of rates and the fall of bond prices which, with the probability that income from bonds will not be sufficient to abandon the precaution of keeping money in cash, leads to a high speculative demand for money and to a low demand for keeping bonds (that is his concept of liquidity preference). Besides, interest rates would be quite low during periods of depression. Speculators would be unwilling to keep tied up reserves so that their demand for money would absorb every offered amount. Every increase in the offer of money would be balanced by a corresponding increase in demand, and interest rates would not fall. In such a case monetary policy would

be totally inefficient (Screpanti and Zamagni, 1995, pp. 268–9). Fr(
interpretation, it follows that a situation is possible when there is unen
and surplus capacity in the economy, and as monetary policy cannot re:
problem, fiscal policy and public investment become a necessity.

Secondly, in order to increase employment, it is necessary to increase
effective demand and that is possible in two ways – by increasing the propensity
to spend (which might be obtained by a redistribution of income) or by an increase
in investments (Chick, op. cit., pp. 317–8). Investments can be increased in two
ways – by an increase in the marginal efficiency of capital, which really means
an increase in profit expectation, or by a lower interest rate. When demand cannot
be increased in the above mentioned ways (for example, when interest rate is
low enough, as it was then), the only possibility is to fill the gap between
potential output and current demand with government spending. Keynes was
very clear regarding the financing of government spending, that is public
works. The source for that to him was new money. The effect of spending would
in his opinion lead to an increase in employment and a decrease in the cost of
compensation for unemployment. Demand as well as employment would be
further increased by the effect of multiplier, and if income grows sufficiently,
taxes may rise as well and the deficit caused by financing of public works would
not be as expensive for the government as it might seem. On the other hand, the
effect on prices at the very low level of output would be minimal.

Besides, the growth of income can change the expectations of investors, who
might then increase their investment.

The derived estimate that fiscal policy is successful unlike a monetary one,
is not emphasized as a general principle because every element in such an
approach depends on the actual situation in various economies.

Accordingly, the government comes into play temporarily, that is when it is
necessary. Keynes tries to prove that there are fields of activity in which private
initiative is indispensable and in which the government should not interfere, but
there are also activities in which the government acts more efficiently than the
private sector.

During his lecture in Germany in 1926, Keynes had already pointed to the
indispensability of government intervention, specifying that 'technically social'
services should be separated from those which are 'technically individual'. The
most important agenda of the state are not those belonging to the scope of action
of an individual, which he already fulfils, but those functions which are outside
that scope, which nobody fulfils and which nobody will fulfil if the government
does not take them over. It is important that the government does not do what
individuals have already been doing, whether it does better or worse than an
individual, but that it does what, at the present, nobody does (Keynes, 1994, p. 79).

The role of the government expands to the mutual adaptation of the inclination
to spend and of the encouragement to invest. Keynes emphasizes in his *General*

Theory that such expansion of the role of government might seem to some as a great restriction of individualism. However, he defends this as the only feasible way of avoiding the destruction of the entire existing system of economic life, but also as a precondition for successful entrepreneurial activity of the individuals (Keynes, 1987, p. 214). An active role of government does not, by any means, cause an overall suppression of the market mechanism. With the intervention of state authorities to harmonize the inclination to spend with the attractions of investment, there are no additional reasons for the socialization of economic life (Keynes, *ibid.*, p. 213).

Keynes emphasizes that the ultimate goal should be to choose those variables which central government can control consciously, and govern them, and that, in the kind of society we live in (Keynes, *ibid.*, p. 145). That means that government intervention is indispensable to save the whole system, and the choice of variables depends on their effectiveness and applicability in the given situation (Heilbronner and Thurow, 1995, p. 33). It is normal to discuss the effectiveness of various variables. The monetarists point out the key role of regulating the money supply, while orthodox Keynesians emphasize government spending and the level of investment. These differences are of less importance in reality. As Modigliani (1991, p.17) points out, these differences are of secondary importance and they can be reduced to emphasis and not to principle. The basic and most important difference is in an attitude towards the need for a stabilization policy and the right role of the government that does not come from analytical differences, but is primarily concerned with the difference in empirical estimates of the value of some crucial parameters of the system, and, in the same measure, with differences in social attitudes and views.

We have to bear in mind also that Keynes's *General Theory* was, above all, a tract about the Great Depression, and that Keynes did not give general policy signposts for the functioning of the economy, neither did he provide a programme for the future development (Galbraith, 1995, p. 197). It is true that he emphasized in his essay 'Economic Prospects of Our Grandchildren' (1930), that 'economic problems are not permanent problems of humanity and that the chances are that they may be resolved in some hundred years (the forecast, after more than sixty-five years, which seems to have proved so far unrealistic) (Keynes, 1987, p. 87–8)'. But the fundamental thing in his work is the explanation and the solution of the problem which faced humanity at that time, and that was unemployment. His *General Theory* rests on five key suppositions founded on the world as Keynes looked at it, and we have to distinguish whether our world is significantly different. These suppositions are: unemployment is the rule; there is wide stability of prices; the availability of money is completely inflexible; resources of capital and technique are given; population does not increase significantly; and the capital resources are insufficient.

The role of the government, 50 years after his death, has essentially changed. The government does not behave as a temporary agent in action when it is necessary but participates in production on a long-term basis. Beginning with the government which increases effective demand by government spending, that is by public works, the role of government in contemporary economies has expanded in several fields.

Government's role in modern economy

The market is not the only and almighty regulating mechanism that obtains optimal results and provides answers to the basic economic questions, how and for whom to produce. It is able to do this only if some very restrictive preconditions are fulfilled. These preconditions are necessary for the unity of interests at various levels and for concordance between individual and social optimum, and they refer to tastes, resources and competition.

The following preconditions must be fulfilled for the effective action of the market as an automatic regulator of the economic system: the quantity of disposable resources, technology and tastes are given as a constant; demand is the result of real social needs; diminishing returns dominate the production, that is there is no economy of scales; the producers seek to maximize both the profit and the consumer's utility within the limits of disposable income; conditions of total competition reign in the market. These preconditions are general but not fulfilled in reality. Economists agree that there is a built-in dynamic inefficiency in the market that results due to the time lag between the decision-making process and the outcomes. It is for this reason that any market information is reliable only in the short run.

Besides, there are situations where the market as the allocator of resources fails, even in perfect conditions; that is, there are situations which the market mechanism cannot, by definition, resolve and they are known in literature as market failures. Two such cases are the phenomena which prevent the re-establishment of an equilibrium – indivisibility of factors and products, and the economy of scales, and another two causes leading to a suboptimal equilibrium – the externalities and the public goods.

Precisely due to the above mentioned drawbacks of market mechanism in the allocation of resources in all world economies, a simultaneous action of the market mechanism and government intervention is necessary. Additional regulation, in tandem with the market, is necessary for the success of the economic system, and therefore the involvement of government is of special importance.

We can generally speak about three economic functions of government, and those are: advancing efficiency, equity and stability.[2] The government fulfils its function of advancing efficiency seeking to correct market imperfections and failures, whereas, by advancing equity, it seeks to correct great income inequalities which are unacceptable either morally or politically. The government fulfils the function of advancing stability, that is to say curbing inflation and unemployment and increasing economic growth, in the first place by fiscal and monetary policy, where Keynes's theory remains one of the fundamental approaches (especially if we take into account particular countries in specific circumstances).

The question can well be asked: how actively should the government participate in economic life, or in which direction is its involvement most desirable?

The experiences of the 1970s and the 1980s demonstrates that government that tried to take over key points in their economies have shown a descending trend and a stagnation of growth. Conversely, higher rates of growth were obtained by those countries where the intervention of government in the economy was less, with the outstanding examples of the Asian 'tigers' (Hong Kong, Singapore and Taiwan). Consequently, government administration should abandon its function of the production and allocation of goods and services – those activities which are best fulfilled through market competition. Governments should try to create a free market environment in which it allows free action of the market, intervening efficiently only when and (where) the market proves to be inadequate.[3]

The growth experience of various countries proves the importance of six growth factors (accumulation of physical capital; best possible use of human capital; intensive research, development and innovations; better management and organization; improved physical and social infrastructure; and optimal allocation of output between immediate production sectors), pointing out also the role of stimulating the process of growth by competition and the possibilities for government action, for example in its concern for education and physical and social infrastructure. However theory and experience show very little that public ownership of the means of production is an indispensable or useful element (Stern, 1991, p. 131).

Consequently the involvement of the government is of special significance in relation to human capital, scientific research, improving the infrastructure (physical and social), creating the best environment for encouraging enterprising spirit, stability of economic movement, growth of the overall factors of productivity and the advancement of global competition.[4]

This is a general consideration and claim. The fact is that there are differences in the size of the involvement of government measured by the percentage of the gross domestic product (GDP) in various countries. In some countries, the government is generally occupied with legal structure and some goods and services, such as roads and national defence, which are difficult to provide in the private sector. On the other hand, the government in some countries is involved in all kinds of activities from the management of air companies, hotels, theatres, radio and television to the production of iron. Among the developed and fast growing countries of the world the total government (current and capital) expenditure (as a percentage of GNP) in 1994 ranged from a high in The Netherlands – 52.9 per cent, Belgium – 50.4 per cent, Sweden – 51.0 per cent, Norway – 49.8 per cent, France – 47.4 per cent, UK – 42.7 per cent, Germany – 33.6 per cent, to a moderate percentage in Australia – 28.2 per cent, and in the US – 23.0 per cent, and to a significantly low share in the GNP to 17.6 per cent in Singapore, 18.9 per cent in South Korea and 15.3 per cent in Thailand.[5]

However it is also a fact that the process of privatization, both of state enterprises and great public systems (particularly in traffic and communications) has been present, since the 1980s, in some developed countries – notably the US, France, and the UK.[6] The experience of these countries shows that private firms are more efficient than public ones, and consequently the government should abandon the function of production as it is best performed through market competition.[7] The government should withdraw from the economy as the basic allocation mechanism, that is as the largest owner and entrepreneur, and the focus of economic policy should be transferred from a short-term regulation of the amount of spending to the structural effects on the supply side, including – as already emphasized – assisting in education and investment in human capital, advancement of the physical and social infrastructure, stimulation of research and innovation, and in creating a suitable institutional and legal environment for the development of entrepreneurship and the stability of economic activity.

Government's role in developing countries
The role of government in economic development of the developing countries is a theme of many discussions. Theoretical research in economics carried out immediately after World War II points out that the main function of the government is promoting industrialization through planning and direct involvement in production process. The justification for such an approach was that market failures in the developing countries were on the increase and that government had to substitute for the market in numerous ways.[8] Later, opposite views appeared which minimized the role of the state. However, on the basis of theory and experience, it can be proved that the role of the government cannot be minimal. Only one question arises: towards which fields should the direction of its actions be orientated?

Before we consider this, we should bear in mind that this is the general view of the role of government in the developing countries. The fact is that developing countries differ from each other in many things. Although over 85 per cent of the world population live in the developing countries, they only earn 22 per cent of the world income. In 1992, the gross national product (GNP) per inhabitant in the 37 poorest countries was on average US$390 only, and in the 23 richest countries US$22 160, while the average life expectancy in the 10 poorest countries of the world was 48 years, and in the 10 richest countries 77 years. Also there are great differences within the poor countries themselves. For example, GNP per capita in India is US$310, Bangladesh US$220, Ethiopia US$110 and in Mozambique only US$60. Further the countries differ in the level of industrialization achieved, the existence and size of the market, the development of infrastructure, health services, education and so on, which largely condition the direction and the intensity of government actions in various countries.

Under such conditions, generally speaking, the role of the government cannot be minimal, but it is certain that the main direction of its activity should not be in production but in the fields of health care, education, protection of the poor, infrastructure (physical and social) and in management and organization, that is in securing such an environment which will stimulate the spirit of entrepreneurship. These directions of action are valid for all contemporary economies, including the developing countries.[9]

A lack of infrastructure, together with weakness of management and economic organization, cause – probably significantly – a low factor productivity in developing countries. It is difficult to expect efficiency of the factors and businesses in those countries where the supply of electrical energy and water is unreliable, telephone and postal services weak, and the traffic slow and dangerous. Social infrastructure has a special significance referring more to the way the business is run than to human capital (in the field of literacy, technical knowledge and so on.). A system without a complete business morality where individuals see the source of profit in various forms of corruption, or where bureaucracy is obstructionist, or where ownership rights have not been clearly defined, can bring about an uneconomical allocation of resources, accompanied by expenses and distortions of stimuli that can be serious obstacles to growth. The weaknesses of management, organization and infrastructure can explain the phenomenon of unproductive use of scarce capital, and why some countries, such as India in the 1960s and the 1970s, did not score higher growth rates although having successfully boosted their rates of saving.

On the one hand, in the majority of developing countries, the system of industrial licensing, restrictions on export and import, control of prices, inappropriate employment laws, the founding of enterprises and ownership rights have weakened the force of competition, slowed down technological progress and the growth of productivity (Weiss, 1995, p. 7). We often hear that curbing of the labour market has helped developing countries in bringing about the competitive pressure to export, and that it is necessary by all means for successful economic growth and development. However the experience of the Asian 'tigers' of East Asia is worth mentioning. Significant results have been obtained in achieving and maintaining full employment, growth of real wages, improvement of the structure of employment, decreasing income inequalities and lowering the rate of poverty. The economic growth produced by the rise in exports was not based on the curbing of wages, that is on the curbing of the labour market but, on the contrary, that growth was accompanied by an improvement of the conditions in the labour market (Fields, 1994, pp. 397–403).

On the other hand, we have to bear in mind that the countries which recorded highest rates of growth were those with the greatest rise of productivity, whereas economic growth was stagnant in the countries with only a small rise in productivity. The question can be asked: what does lead to a rise in productivity? That is surely technological progress. However technological progress is influenced by: history, culture, the system of education, institutions and applied policies. The term technology is quite broad and it is applied through investment in physical and human capital. Therefore investment in human and physical capital and the strengthening of market competition are significant potential sources of local growth. The research undertaken on the sample of 60 developing countries for the period 1965–87, correlates the rise of productivity and output with education and economic policy. It shows that education of labour contributes significantly to a rise in productivity and output, as well as a successful environmental policy. Also, besides its individual effect on productivity and growth, there is an interaction effect when education and policy are combined. Experience shows that investment in people, together with increasing quality and quantity, is another kind of infrastructure which is comprised basically in a development programme and which is within the competence of the government, creating the best environment for the rise of productivity and the advancement of entrepreneurship. This includes a list of activities such as advancing the development of the market and a competitive micro economy; a clear definition and protection of ownership rights, attracting foreign capital; openness; a stable macro economy, and improved management and so on.

Endnotes

1. Keynes states, in the preface to the *General Theory* that the main aim of his book is to deal with difficult questions of theory, and only the secondary intention is to apply this theory to practice (Keynes, 1987, p. 13). In fact, the *General Theory* gave less space to systematic discussion economic policy issues than any other Keynes's book (see for details Leijonhufvud, 1983, p. 268).
2. This division can be found in the introductory text books of *Economics* (see for example Samuelson and Nordhaus, 1995, pp. 30–35). The traditional role of the government in a market economy revolves around five basic tasks: providing certain goods and services such as national defence, raising taxes to pay for these services, redistributing income, regulating business, and making and enforcing the law (see Baumol and Blinder (1994, p. 42).
3. See, for example, Jurin (1992, p. 31–2) for the interpretation.
4. In the OECD and EU countries, it is now generally accepted that industrial policy should not get involved in the market mechanism, instead it should increase the market's efficiency through horizontal policies – policies which seek to increase the quality of important product inputs

136   John Maynard Keynes

(education, research and development, telecommunications and so on). Through such measures, policy makers in these countries seek to improve the general economic environment and produce effects benefiting all market agents. Such a market-oriented industrial policy does not threaten the allocation of resources and reduces state intervention to its lowest possible level (Kesner-Škreb 1995, p. 387).

5   The data is based on the statistics of the World Bank (*World Development Report*, 1996). However it is interesting to note that the total government spending in the US in 1929 amounted to 10.1 per cent of GDP, whereas in the period between 1930 and 1970 it rose significantly, and in 1970 it amounted to 30.8 per cent. Since then its share has continued to rise but at a slower rate and, in 1993, it amounted to 34.4 per cent of GDP (see Gwartney and Stroup, 1995, p. 115).

6.   Since the 1980s, almost 50 of the biggest businesses in the UK have been privatized (see for details Bailey, 1995, pp. 291, 296–7).

7.   One should bear in mind here that there are numerous methodological difficulties in comparing the efficiency of nationalized industries and private companies. Thus, it is not easy to make such judgements. Further, political, social, industrial and economic conditions relevant for each industry are not directly comparable at the time of enforcing nationalization and at the time of privatization. Also, the criticism that the monopoly of the public sector is transformed, by privatization, into a monopoly of the private sector is not necessarily true, because a change in the market structure cannot occur overnight. The fact is that the effect of privatization depends on the form of regulation, and on the development of technology and market structures.

8.   See Grabowski and Shields, 1996, p. 267.

9.   The differences in GNP per capita need not be the main indicator of the situation in various countries. Thus, in China, with US$470, the life expectancy is 70 years, and the infant mortality rate 31 per thousand, whereas in Brazil, with US$2.770 per capita income, the life expectancy is 65 years and the infant mortality rate 61 per thousand (Meier, 1995, p. 549).

9.   The data for 1986–7 shows that developing countries show less attention to health care and social security than developed countries (seen as the percentage of the total government spending), while more attention is paid to defence and general public services, education, transport and communications, and other services (*ibid.*, p. 550).

References

Bailey, S.J. (1995), *Public Sector Economics – Theory, Policy and Practice*, London: Macmillan.
Baumol, W.J. and Blinder, A.S. (1994), *Economics – Principles and Policy*, Fort Worth: The Dryden Press.
Chick, V. (1983), *Macroeconomics After Keynes – A Reconsideration of the General Theory*, Cambridge, Mass.: The MIT Press.
Fields, G.S. (1994), 'Changing Labour Market Conditions and Economic Development in Hong Kong, the Republic of Korea, Singapore, and Taiwan, China', *The World Bank Economic Review*, 8 (2),397–403.
Galbraith, J.K. (1995), *Ekonomija u perspektivi – kritička povijest*, Zagreb: Mate.
Grabowski, R. and Shields, M.P. (1996), *Development Economics*, Oxford: Blackwell.
Gwartney, J.D. and Stroup, R.L. (1995), *Economics – Private and Public Choice*, Fort Worth: The Dryden Press.
Heilbroner, R.L. and Thurow, L.C. (1995), *Ekonomija za svakoga*, Zagreb: Mate.
Jurin, S. (1992), 'Strategija gospodarskog razvoja Republike Hrvatske', *Ekonomska misao i praksa*, 1 (1), 31–2.
Kahn, R. (1972), *Selected Essays on Employment and Growth*, London: Cambridge University Press.
Kesner-Škreb, M. (1995), 'Intervencija države u poticanju gospodarske aktivnosti u tržišnim privredama', *Financijska praksa*, 19 (5), 387.
Keynes, J.M. (1987), *Opća teorija zaposlenosti, kamate i novca*, Zagreb: Cekade.
Keynes, J.M. (1994), 'Kraj laissez-fairea' in J.M. Keynes, *Izabrana djela*, Zagreb: Privredni vjesnik i Matica hrvatska.
Leijonhufvud, A. (1983), *O kejnezijanskoj ekonomici i ekonomici J.M. Keynesa*, Zagreb: Cekade.

Meier, G.M. (1995), *Leading Issues in Economic Development*, New York: Oxford University Press.

Modigliani, F. (1991), *Rasprava o stabilizacijskoj politici*, Zagreb: Cekade.

Samuelson, P.A. and Nordhaus, W.D. (1995), *Economics*, New York: McGraw-Hill.

Screpanti, E. and Zamagni, S. (1995), *An Outline of History of Economic Thought*, Oxford: Clarendon Press.

Stern, N. (1991), 'The Determinants of Growth', *The Economic Journal*, **101** (404), 131.

Weiss, J. (1995), *Economic Policy in Developing Countries – The Reform Agenda*, London: Prentice Hall, Harvester Wheatsheaf.

World Bank (1996), *The World Development Report*, Washington DC: The World Bank.

PART III

UNEMPLOYMENT, WAGE AND PRICES

12 Keynes, involuntary unemployment and wage and price inflexibility
John S.L. McCombie

There is a certain irony in the recent renaissance in Keynesian economics that the form of the new Keynesian economics concentrates on the role of price stickiness in explaining involuntary unemployment. In many ways this is reminiscent of the neoclassical synthesis of the 1960s, which attributed unemployment to money wage, and hence price rigidity; and this was often criticized as resulting from money illusion or as an *ad hoc* assumption. Consequently, the *General Theory* (Keynes, 1936), far from being general, was seen merely as a special case of the classical system, although with important policy conclusions and new theoretical concepts, such as the consumption function (Leijonhufvud, 1968).

The quantity-constrained models that arose out of the work of Clower (1965) and Leijonhufvud (1968), and which were the precursors of the new Keynesian economics, seemed to be a rehabilitation of Keynes because the problem of lack of effective demand returned to the centre of the stage. But again, it was argued that this approach required price stickiness. Thus, the purpose of the new Keynesian economics is to provide a satisfactory theoretical rationale for this in terms of optimizing agents and hence remove the charge of *ad hocery* (Mankiw, 1990; Gordon, 1990).

But the post-Keynesians claim that neither this nor the Aggregate Demand/Aggregate Supply (AD/AS) model are Keynes (Davidson, 1992). Firstly, there is no independent role for the lack of effective demand and, secondly, Keynes himself explicitly ruled out money wage and price inflexibility as the *cause* of involuntary unemployment. Mankiw (1994) gives the game away when he suggests that 'the new Keynesian economics is much more in line with the neoclassical synthesis than with Post-Keynesian analysis'.

It is the purpose of this chapter to examine these issues in further depth.

Involuntary unemployment and sticky wages and prices

It became part of the orthodoxy of the neoclassical synthesis that Keynesian unemployment was due to a combination of money and price stickiness. To see this, suppose, for example, that the economy is subject to a deflationary shock which drives the price level down. If there is money wage rigidity, this will cause the real wage to rise. Through the neoclassical short-run production function,

141

this will result in a rise in unemployment. On the other hand, money wage flexibility is likely to remove involuntary unemployment. Suppose real wages are initially too high: then, if the labour market is competitive, money wages will fall. This will lead directly to a less than proportional fall in the price level (hence reducing the real wage) or to an increase in effective demand through the Keynes and the Pigou effect, or both. An increase in effective demand would in turn cause a rise in the price level, leading to a fall in the real wage and hence, through the short-run production function, to a rise in employment.

Consequently, in the early assessments of the *General Theory*, there was much discussion about whether or not the persistence of involuntary unemployment relied on money illusion and sticky prices. This was especially pertinent as Keynes explicitly argued that workers would be more willing to accept a cut in real wages due to a rise in the price level than through a reduction in money wages with prices held constant (*General Theory*, p. 264). The consensus of opinion was summarized by Samuelson (1963) when he wrote that 'had Keynes begun his first few chapters with the simple statement that he found it realistic to assume that modern capitalistic societies had money wage rates that were sticky downward and resistant to downward movements, most of his insights would have remained just as valid'. Such a view opened Keynes to the charge that the *General Theory* was nothing more than a special case of the classical system with the *ad hoc* assumption of sticky money wages and, hence, prices imposed.

Trevithick (1976) provided a justification for workers resisting a cut in money wages while accepting a fall in their real wages due to a general price rise in terms of utility maximization when relative wages are an argument of the utility function. (But see Addison and Burton (1982) for a critique of this view.) But, to a certain extent, this is beside the point. While Keynes did make some passing remarks about the role of wage relativities, it was only that – a passing remark. The reason is that Keynes did not see unemployment as being caused by the rigidity of money wages or by the demand by workers for an excessive real wage. He was quite explicit about this: 'It is not very plausible to assert that unemployment in the United States in 1932 was due either to labour obstinately refusing to accept a reduction in money-wages or to its obstinately demanding a real wage beyond what the productivity of the economic machine was capable of furnishing' (*General Theory*, p. 9). There is no doubt that Keynes was not only sceptical of the possibility of persuading labour to take money wage cuts, but was also concerned that such a policy, even if successful, would be inequitable (see Kahn's (1984, pp. 126–33) discussion) and would be likely to depress further aggregate demand.[1] The fall in nominal interest rates consequent on the fall in prices was likely to be accompanied by a worsening of entrepreneurial expectations; any movement down the marginal efficiency of capital (MEC) schedule (the Keynes effect) would be more than offset by the leftward shift of the schedule itself. Furthermore, writing in 1931, Keynes discounted the Pigou effect, proffering the view that 'there is a degree of deflation which no bank can stand.... Modern capitalism is faced, in my belief, with the choice of finding some way to increase money values towards their former figure, or seeing widespread insolvencies and defaults and the collapse of a large part of the financial structure' (Keynes, 1972, p. 157, cited by Kahn, 1984, p. 133).

As Keynes pointed out, labour could not bargain for the real wage, which was determined by 'certain other forces' (*General Theory*, p. 13), notably the level of effective demand. One interpretation of why this occurs is that a cut in the money wage would result in an equiproportionate cut in prices (because price is equal to marginal prime cost which is determined by the money wage). Thus the real wage would remain unaltered.

However, in Chapter 19 of the *General Theory*, Keynes seems to accept that a fall in money wages would reduce the real wage. In discussing the classical argument, he agreed that 'prices certainly do not change in exact proportion to changes in money wages' (*General Theory*, p. 259) and 'a reduction in money wages will somewhat reduce prices' (*General Theory*, p. 262). Whether or not this would stimulate employment, Keynes considered, depended on a number of factors, including the effect of a possible redistribution of income on the propensity to consume; the effect of lower money wages relative to those abroad; the effect of a collapse in investment as the debt burden of firms increases; the effect of a lower interest rate on investment; and the expectations of the subsequent direction of changes of money wages. The overall conclusion to which Keynes came was that the net effect on demand from an exogenous cut in the money wage was likely to be adverse; hence he argued that rigid money wages should actually be a policy objective. Money wage rigidity was not a behavioural assumption. Consequently Keynes held that even though the real wage may fall in the short run, there is no guarantee that employment will increase.[2]

How is it then that the orthodox textbook interpretation of Keynes still often asserts that his explanation depends upon either downward money wage or real wage rigidity? The answer lies in Chapter 2 of the *General Theory*.

Chapter 2 of the *General Theory*

In Chapter 2, Keynes considered the standard aggregate analysis of the labour market based on the demand for and supply of labour. He argued that the fact that all markets were assumed to clear was based on what he termed the two classical postulates. He showed, to his own satisfaction at least, why the acceptance of both these postulates ruled out involuntary unemployment. He then rapidly proceeded to his own explanation as to why involuntary unemployment could occur in Chapter 3, in terms of the lack of effective demand. He never successfully integrated the analysis of the labour market into his explanation.

This opened the door for the neoclassical synthesis which, as has been noted, effectively reduced the *General Theory* to a special case of the classical theory. I have a certain sympathy with the view that Keynes rushed through the analysis of Chapter 2 (which occupies only 18 pages out of the 400-page book), keen to get on and present his own views of the determination of the level of employment in terms of demand factors.

The difficulty with Keynes's own argument stems precisely from his taking the two classical postulates as his starting point, primarily at the insistence of Harrod (Keynes, 1973a, pp. 533–4). Harrod argued, in effect, that it would be poor rhetoric, in McCloskey's (1985) sense of the term, to abandon the assumption that two independent demand and supply functions jointly determine equilibrium prices and quantities.

The first classical postulate is the traditional neoclassical marginal product theory of factor pricing condition that 'I. *The wage is equal to the marginal product of labour'*. Keynes kept the first postulate while arguing that the second postulate, 'II. *The utility of the wage when a given volume of labour is equal to the marginal disutility of that amount of employment'*, was inapplicable. To assert that the latter postulate held necessarily implied that the economy was fully employed. Consequently, when there was unemployment, the short side of the market (namely, the demand for labour given by the first postulate) determined the actual level of employment.

According to Keynes the first postulate is the result of profit maximization and the existence of diminishing returns. It implies that

> with a given organisation, equipment and technique, real wages and the volume of output (and hence of employment) are uniquely correlated, so that, in general, an increase in employment can only occur to the accompaniment of a decline in the rate of real wages. Thus, I am not disputing this vital fact which the classical economists have (rightly) asserted as indefeasible. In a given state of organisation, equipment and technique, the real wage earned by a unit of labour has a unique (inverse) correlation with the volume of employment. Thus, *if* employment increases, then, in the short period, the reward per unit of labour in terms of wage-goods must in general decline and profits increase. (*General Theory*, p. 17, emphasis in the original, omitting a footnote).

But while a fall in the real wages is a necessary condition for an increase in employment, Keynes considered that it is not sufficient. The choice of the word 'correlation' by Keynes was deliberate as it does not imply causation. It is effective demand that determines the level of employment, which in turn determines the marginal product of labour and hence the wage. Keynes is quite explicit about this: 'the propensity to consume and the rate of new investment determine between them the volume of employment which is uniquely related to a given level of real wages – not the other way around'. Moreover, in

Chapter 19, Keynes explicitly rejects the assumptions underlying the short-run neoclassical aggregate production function.

> For the demand schedules for particular industries can only be constructed on some fixed assumption as to the nature of the demand and supply schedules of other industries and as to the amount of the aggregative effective demand. It is invalid, therefore, to transfer the argument to industry as a whole unless we also transfer our assumption that the aggregate effective demand is fixed. Yet this assumption reduces the argument to an *ignoratio elenchi* (*General Theory*, p. 259).

Thus, according to Keynes, a fall in the money wage will only increase employment if it is '*accompanied by the same aggregate effective demand as before*' (*General Theory*, p. 259, emphasis in the original), but there is no guarantee that this will be the case (Davidson and Smolensky, 1964). However this important qualification was completely overlooked in the neoclassical synthesis, possibly because it did not come in Chapter 2 but much later in the *General Theory*. Nevertheless its existence has been repeatedly pointed out by the post-Keynesians (for example Thirlwall, 1983).

Consequently the unique direction of causation from the level of employment to the real wage was also lost in the neoclassical synthesis, which adopted the traditional neoclassical one-sector short-run production function with capital labour substitution. In other words, as more labour is employed, capital is spread more thinly over those employed. A unidirectional causation in these circumstances becomes untenable and could be dismissed on the grounds that Keynes had simply not appreciated the simultanity in his implicit model.

For sake of argument, suppose that the real wage is above its market clearing level and unemployment exists. If there is an *exogenous* fall in the real wage, then, given that firms are profit maximizers, the level of output must automatically increase, *pari passu*, as the economy moves down the labour marginal productivity curve. The volume of output (the area under the marginal productivity curve) must also increase and, in effect, Say's law holds: the increase in supply necessarily creates its own demand. For expositional ease, let us assume a classical savings function so that workers consume all they spend and all profits are invested. As the real wage falls and employment increases, investment will automatically increase. The neoclassical interpretation of Keynes's demand and supply-side model is, in a sense, over-determined since changes in the level of investment are also determined by fluctuations in 'animal spirits'. These, in turn, determine shifts of the MEC schedule and changes in the rate of interest, which cause movements along the MEC schedule. But there is no mechanism in the model by which a fall in the real wage will necessarily cause 'animal spirits' and the rate of interest to change in such a way as to induce exactly the required increase in investment. With the use of the short-run production function and a fall in the real wage rate, these considerations are effectively ignored. The whole demand side – the centre piece of the *General Theory* – has become irrelevant, since the fall in the real wage, by itself, will generate the requisite demand to purchase the increased supply.

The only way for a fall in the real wage not to lead to an increased output is for the first postulate to be violated or amended; this will be discussed below. But if we accept the conventional production function, the whole of the *General Theory* depends on a mechanism that prevents real wages from adjusting downwards, that is a market imperfection of some sort.

This is carried over to the textbook discussion of the Keynesian model in terms of the AD/AS model. A typical story goes as follows. Consider the economy initially in equilibrium. There is a deflationary shock and prices fall as the AD curve shifts down to the left. Money wages are assumed to be rigid (because of, say, the wage relativities argument) and hence real wages rise. Through the short-run production function, employment falls with a fall in the price level and so we have a positively sloped 'Keynesian' AS curve (as opposed to the vertical classical AS curve) in price output space. Thus, in most macroeconomic textbooks, the cause of 'Keynesian' unemployment is the *assumption* of downwardly rigid money wages. To bring the economy back to full employment requires the real wage to be lowered. Consequently, increasing demand shifts the AD curve back to the right and drives up the price level, reducing the real wage. Thus Keynesian involuntary unemployment is caused by rigid money wages which, in the absence of government intervention to, for example, increase expenditure, prevents the real wage from falling in the presence of excess labour supply and from clearing the labour market. No wonder the consensus was (is) that Keynes was merely a special case of the classical system with an *ad hoc* restriction imposed upon it.

There is only one problem with this analysis – it is not what Keynes had in mind. He made this quite explicit in the course of his article 'The Relative Movements of Real Wages and Output' published in 1939. Since the 'Keynesian' supply curve has become such an established textbook explanation of Keynesian unemployment, it is worth quoting Keynes's implicit rejection of this.

> I was already arguing at that time [c. 1929] that the good effect of an expansionist investment policy on employment, the fact of which no one denied, was due to the stimulant which it gave to effective demand. Prof. Pigou, on the other hand, and many other economists explained the observed result by the reduction in real wages covertly effected by the rise in prices which ensued on the increase in effective demand. It was held that public investment policies (and also the improvement in the trade balance through tariffs) produced their effect by deceiving, so to speak, the working classes into accepting a lower real wage, effecting by this means the same favourable influence on employment which, according to these economists, would have resulted from a more direct attack on real wages (*e.g.*, by reducing money wages whilst enforcing a credit policy calculated to leave prices unchanged).

Thus the irony is that Keynes ascribes to the classical economists the exact chain of events sketched out above with respect to the 'Keynesian' AD/AS model.[3]

Real wages over the trade cycle

Shortly after the publication of the *General Theory*, two articles published in the *Economic Journal* by Dunlop (1938) and Tarshis (1939) suggested that, far from real wages moving contracyclically over the trade cycle, they in fact moved procyclically. This was at variance with both Keynes's assumption and the relationship predicted by the short-run production function. Recent research suggests that either real wages are slightly procyclical or are roughly constant over the trade cycle.[4] In either case, this is enough to contradict the neoclassical foundations of the AS curve, unless one is prepared to accept the real business cycle theory's implausible assumption of substantial technological shocks over the cycle. Keynes was reluctant to abandon immediately the conventional wisdom and accept a procyclical real wage.[5] Nevertheless, if real wages are not contracyclical, then a fall in the real wage neither is associated with nor causes an increase in employment. Hence as Keynes (1939, p. 40, omitting a footnote) noted if 'it proves right to adopt the contrary generalisation, it would be possible to simplify considerably the more complicated version of my fundamental explanation which I have expounded in my 'General Theory''. If Keynes had adopted this contrary generalization, it would have prevented the emasculation of his theory by the neoclassical synthesis.

McCombie (1985–6) demonstrated that one way of reconciling the procyclical movement (or constancy) of the real wage over the trade cycle with the marginal productivity curve of labour was to allow for the occurrence of excess capacity, in the sense of idle machinery, as the economy moves into recession.

The conventional short-run production function approach normally assumes that capital is always fully utilized; it is only employment that is laid off. Since most of the capital stock is already purchased (although some may be rented), there is no saving to be had from leaving it idle. Consequently, given the possibility of capital-labour substitution, a profit-maximizing firm will economise on labour (where it saves the wage costs) and fully use its capital. Weeks (1989, p. 127), although presenting a critique of neoclassical macroeconomics, accepted that 'neoclassical theory reaches profound truth when it ignores the possibility of unemployed capital'.[6] But, labour is a 'quasi-fixed factor of production' (Oi, 1962). There is a fundamental asymmetry between capital and labour. Labour, once made redundant, may be lost to the firm when it needs to expand its labourforce during a subsequent upswing. This loss of firm-specific skills means that there are retraining costs as well as hiring costs. The firm does not have to bear such costs when bringing equipment and machinery back into production. Consequently it may be optimal for a profit-maximizing firm to lay off both capital and labour (that is the flow of capital and labour services both fall) as the economy moves into recession. The possibility of less-than-full utilization of capacity substantially alters the analysis. Take, for example, the case where the real wage is above the market clearing level. Let us assume that it falls exogenously. To begin with, let us further assume that firms adopt a cautionary attitude and retain the existing level of employment and output, while waiting for demand to change. If investment also remains constant, the fall in consumption, consequent upon the decline in the real wage, will lead to an accumulation of unwanted inventories. Production will be cut back, with both labour and capital being laid off. The marginal product of labour, which is a function of the level of the utilized capital stock (strictly the flow of capital services), will shift to the left, so that employment may actually decrease as the real wage falls towards the market clearing level. (It is, nevertheless, theoretically possible for employment to increase as capital becomes progressively more underutilized (see McCombie, 1985–6). Moreover it should be noted that the first classical postulate is still fulfilled.

There is some textual evidence in the *General Theory* that Keynes appreciated the existence of less-than-full capacity utilization. For example, on p. 42, footnote 2, he writes of 'a surplus of equipment identical in type with the equipment in use'. However, the exegetical evidence is scant and it is clear that the role of the underutilization of capital was not at the forefront of Keynes's mind when he wrote the *General Theory*. But what this discussion has shown is that even retaining the first classical postulate, it is not necessary to assume real wage rigidity to generate involuntary unemployment.

The importance of this approach is that a fall in the real wage is no longer *even* a necessary, let alone a *sufficient*, condition for an increase in employment; it all depends upon what is happening to the level of aggregate demand.

The new Keynesian models

The roots of these models go back to the pioneering work of Clower (1965) and Leijonhufvud (1968), which was an attempt to explain involuntary unemployment within a Walrasian mechanism. As is well known, all that was required was the absence of an instantaneous market clearing price vector (that is no Walrasian auctioneer). With false trading, quantity adjustments occur. The heart of the problem can be summarized by Clower's dictum that goods buy money and money buys goods but goods do not buy goods. In other words, if there is a barter economy, there can be no effective demand failure because each offer to supply an extra hour of labour is simultaneously an offer to buy the equivalent amount of extra goods.[7] This would seem to capture the distinction Keynes was trying to make in the draft of the *General Theory* when he drew a distinction between an entrepreneurial and a co-operative economy. The subsequent quantity-constrained models (Barro and Grossman, 1971; Malinvaud, 1977) became essentially fixed-price or temporary equilibrium models. This approach used the one-sector short-run aggregate production, but because the first classical postulate was abandoned, the real wage could be below the marginal productivity of labour. But these models still required price rigidity (and, hence, money wage rigidity) since if prices fell the real balance effect would come into play causing an automatic return to full employment.

The problem within an optimizing framework was to explain why the opportunity from mutually profitable trade did not occur. If all opportunities for profitable trade were taken, then any existing employment would be voluntary. It was dissatisfaction with the explanation of why wages and prices could be sticky that led Barro, one of the pioneers in developing the disequilibrium model, ultimately to reject it as a satisfactory explanation. (The 'nontheory of price rigidities', as he called it (Barro, 1979).) The rise of the new Keynesian theory in the late 1980s was precisely to rectify this deficiency, that is to provide a theoretical justification for wage and price stickiness within an optimizing or neo-Walrasian framework and also to place Keynesian economics on firm micro-foundations. The initial justification for sticky prices was contract theory, which provided a rationale for nominal wage stickiness. For Barro, the difficulty was that if all parties correctly perceived that the marginal value product of labour exceeded the wage, then there would be scope for a mutual improvement through renegotiation.

However, other explanations for price stickiness were soon forthcoming including the efficiency wage argument, the insider-outsider argument and menu costs.[8] Yet the question naturally arises: can these market rigidities really explain the dramatic fall in output in the Great Depression, when there was certainly no evidence of downward money or price rigidity? The new Keynesian economics has, like the neoclassical synthesis, obscured the central message of the *General Theory*, namely, the importance of effective demand.

Concluding comments

In this chapter, it has been argued that one reason for the distortion of the main message of the *General Theory* was the use of the short-run neoclassical production function, and that there was some evidence that Keynes accepted this in Chapter 2. The production function implies that if unemployment is due to the real wage being above the market clearing level, then a fall in the real wage *must* by the logic of the model lead to a decrease in unemployment. If money wages are downward sticky, then the remedy is to drive up the price level and this was the role to which effective demand was relegated in, for example, the AD/AS model. But it is clear from his Keynes's 1939 paper that, notwithstanding any textual evidence in the *General Theory*, this not what he had in mind. The quantity constrained models, by abandoning the first postulate, re-emphasize the key role of effective demand. But these and subsequent models are unsatisfactory to the extent that they assume the full utilization of capital and give undue prominence to price stickiness. An alternative model was discussed which still retained the first postulate, but allowed for variations in the capacity utilization rate. The policy conclusion is that attempts to cure unemployment by attempting to increase wage flexibility by deregulating the labour market, by itself, is unlikely to be successful. Keynes is as relevant today, as he was 60 years ago.

Endnotes

1. Both money wages and prices fell sharply in the Great Depression.
2. It has been argued that, for an individual country, a fall in real wages would increase overseas demand for its exports and hence lead to an increase in employment. However, there is much evidence that, in international trade, price competitiveness is relatively unimportant – it is non-price competitiveness that matters (McCombie and Thirlwall, 1994).
3. However, part of the confusion may have arisen from Keynes himself. His well-known definition of involuntary unemployment is: '*Men are involuntarily unemployed if, in the event of a small rise in the price of wage-goods relatively to the money-wage, both the aggregate supply of labour willing to work for the current money-wage and the aggregate demand for it at that wage would be greater than the existing volume of employment*' (*General Theory*, p. 15, italics in the original). As Hawtrey (in Keynes, 1973b, p. 31) noted in a letter to Keynes in 1936, Keynes's definition 'implies that if employment can be increased by some other method and not by this [rise in the price level] then employment is not involuntary.' Hawtrey continued: 'if that were so, the "small rise in the price of wage goods relatively to the money wage" would have to be read in the narrow sense to exclude the case where the relative rise is due to a fall in the money wage. But you nowhere say this expressly.' It is clear Keynes gave careful thought to his definition of involuntary unemployment as, in the galley proofs, he defined it with respect to the *level* of money-wages in terms of wage goods.
4. See Coddington (1983, pp. 26–38) for a discussion of how difficult it is to determine empirically whether a worker without a job is voluntarily or involuntarily unemployed. Questionnaires are likely to be misleading because few drawing benefits are likely to admit to being voluntarily unemployed. The possibility of involuntary unemployment is best reviewed as a paradigmatic assumption (Kuhn, 1962) or part of the Lakatosian (Lakatos and Musgrave, 1968) hard core of the Keynesian approach. In this sense, it is either not tested or not testable. Conversely, the impossibility of involuntary unemployment should be viewed as, by assumption, an irrefutable central tenet (or part of the hard core) of the New Classical Economics. This leads to the explanation of employment fluctuations in terms of inter-temporal utility maximization and hence optimal.
5. Keynes (1939, pp. 42–3) conceded though that if, 'we are to make any single statistical generalisation. ... we shall not often go far wrong if we treat real wages as substantially constant in the short period'.
6. However, Weeks continued that this is 'for the wrong reason'. He argued that 'no exchange is needed to occur for capital to be employed, while labour requires a successful sale and purchase'.
7. There is one difficulty with this as a complete explanation of involuntary unemployment. Even if workers could communicate their notional demands, these would be for consumer goods. This would not be a necessary and sufficient condition for full employment because there would have to be an appropriate increase in investment. There is nothing in the Clower–Leijonhufvud model that ensures that this will occur.
8. There is not space to deal here with the shortcomings of these various theories. A good survey is to be found in Sawyer (1996).

References

Addison, J.T. and J.Burton (1982), 'Keynes's Analysis of Wages and Unemployment Revisited', *The Manchester School*, 50, 1–23.

Barro, R.J. (1979), 'Second Thoughts on Keynesian Economics', *American Economic Review, Papers and Proceedings*, 69, 54–69.

Barro, R.J. and H. Grossman, (1971), 'A General Disequilibrium Model of Income and Employment', *American Economic Review*, 61, 82–93.

Clower, R.W. (1965), 'The Keynesian Counter-Revolution: A Theoretical Appraisal', in F.H. Hahn and F. Brechling (eds), *The Theory of Interest Rates*, London: Macmillan.

Coddington, A. (1983), *Keynesian Economics: The Search for First Principles*, London: Allen and Unwin.

Davidson, P. and Smolensky, E. (1964), *Aggregate Supply and Demand Analysis*, New York: Harper Row.

Davidson, P. (1992), 'Would Keynes be a New Keynesian?', *Eastern Economic Journal*, 18, 449–63.

Dunlop, J.T. (1938), 'The Movement of Real and Money Wages', *Economic Journal*, 48, 413–34.

Gordon, R.J. (1990), 'What is New Keynesian Economics?', *Journal of Economic Literature*, 28, 1115–71.

Kahn, R.F. (1984), *The Making of Keynes' General Theory*, Cambridge: Cambridge University Press.

Keynes, J.M. (1936), *The General Theory of Employment, Interest and Money*, London: Macmillan.

Keynes, J.M. (1939), 'Relative Movements of Real Wages and Output', *Economic Journal*, 49, 35–51.

Keynes, J.M. (1972), *Essays in Persuasion, The Collected Writings of John Maynard Keynes*, vol. 9, in D.E. Moggridge, (ed.), London: Macmillan.

Keynes, J.M. (1973a), *The General Theory and After, Part I, Preparation, The Collected Writings of John Maynard Keynes*, vol. 13, in D. Moggridge, (ed.), London: Macmillan.

Keynes, J.M. (1973b), *The General Theory and After, Part II, Defence and Developments, The Collected Writings of John Maynard Keynes*, vol.14, D. Moggridge, (ed.), London: Macmillan.

Kuhn, T.S. (1962), *The Structure of Scientific Revolution*, Chicago: Chicago University Press.

Lakatos, I. and A. Musgrave (eds) (1968), *Criticism and the Growth of Knowledge*, Cambridge, UK: Cambridge University Press.

Leijonhufvud, A. (1968), *On Keynesian Economics and the Economics of Keynes*, Oxford: Oxford University Press.

Malinvaud, E. (1977), *The Theory of Unemployment Reconsidered,* Oxford: Blackwell.

Mankiw, N.G. (1990), 'A Quick Refresher Course in Macroeconomics', *Journal of Economic Literature*, 28, 1645–60.

Mankiw, N.G. (1994), Interview, in Snowdon, B., H. Vane, and P. Wynarczyk, *A Modern Guide to Macroeconomics*, Aldershot: Edgar Elgar.

McCloskey, D.N. (1985), *The Rhetoric of Economics*, Madison: University of Wisconsin Press.

McCombie, J.S.L. (1985–6), 'Why Cutting Real Wages Will Not Necessarily Reduce Unemployment – Keynes and the 'Postulates of the Classical Economics', *Journal of Post Keynesian Economics*, 8, 233–48.

McCombie, J.S.L. and A.P. Thirlwall (1994), *Economic Growth and the Balance-of-Payments Constraint*, Basingstoke: Macmillan.

Oi, W.Y. (1962), 'Labor as a Quasi-Fixed Factor', *Journal of Political Economy*, 70, 538–55.

Samuelson, P.A. (1963), 'A Brief Survey of Post-Keynesian Developments', in R.E. Lekachman (ed.), *Keynes' General Theory: Reports of Three Decades,* London: Macmillan.

Sawyer, M.C. (1996), 'The New Keynesian Macroeconomics: A Partial Critique', Paper presented to the Post Keynesian Workshop, Knoxville, Tennessee, July.

Tarshis, L. (1939), 'Changes in Real and Money Wages', *Economic Journal*, 49, 150–4.

Thirlwall, A.P. (1983), 'Comment' in G.D.N. Worswick and J. Trevithick, (eds), *Keynes and the Modern World*, Cambridge: Cambridge University Press.

Trevithick, J.A. (1976), 'Money Wage Inflexibility and the Keynesian Labour Supply Function', *Economic Journal*, 85, 327–32.

Weeks, J. (1989), *A Critique of Neoclassical Macroeconomics*, Basingstoke: Macmillan

13　Inequality and unemployment: an analysis across time and countries

James K. Galbraith

What is the relationship between inequality and unemployment? A standard view holds that these two variables move in opposite directions. The intuition behind this view is that flexible labour markets, characterized by a wider dispersion of earnings, will clear more readily and so yield lower rates of unemployment. Loose comparisons between Europe, where wage structures are said to be compressed and unemployment is high, and the US, where the reverse is true, have bolstered this belief over the past decade.

Very recently, though, systematic evidence has been brought to bear. In a recent study, the Organization for Economic Cooperation and Development (1996) reports that low-skilled workers are unlikely to face significantly higher rates of unemployment in countries with more equal wage distributions. Papers by Card, Kramarz and Lemieux (1994) covering France, Canada and the US, and by Nickell and Bell (1996) covering Germany, the UK and the US, have also cast doubt on the idea that equality *per se* is a cause of unemployment.

The OECD finding was instantly controversial. An article in *The Economist*[2] attacked it, raising questions about the evidence and reformulating the standard view:

> By itself, the lack of a positive correlation between high levels of inequality and low unemployment proves nothing.... A more direct test of the value of flexible labour markets is how they respond to shifts over time... A comparison of changes in unemployment and changes in inequality... over the past decade and a half show a much closer correlation. *Countries that have allowed the relative wages of low-skilled workers to fall have, in general, seen the smallest increases in unemployment* (Emphasis added).

The Economist supported this conclusion with a scatter chart covering ten countries over a single time frame, 1980 to 1995, plotting the change in the 50/10 per centile wage ratio against the movement of unemployment. Their emphasis on change over time is surely both correct and useful. But, as I will show in this chapter, otherwise the position quoted fails to withstand examination. And even the cautious OECD study finding of 'no correlation' between unemployment and relative equality understates the actual direction of the evidence.

This chapter will show, for countries mainly from Europe and North America,[3] that:

- For most countries, the time-series relationship between unemployment and wage inequality is usually *positive* and in some cases strongly so. A few smaller countries have slightly compressed their wage structures while experiencing large increases in unemployment, resulting in a negative correlation. In no case has any country systematically reduced unemployment while increasing inequality in the wage structure.
- Year by year from 1970 to 1992, the correlation across countries between levels of unemployment and levels of inequality is overwhelmingly positive, not negative or even zero (as the OECD study apparently found). This correlation does start out negative, and stays so from 1970 to 1973. But after 1974 it is positive for every year up to the end of the data set, and the correlation coefficient is itself associated with the overall level of unemployment in the OECD. That is, higher average unemployment produces a stronger positive association between unemployment and inequality across countries.
- Year by year, the correlation across countries between the *change* of unemployment and the *change* of inequality is sometimes positive and sometimes negative. The average value of the correlation coefficient across all years is virtually zero, with a high standard deviation. Thus a rising level of unemployment can accompany a rising or falling degree of inequality in the wage structure. There is no consistent pattern, except that when overall unemployment is high, the relationship between changes is more likely to be positive.
- There is a complex pattern of international interdependence both in wage structures and unemployment rates, and these patterns of interdependence are only partly overlapping. There are strong elements of geographic affinity in both patterns.

In this chapter we discuss some issues of theory, data, and method, and present a benchmark estimate of inequality in the wage structure for the US; present year-by-year time-series measurements of inequality in the manufacturing wage structure for 21 OECD countries. These measures are self-consistent within countries and across time, but they are not comparable across countries. The section then shows how for 13 of these countries the measurements can be converted to estimates of the change in the overall inequality of family income, measured by the Gini coefficient, by benchmarking to available Gini estimates from the Luxembourg Income Surveys. Thus it is possible to reverse-engineer annual estimates of earnings inequality, comparable across countries, for a wide variety of countries going back to the early 1970s in most cases. We further present an analysis of the correlation between unemployment and inequality, with the main conclusions as outlined above. Final sections present an analysis of international patterns of interdependence and offer conclusions and avenues for further research.

Theory, data, method

Strictly speaking, the neoclassical theory of income distribution does not predict any pattern of association between wage dispersion and unemployment. The theory merely says that compensation will follow the marginal productivity of labour. In the purest setting, there will be one single wage rate (the law of one price, in effect); in models with heterogeneous labour wages may vary with risk, skill, compensating differentials and other factors.

A systematic inverse relationship between degrees of inequality and levels of unemployment will therefore emerge only if there exists some natural common distribution of underlying wage determinants across countries, and if some countries 'unnaturally' compress their wage structures, producing unemployment, while others do not. There is no particular evidence for either part of this proposition, neither that skills and other wage determinants are similarly distributed across countries, nor that wage compression in some countries is 'unnatural' compared to that in others. Nevertheless, as noted above, something like this seems to be a widely held view of the contrasting experience of Europe and the US in recent years.

Theories derived from Keynes have a different implication. In the Keynesian case, rising unemployment may *cause* an increase in the dispersion of hourly wages, simply by breaking down the common inflexibility of relative nominal wage rates that characterizes periods of full employment. Keynes (1936) emphasizes the importance of relative pay differentials to workers. It is an easy implication that some workers – those strongly unionized, for instance – defend themselves more effectively than others.

Thus, were one to find a consistent inverse association across countries or through time between levels of unemployment and inequality, that would tend to support the prevailing view. It would be possible for an inverse relationship to hold and the inference to be false. Still, in that case, given the simple theoretical story behind the prediction, the burden would then fall on sceptics to develop a competing and superior theory.

As *The Economist* argued, an inverse correlation between *rates of change* of inequality and of unemployment would strongly support the standard view. Since forces affecting rates of change abstract from structural differences between countries, such a finding would provide stronger evidence than an inverse correlation of levels, and would be sufficient to make the case for the standard view in the face of no correlation across levels. It would also support a policy argument that wage flexibility should be increased in order to fight unemployment.

A finding of no association between levels of inequality and unemployment would be inconclusive. Perhaps some countries are more equal than others simply because they are more internally homogeneous. Perhaps those who are visibly compressing their wage structures are merely reflecting in law a more equal underlying distribution of skills and risks, and therefore a public preference for equality borne of an egalitarian social structure. In such a case, the standard view might still be true, as *The Economist* argued, or it might be false.

On the other hand, findings of *positive* association, either between hourly wage inequality and unemployment levels, or between changes in these variables, either across countries or through time, would be hard to square with the standard view. In the cross-country case, we would have to find a reason why countries with more heterogeneous labour also had less efficient labour markets. Such a thing is possible, surely, but no easy explanation comes to mind. A finding of positive association between unemployment and inequality would, however, be consistent with the alternative Keynesian view, according to which movements of aggregate demand move unemployment and inequality in the same directions.

The next question is, what to measure? Hourly average wages are the pay variable of theoretical interest, because the theoretical issue is the relationship between unemployment and an hour's wage. But most data sets dealing with inequality rest not on the structure of individual hourly wages but on the distribution of family *incomes*. Factors affecting family income, such as changes in the demographic composition of families, have to be sorted through quite carefully before a measure based on incomes can be taken to be closely related to wages.

Another problem concerns the measure of inequality employed. Partial measures, such as a ratio of earnings at the lowest decile to those at the median – a measure used in the OECD study – can be unrepresentative of the structure of wages as a whole. Unemployment, after all, occurs throughout the structure of wages; the phenomena of downsizing and technological obsolescence can hit the highly placed and the highly skilled. Equally, changes in the minimum wage will be more important to a low-to-median ratio than they may be to the entire distribution. Ideally, then, one should seek a summary measure of inequality that covers the entire distribution of wages, based on individuals rather than families, on hours worked or a close approximation thereof, and if possible excluding non-wage sources of income.

We propose a direct measure of the change in inequality in wage structures that nearly meets these criteria. Our measure is based on the work of Henri Theil (1972), whose measure of dispersion, derived from theories of information and entropy, is known as Theil's T. T has the very useful property of decomposability. For any set of mutually exclusive groups, T is the sum of the inequality between groups and the inequality within them. Thus a lower-bound estimate for T, T' or the between-group component of T, can be computed from grouped data (see the Appendix for details). If grouped data are collected on a sufficiently detailed and consistent basis over time, then change in annual T' can serve as a time-series estimate of changes in inequality.

This insight greatly broadens the potential sources of data from which measures of inequality can be computed. In particular, it makes possible the use of *industrial* data sets, with measures of average annual earnings per employee by industry, for this purpose. Industrial classifications are, after all, merely sets of mutually exclusive groups. Their major limitations for this purpose are two-fold:

1. such data sets may have some sources of within-group inequality that do not vary between groups, and
2. the quality of industrial data is much better for manufacturing than for services; many such data sets do not cover the services sector at all.

We have examined both of these issues very extensively with regard to the US, using three alternative measurements of cross-industrial wage dispersion. The first is based on the Annual Survey of Manufactures for the years 1958–92; in our analysis we reduced 139 three-digit industries into 23 internally homogeneous groups through methods of numerical taxonomy beyond the scope of this chapter.[4] Hourly wage data are used in this analysis, and employment weights are from the same source. The second is the OECD's Structural Analysis Database (STAN), which at its finest level of disaggregation breaks the industrial structure into about 40 mutually exclusive groups, with the useful property that the same classification scheme is employed across all covered OECD members. STAN data on annual earnings per employee compiled in this way are now available from 1970 to 1992, with annual updates. The third US data set was compiled from 1920 to 1947 by Thomas Ferguson and myself from data originally collected by the National Industrial Conference Board and other sources; it covers a wide range of services as well as manufacturing, and a full analysis of that material will be presented in a separate publication (Ferguson and Galbraith, 1996).

These analyses show that our post-war measures of T' based on hourly wages or annual earnings are very good proxies for each other. They also closely mirror changes in inequality more broadly measured, for example by the Current Population Survey's annual estimate of a Gini coefficient for family incomes in the US. The Bureau of Labor Statistics has produced an annual series of the Gini coefficient, based on quintiles of the Current Population Survey of family incomes and going back to 1947. For the period 1958 to 1992, the correlation coefficient between this series and T' estimated from the ASM is 0.86. For 1970

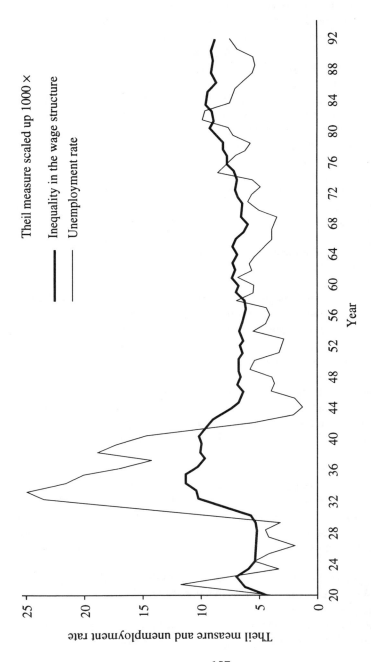

Sources: Census Reports for 1958–92, CPS-based Gini coefficients for 1947–58 as published by the Census Bureau, Conference Board and other industrial wage series for 1920–47, and author's calculations. Unemployment rate is from Robert Gordon (1986).

Figure 13.1   Inequality and unemployment, US, 1920–92

157

to 1992, the correlation between T' estimated from the STAN database and the CPS Gini is 0.92. These correlations indicate that both series provide high-quality approximations of measurements otherwise obtainable only from expensive, and for many countries, non-existent annual micro-data.[5] We have also found positive correlations between T' for the UK and Sweden and annual Gini series reported by Carnoy *et al.* (1996).

Why is this so? The reason apparently is that with a sufficiently fine disaggregation of industries, most sources of variation within industries also show up as between-group variation between some industries and some others. The dispersion of wages across the industrial classification structure covaries in a reasonably faithful way with the income distribution. We have also discovered that the forces that affect the manufacturing wage structure also affect the dispersion of wages between manufacturing and services. This is partly because many activities classed as services are linked to manufacturing, and partly because the economy is unitary: the same large forces affect all sectors, however they may be classified by government accountants.

Using the first of these correlations to plug the gap in our data for T' for the years 1947–58, and benchmarking the 1920–47 series to the estimated 1947 values, I have computed a complete series for wage inequality in the US from 1920 to 1992. This series is presented as Figure 13.1, alongside a measure of the unemployment rate. The correspondence of the two series is very strong, and in fact some 55 per cent of the variation in T' over the entire period is explained just by the movement of unemployment. This figure constitutes the first exhibit in our case that unemployment and inequality are positively associated.

Measurements of wage inequality in the OECD

Figure 13.2. shows annual time-series estimates of the inter-industry dispersion of annual earnings for all the countries represented in the STAN database, for all years with sufficient usable data. This is the fundamental data set of the present study.

There are some problems with the data. Most notably, the sharp drop shown in wage inequality in Belgium in the early 1970s does not appear plausible, and does not show up when the same analysis is run at a higher level of industrial aggregation (for example, a two-digit decomposition). We therefore are inclined to regard that discontinuity as a data defect. A less visible defect apparently produces discontinuity in the data for France in 1977.[6] Still it is remarkable how few such defects hit the eye.

Overall the series appear broadly in accord with the stylized facts of the time and place. We observe that increases in inequality in Northern Europe appear quite low; in solidaristic Scandinavia wage structures have been almost undisturbed. In France in the 1970s, a known time of turmoil, inequality increases, as it does in Greece. In Canada, the US, Mexico and New Zealand

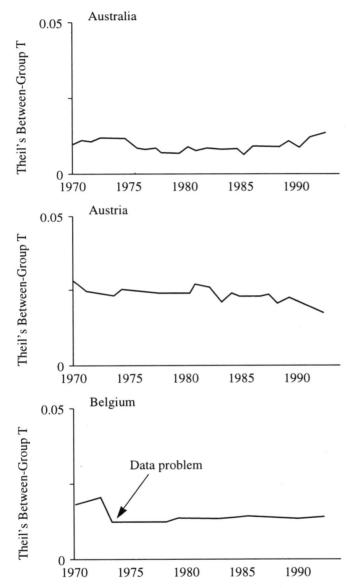

Source: Computed from the OECD STAN Database using the group decomposition of Theil's T statistic, computations by James Galbraith and Lu Jiaqing, with help from Jen Steele.

Figure 13.2   Wage inequality in the OECD, 1970–92 (lower bound estimates of Theil's T)

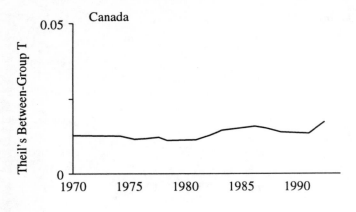

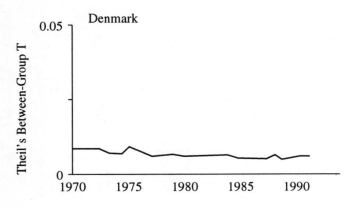

Figure 13.2   continued

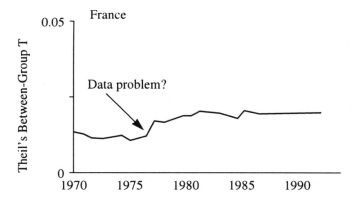

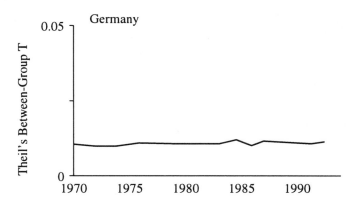

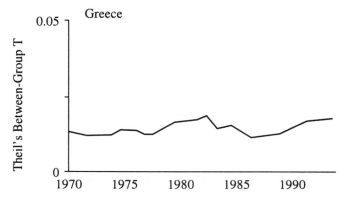

Figure 13.2 continued

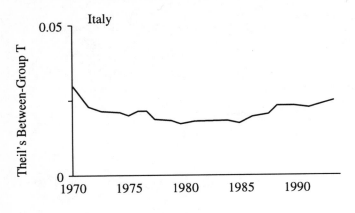

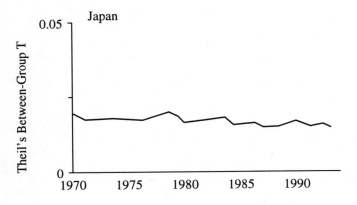

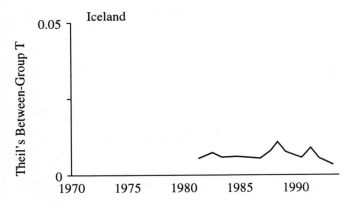

Figure 13.2   continued

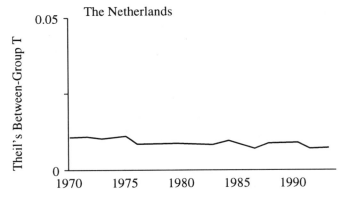

Figure 13.2   continued

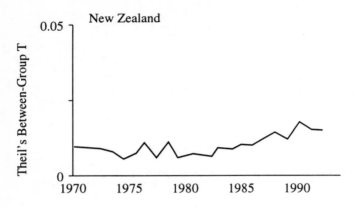

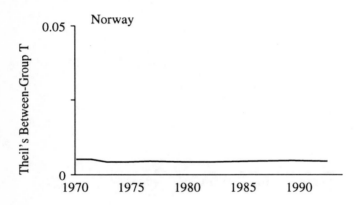

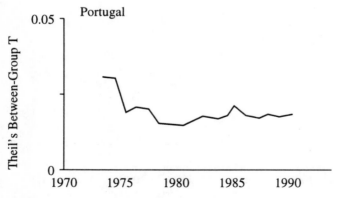

Figure 13.2   continued

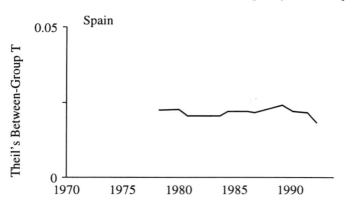

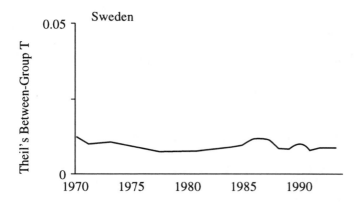

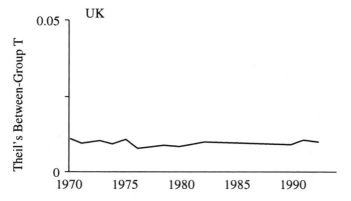

Figure 13.2   continued

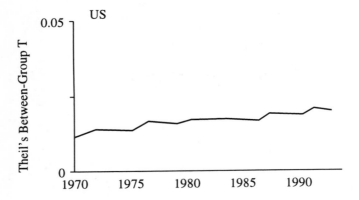

Figure 13.2   continued

there are sharp increases in inequality, especially towards the end of the period. The same is somewhat true of Italy. In Portugal, following the revolution in 1974, inequality declined, the same happened in Spain under the Socialist government a decade or more later. A very few countries, notably Denmark and Austria, show steadily declining wage dispersion over the period.

Again the level values of these series are not strictly comparable across countries. A finding that country A has a higher value of T' than country B does not necessarily imply that overall income inequality was greater in country A. Non-comparabilities may be due to cross-country differences in the composition of industrial employment, to cross-country differences in the proportion of total employment in covered manufacturing, and to cross-country differences in the allocation of non-wage incomes. However, given the very high correlation between T' and the movement of inequality in family incomes observed in the US, we do expect that *movements* in T' will prove a good proxy for the trend of inequality in most countries.

Fortunately, we have benchmark measures of inequality that are, in fact, designed to be comparable across countries. These are the Gini coefficients of the Luxembourg Income Studies, now available for scattered years for at least 13 countries of the OECD's 22. It is therefore possible to benchmark T' to the known level of the Gini for each of these countries. The simple assumption that the two series co-vary closely, known to be correct for the US, yields a kind of reverse-engineered annual Gini coefficient for the 13 countries, which we can call a Theil-Gini or $T'G$ measure of inequality. Estimates of the Theil-Gini coefficient are presented in Figure 13.3, and a table of values is given in the Appendix.

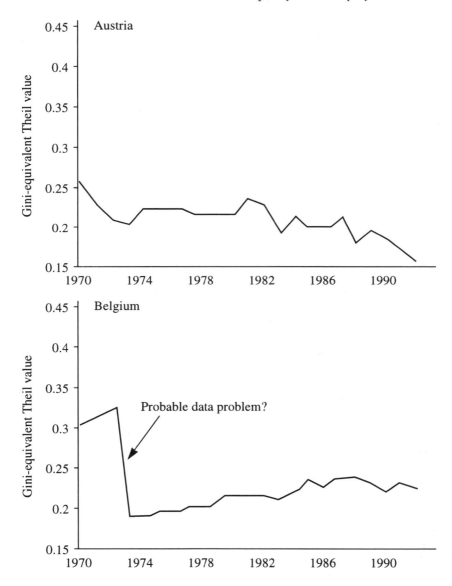

Source: Between-group Theil inequality statistics computed from the OECD STAN database by Galbraith and Lu using industrial wage data, adjusted to the equivalent level-measures of the LIS Gini coefficients, as reported by Niggle (1996), which are available for selected years and therefore make possible inter-country comparisons of levels of inequality.

Figure 13.3   Inequality compared (LIS-adjusted group-Theil statistics)

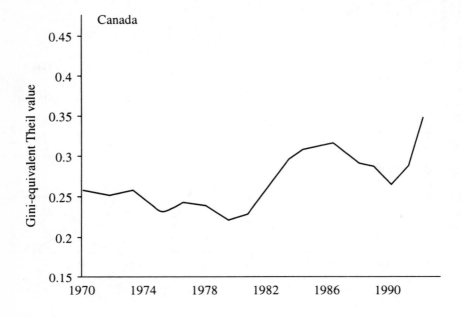

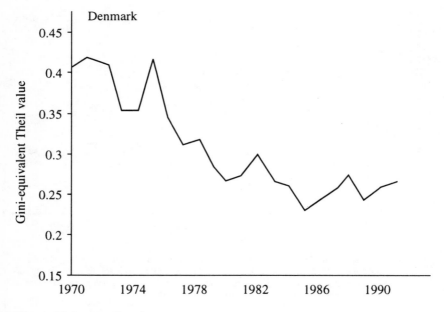

Figure 13.3   continued

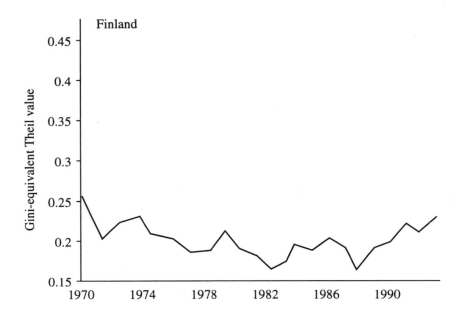

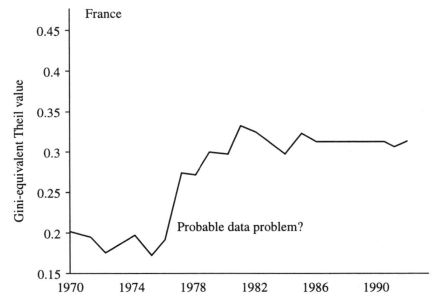

Figure 13.3   continued

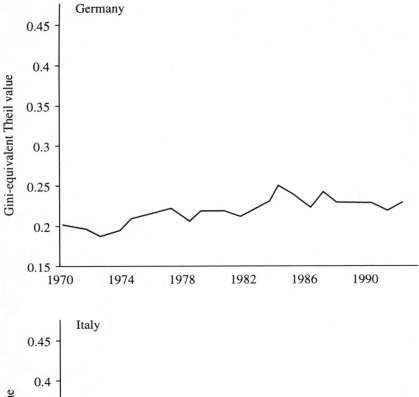

Figure 13.3   continued

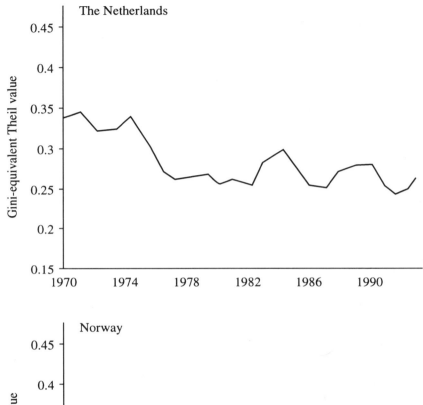

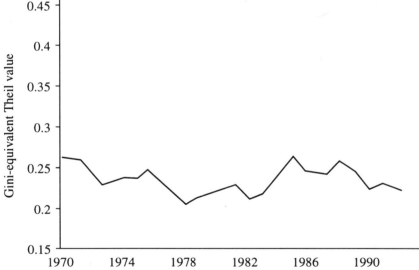

Figure 13.3   continued

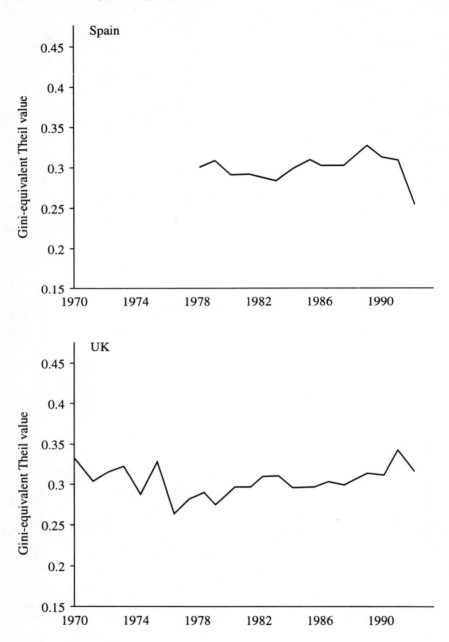

Figure 13.3   continued

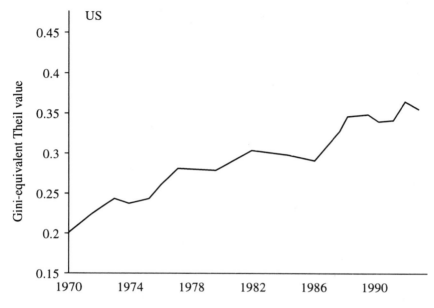

Figure 13.3 continued

As a final exercise in this vein, we were tempted to exploit the additivity of the Theil series to produce an approximate meta series for changing inequality in Europe, incorporating both within-country and between-country components of wage inequality and adjusted to Gini-equivalent values. However, this effort did not succeed; the issues involved are also discussed in the Appendix.

Unemployment and inequality

To return to the opening question of this chapter, what is the relationship between inequality and unemployment? Figure 13.4 presents some evidence in the form of representative time trends for both series in eight OECD countries. In each case, unemployment is the thin line, inequality is the darker one; the inequality coefficient is scaled, usually by factor of 1000, to facilitate visual comparison. The patterns obviously vary. In some cases – Germany, France, Canada, Australia – the correspondence between the two series appears to be positive. In the case of Japan, the series move in opposite directions, as wage dispersion declines while unemployment rises. In the case of the UK, the series bear no apparent relationship to each other. For the US it is hard for the eye to tell.

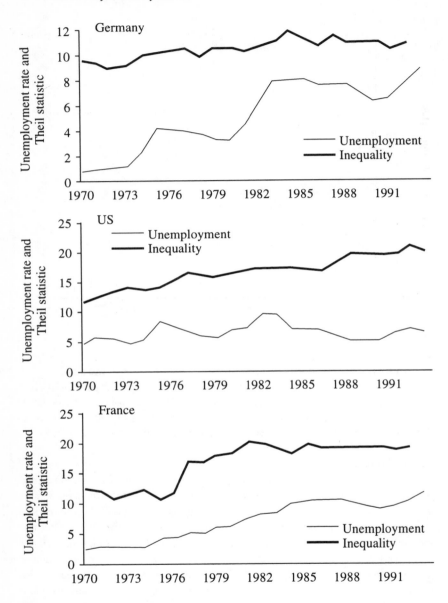

Source: Computed by James K. Galbraith.

Figure 13.4   Unemployment and inequality in selected OECD countries, 1970–92

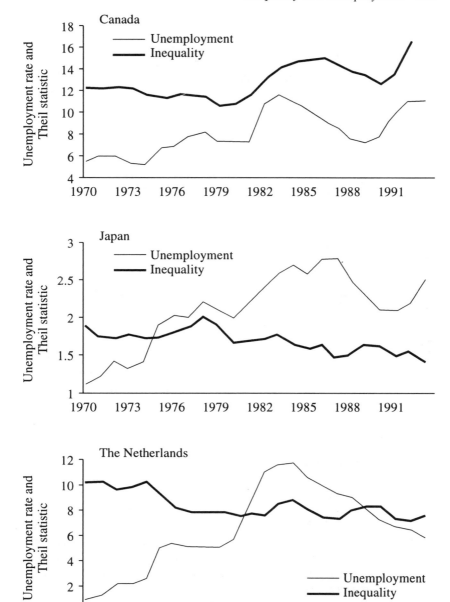

Figure 13.4   continued

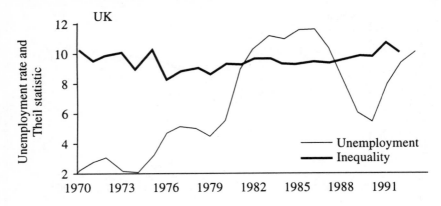

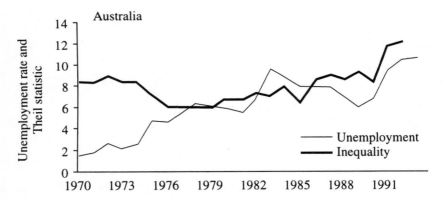

Figure 13.4   continued

Figure 13.5 attempts to bring some order to this analysis. It shows an array of correlation coefficients between time-series measures of inequality and unemployment, ranked from lowest to highest across the 18 countries for which internally consistent time-series on both variables are available.

As the top half of the figure shows, Germany, France, New Zealand, Canada, Australia, the US and Greece show a positive correlation between inequality and unemployment. In general, countries which experienced large increases in inequality, notably France, New Zealand, Canada, Australia and the US, also experienced higher unemployment, and in general the movements occurred at the same time. The association is also strongly positive in the case of Germany, although the increase in wage dispersion in Germany is comparatively small.

Denmark, the Netherlands, Austria, Japan, Belgium, Finland, Norway and Sweden show a negative correlation between inequality and unemployment. For

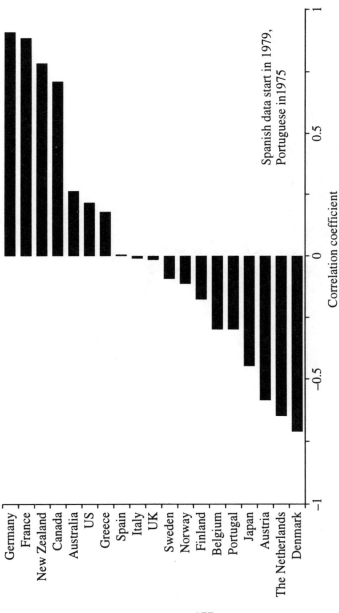

Source: Inequality measure is a between-group Theil statistic computed from manufacturing data as described in text, from OECD STAN database; unemployment data are from OECD Historical Statistics.

Figure 13.5(a)   Inequality and unemployment (1) (correlation of time series, 1971–92)

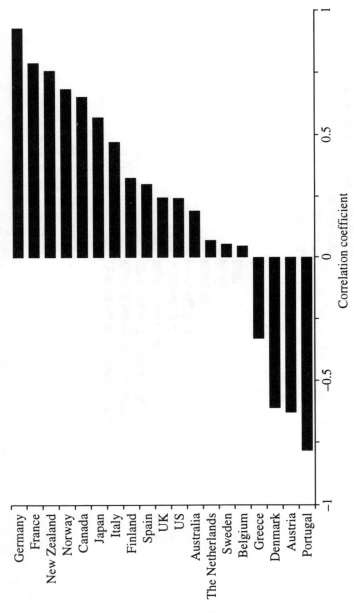

Source: Correlation for 1970–92 based on between-group Theil coefficients calculated with fixed 1970 employment weights. This eliminates distortion due to correlation of unemployment and changing composition of employment in some countries.

Figure 13.5(b) Inequality and unemployment (2) (fix-weighted between group T')

178

three countries, Italy, Spain and the UK, the correlation is essentially zero. The negative correlation is thus present mainly in those countries which succeeded in holding constant or even compressing their distribution of wages over this period.

The top half of Figure 13.5 is based on measures of inequality for which the underlying employment weights are allowed to vary from year to year according to actual shifts in the composition of employment. This permits accurate tracking of changes in wage dispersion in the manufacturing sector, but it introduces a bias into measures of the change in the structure of wages *per se*. For, as it turns out, there is a systematic association in many countries between changes in the composition of employment and changes in unemployment: as unemployment rises, people who are further away from (presumably, below) the mean of the wage structure are more likely to lose manufacturing jobs, and to be displaced into services or into unemployment. This source of bias is very small for the US, but quite substantial in a number of other countries, particularly smaller ones.

The bias can be removed, yielding a measure of wage dispersion affected only by changing average within-industry wage rates, by fixing employment weights in the calculation of the between-group Theil statistics at their 1970 values. The resulting fixed-weight inequality estimates are correlated to the unemployment rate in the bottom half of Figure 13.5. The results are striking. In eight countries, the correlation through time switches from *negative* to *positive*. In only one, Greece, the correlation moves the other way. In other words, when one considers only movements in relative wages, and not offsetting movements in the composition of manufacturing employment, the verdict that *rising* unemployment leads to *greater* inequality becomes stronger.[7]

What accounts for the distribution of countries into positive and negative correlation cases and for the pattern of shifts from negative to positive correlations as one moves from variable to fixed employment weights? Several somewhat interconnected hypotheses suggest themselves. The economies with pronounced negative correlations between unemployment and inequality in the top half of Figure 13.5 and a tendency to flip to positive in the bottom half appear, on the whole, to be economies with a certain dualism in manufacturing, marked by strong and relatively stable, high-wage export sectors (Norway, Japan, Italy, Finland). In such countries, unemployment may rise more sharply among lower-wage manufacturing workers, even as their relative wages fall. This would diminish the weight of such workers in overall wage dispersion and account for the bias towards equality in the variable-weighted inequality measures for such countries. Large economies that sit, so to speak, at the centre of their own economic basin (Germany, France, the US) tend to show a positive correlation with unemployment on both inequality measures. So do the Anglo-

Saxon economies (New Zealand, Canada, Australia, the US). In these countries unemployment may be more nearly an equal opportunity proposition.

One might object that correlations across time of annual measures present a misleading picture, that one should instead examine the cumulative association of changes in inequality and changes in unemployment over a longer period. This is the procedure favoured by *The Economist*, which presented data for ten countries showing the difference between changes in inequality and changes in unemployment beginning in 1980 and ending in 1995.

Such a procedure is however quite treacherous, for the correlation across countries of cumulative changes in unemployment and inequality turns out to depend critically on the choice of starting year. Figure 13.6 illustrates how the correlation coefficients vary, as one moves the starting dates forward from 1971 to 1991, with the ending date held constant at 1992. The comparison covers 18 countries, including all ten in *The Economist's* scatterplot, and the results are consistent with what *The Economist* found for the dates it chose. For a starting date in 1980, the correlation over subsequent years between changing unemployment and changing inequality appears mildly negative, on the order of –0.25. But this is a rare case; 1980 was a year of high unemployment in the

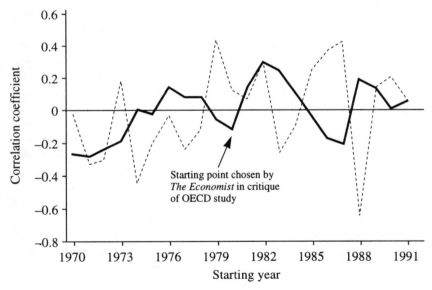

Note: Thick line shows correlation coefficient for cumulative changes in inequality and unemployment across countries from alternative starting dates through 1992. Dotted line shows correlation of year-to-year changes. Both series have average values near zero.

Figure 13.6 Annual and cumulative changes (inequality and unemployment)

US – 7 per cent – and low unemployment in the rest of the OECD – 5.1 per cent. For many other starting dates, arguably more representative, the cumulative correlation across countries is positive. And the average across years of these correlation ratios is statistically not different from zero.

For completeness, I calculated the relationship between the annual rate of change of inequality and the annual rate of change of unemployment, across countries, by year from 1971 to 1992. These correlation ratios of year-to-year change (dotted line in Figure 13.6) fluctuate erratically from one year to the next. There is no consistent pattern, and on average across years the correlation of these movements is zero. Unemployment can rise or fall, without any systematic movement of inequality either up or down.[8] However, this correlation ratio is itself positively correlated with unemployment ($\rho = 0.23$): when overall unemployment is higher, a rise in inequality is more likely to be associated with increasing than with declining unemployment.

Note: The above figure shows that as unemployment rises, the cross-country correlation between unemployment and inequality becomes stronger. Overall correlation between these two series is .89.
Correlation ratio scaled X10 for visual comparison. See Fig 13.8 for list of countries and explanation of inequality measure.
Source: Computed by James K. Galbraith.

Figure 13.7   Unemployment and inequality (correlation across 13 OECD countries)

The more revealing procedure is illustrated in Figure 13.7, which shows the annual correlation ratios across countries between the level of unemployment and the level of inequality, for the 13 countries for which LIS-benchmarked Theil-Gini coefficients have been computed. This figure answers two fundamental questions. Firstly, do countries with less inequality have more unemployment? And secondly, how has this relationship changed over time?

The figure shows that there was a time, back in the early 1970s, when low-wage-inequality countries, notably the US in those years, suffered high unemployment compared to fully employed but less-equal Europe. But that negative association disappeared with the first oil shock and the mid-1970s' recession. Since then, the relationship has always been positive, and it has become more positive as unemployment rose throughout the OECD. The meta-correlation between the time-series of correlation coefficients (dark line) and the OECD unemployment rate (thin line) is .89, which seems high enough.

Thus we are at the situation foreshadowed in the introduction. There is a *positive* cross-country association between levels of unemployment and inequality. The within-country time-series correlation is positive for the larger, market-oriented countries, though negative for the corporatist cases. There is no meaningful cross-country association between movements of the two variables, either year to year or cumulatively.

All three findings are consistent with the Keynesian view, and difficult to reconcile with the standard, *ad hoc*, pseudo-neoclassical vision. Ironically an implication of these results is that the best way to restore the standard worldview would be for the large, market-oriented and inequality-unemployment sensitive countries to embark on a programme of global reflation. This would reduce both unemployment and inequality in the market-oriented countries, reducing the positive cross-country correlation between the two variables that presently exists.

International interdependence

Our final exercise is a search for international patterns in the movement of inequality and unemployment. This search is facilitated by techniques of numerical taxonomy, specifically cluster analysis, where the criterion observation is the path through time, for each country, of the variable in question. In our case we use the annual rate of change of T', and the annual rate of change of unemployment. With either variable, the effect is to compose a taxonomy of nations, based on the closeness of their historical behaviour with regard to, first inequality and then unemployment.

We compute a matrix of Euclidean distances between the vectors of rates of change, one for each country. We then construct a hierarchical table of association between countries according to the distance between them in this $(t - 1)$ dimensional phase-space, where (t) is the number of years for which one has observations. A standard agglomerative clustering method that minimizes, at each step, the ratio of variance within groups to variance between groups (Ward's method), produces a tree diagram illustrating the covariation of each variable across the countries under analysis.

Figure 13.8 is such a tree diagram. Its geographical patterns emerge with great clarity. To be very precise, there is a North American pattern of (rising) inequality, to which the US, Mexico and Canada all belong, and which has also influenced wage structures in Japan. Over on the right side of the diagram, we see a similar North European orbit, including Austria, Norway and the Netherlands in close association with Germany, and, a little further out, Greece. Sweden and Finland form a Scandinavian pair in some association with the North European block; France is a bit more separate still. The UK, Italy and Denmark appear closer to the North American pattern of wage inequality. Finally, Korea, Australia and New Zealand each follow patterns of their own, not closely tied to any other country in this sample.

Figure 13.8 suggests that the dispersion of wage structures is a transnational affair. It appears to be strongly influenced by geographical propinquity, trading patterns and perhaps other forms of transnational association. The existence of a Central European and of a North American inequality basin, so to speak, is an especially striking finding. Small countries apparently do not control their own fates, so far as wage structures are concerned.

Transnational patterns also characterize changes in unemployment, as Figure 13.9 illustrates. But the patterns are different. Once again there is a North American basin (unemployment data for Mexico were not readily at hand at the time this was written). But now the UK joins the Netherlands, Germany, Sweden and Finland in a North European cluster. And there is a distinct South European cluster, including Italy, France, Belgium, Spain, Greece, and Austria, but also Japan. This cluster, however, has a behaviour of unemployment rates which appears closer to the American orbit than to the North European one, and indeed more resembles the American pattern than the North European countries resemble each other. Norway, Portugal, Australia and Denmark are the outliers on this one.

Overall, inter-country percentage fluctuations of unemployment, as measured by the linkage distance on the vertical axis, are about twice as large as inter-country percentage variations of inequality. And it would appear that wage structures and business cycles operate in overlapping basins. The wage structures of small countries appear to be quite tightly linked to their near neighbours, with Central European norms radiating out over much of the rest of Europe. As for unemployment, the North American pattern seems to rule most of the Western world.

Table 13.1 (a,b) in the Appendix summarizes these findings in a rough three-by-three table. Changes in unemployment (across the top), and changes in

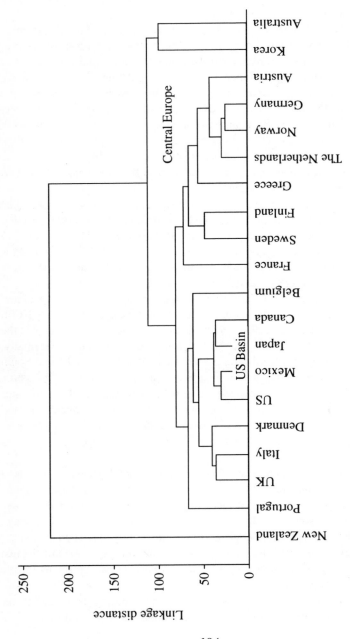

Source: OECD STAN database, 1971–92

Figure 13.8 *Patterns of change in wage inequality cluster analysis/Ward's method/Euclidean distances: changes in between-group Theil entropy measures of inequality*

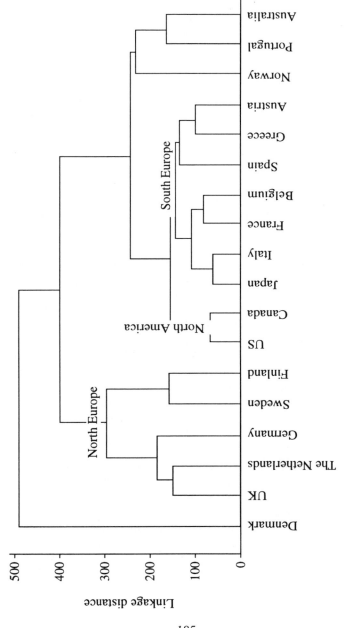

Source: OECD historical statistics 1961–93

Figure 13.9   Patterns of change in unemployment cluster analysis/Ward's method/Euclidean distances

inequality (down the side) are divided into three possible patterns: North American, North European (for unemployment) and Central European (for inequality), and Other. Countries are classed according to where they seem to best fit in the resulting 3 x 3 classification scheme. The result, while by no means definitive, seems a reasonable first cut at how patterns of international influence actually seem to run in the world.

Conclusions and further research
The most important conclusion of this chapter is that it is possible and rewarding to exploit existing sources of wage and earnings data by industry to develop annual time-series measures of changing inequality in the wage structure. It appears that these measures do in fact usefully illuminate some of the central macroeconomic questions of our time. Correspondingly studies that purport to draw deep conclusions from purely cross-sectional data, or from isolated point-to-point comparisons through time, or from small groups of countries may be helpful, ought perhaps to be regarded sceptically.

Secondly, the data are consistent with the Keynesian proposition that higher unemployment produces higher inequality, suggesting especially that a full employment policy will reduce inequality. While full employment policies in small countries run into balance-of-payments constraints, a full employment policy in the larger economies, not so constrained, would appear to have clear-cut spillover effects on their smaller neighbours. Thus a co-ordinated global reflation led by the US and seconded by Germany may be the only feasible path towards global full employment. Thirdly, this study raises the question whether there is anything sensible that a small country can do on its own about either its wage structure or its rate of unemployment. These variables in a small, open economy appear to be substantially dependent on the winds blowing from larger countries, with the strongest winds on unemployment blowing from the direction of the US. There is no case anywhere in this evidence for the proposition that a country can reduce its unemployment rate by increasing the dispersion of its wage structure.

As for further research, there are many more countries with reasonable data on wages and employment across years and industries, and for whom computation of T' is therefore possible. As the Luxembourg Income Study expands its coverage, these estimates can be benchmarked and made comparable across countries. With Gini coefficients (or, better yet, sample-based Theil statistics) for multiple years, the ability of the Gini-adjusted Theil measure to track overall family income inequality through time can be checked. Further analysis of the determinants of wage inequality is warranted, taking account of the effects of changes in exchange rates, inflation rates, and other macroeconomic variables.

Endnotes

1. This chapter is a product of a collaborative project on wage structures at the Lyndon B. Johnson School of Public Affairs of the University of Texas at Austin, and owes a great deal to the work of the following Ph.D. students in public policy: Maureen Berner, Amy Calistri, Pedro Conceicao, Vidal Garza-Cantu, Junmo Kim and especially Lu Jiaqing, who executed the inequality calculations. I also thank Jen Steele for research assistance. The project is funded in parts by the Twentieth Century Fund, the Policy Research Institute at the University of Texas, and the Center for the Study of Western Hemispheric Trade. I thank Larry Mishel, Elke Muchlinski, Stephen Nickell, Robert M. Solow, Myron Tegze, Roger Tollison, Kresimir Žigić and participants in the conferences and seminars at the Berkeley Roundtable on the International Economy, in Dubrovnik, at CERGE in Prague, and at the Southern Economics Association meetings in Washington DC, for valuable comments.
2. 'Jobs and wages revisited,' *The Economist*, 17 August 1996, p. 62.
3. Countries covered are Austria, Belgium, Canada, Denmark, Finland, France, Germany, Italy, The Netherlands, Norway, Spain (data began in 1979), the UK and the US. Some parts of the analysis bring in information from Australia, Greece, Japan, Portugal, Sweden and New Zealand.
4. See Galbraith and Calmon, 1990, 1994, 1996 for a general description of methods, and Ferguson and Galbraith, 1996, for a detailed explanation of this research.
5. Further issues and qualifications concerning Theil-based inequality measures and their use to make cross-country-comparable level estimates of overall inequality in incomes are discussed in the Appendix.
6. This defect emerged from a comparison of and apparent inconsistency between fixed and variable-weighted Theil measures.
7. The shift from a variable to a fixed-weighted measure doubles the estimated increase in wage in equality in the UK after 1979, about 8 to over 16 per cent, making the rise of inequality in the UK much more comparable to that in the US than the variable-weighted measures indicate.
8. The same lack of clear association applies when fixed-weighted inequality measures are substituted. In that case 12 countries show a positive correlation, 7 show a negative one, the average across countries is less that –0.02, 12 countries have correlation coefficients less than 0.15 in absolute value, and only one country shows a correlation of movements greater than 0.4 (absolute value).

References

Card, David, Francis Kramarz and Thomas Lemieux (1994), 'Changes in the Relative Structure of Wages and Employment: A Comparison of the United States, Canada and France', mimeo, Princeton University.

Carnoy, Martin, Manuel Castello and Chris Benner, (1996), 'What is Happening to the US Labor Market?', mimeo, Stanford University.

The Economist, 'Jobs and wages revisited', 17 August 1996, p. 62.

Ferguson Thomas and James K. Galbraith (1996), 'The Wage Structure, 1920–1947'. mimeo, Austin: University of Texas for the Harvard Economic History Seminar, 8 March.

Galbraith, James K. and Paulo Du Pin Calmon (1990), 'Relative Wages and International Competitiveness', L.B.J. School of Public Affairs Working Paper No. 56.

Galbraith, James K. and Paulo Du Pin Calmon (1994), 'Industries, Trade and Wages', in M. Bernstein and D. Adler, *Understanding American Economic Decline*, New York: Cambridge University Press, pp. 161–98.

Galbraith, James K. and Paulo Du Pin Calmon, (1996), 'Wage Change and Trade Performance in U.S. Manufacturing Industries', *Cambridge Journal of Economics*, **20** (4), 433–50.

Gordon, Robert J. (1986), *The American Business Cycle: Continuity and Change*, Chicago: University of Chicago Press.

Grubb W. Norton and R.H. Wilson (1992), 'Trends in wage and salary inequality, 1967–1988,' *Monthly Labor Review*, 23–9.

Keynes, John Maynard (1936) *The General Theory of Employment Interest and Money*, London: Macmillan and Co.

Nickell Stephen and B. Bell (1996), 'Changes in the Distribution of Wages and Unemployment in OECD Countries', *American Economic Review*, May, 302–8.

Niggle, Christopher (1996), 'New Evidence from the Luxembourg Income Surveys', mimeo, Redlands University.

OECD (1996), 'Earnings Inequality, Low-Paid Employment and Earnings Mobility', *OECD Economic Outlook 1996*. Cited in *The Economist*, infra.

Theil, Henri (1972), *Statistical Decomposition Analysis: With Applications in the Social and Administrative Sciences*, Amsterdam, The Netherlands and London, UK: North Holland Publishing Company.

Wolff, Edward N. (1994), *Top Heavy: A Study of the Increasing Inequality of Wealth in America*, New York: Twentieth Century Fund.

Appendix: The Theil measure and Gini-equivalent estimates

Originally drawn from information theory, Theil's T has the following formula:

$$T = (1/n)\Sigma(Y_i /\mu)\log(Y_i /\mu) \tag{1}$$

Here, n is the number of individuals, Y_i is each person's income, and m is average income for the whole population. 'Log' is the logarithm in base 10.

Notice that, whenever a group population consists of equal individuals, the final terms in T all reduce to log $(y_i /m) = \log(1)$, which is equal to zero. Thus T overall is zero for the case of perfect equality. And T increases, as deviations away from the average value increase. Since deviations of (y_i/m) below the mean have values between zero and one, whereas deviations above the mean are unbounded, T increases as more of the observations move away from the average. Thus T is a reasonable way to measure the degree of dispersion about the average value for any group of observations, and that is, after all, what inequality is. The formula for computing T from grouped data is:

$$T = \Sigma(p_i \mu_i /\mu)\log(\mu_i /\mu) + \Sigma(p_i u_i /\mu)T_i \tag{2}$$

where now p_i is the proportion of workers employed in the i-th group, m_i represents the average income for the i-th group, m represents average overall income, and T_i is the Theil T as measured strictly within the i-th group. Thus the grouped Theil statistic is the weighted sum of that part of inequality that occurs between groups (on the left of the above expression) and a part that occurs within groups (on the right).

The formula for T', the between-group-Theil statistic, is just the first element in the forumula for computing the Theil T from grouped data:

$$T' = \Sigma(p_i \mu_i /\mu)\log(\mu_i /\mu) \tag{3}$$

Since the within-group element in variation is omitted, this is obviously a lower-bound estimate of dispersion.

Our estimates of T' for individual OECD countries use average annual earnings in 40 manufacturing industries, weighted by employment in those industries. To compute a cross-country comparable Theil-Gini coefficient for a single country, the T'G index, we assume that T' is perfectly correlated to the unknown series of Gini coefficients (a fact known to be nearly true for the US). We then benchmark the T' series to the known value of the Gini for whatever year it may be available from the Luxembourg Income Survey. To do this we simply scale up the whole T' series so that it matches the known Gini in the known year. The proportionately adjusted values of T' in other years give an estimate of what the Gini might have been, if a survey had been taken in those years.

We find that a series so constructed from the STAN for the US is highly correlated with an actual measure of the Gini coefficient for variations in family income, based on the Current Population Survey, for the years 1970–92 ($\rho = .92$). However, several cautions are in order. Firstly, our benchmark value for the US Gini coefficient from the Luxembourg Income Survey, 0.343 in 1991, is well below the Census estimate of .397 for that year. Correspondingly, all other values in our series will be lower. We have not inquired into the sources of this discrepancy.

Secondly, our measure of T' and T'G for the US rises more rapidly than the CPS series in the 1970s, and less rapidly in the 1980s. Indeed and T' and T'G stabilize in the mid-1980s, several years before the same effect is observed for household incomes. This may be because wage incomes grew more unequal in the 1970s, while non-wage incomes actually contributed to a reduction in household income inequality, through the expansion of social security and other entitlement programmes in those years. In the 1980s, on the other hand, a huge rise in interest incomes flowed mainly to wealthier Americans, so that non-wage incomes would work to increase inequality, relative to the trend in wage incomes. Meanwhile declining unemployment, inflation and a declining value of the dollar all worked to stabilize the dispersion of wage incomes (but that is a story requiring a separate discussion).

Thirdly, our T'G series for the US has about twice the standard deviation of the CPS-Gini series. Our series increases much more sharply than the CPS series, and therefore projects back over 20 years to much lower estimated Gini values in the early 1970s than does the Census series. This turns the US into a low-earnings-inequality country, relative to much of Europe, as recently as 25 years ago.

We think this result is plausible in historical context. Inequality in US wage incomes in 1970 would have been much lower than inequality in overall family incomes, due to the highly skewed distribution of non-wage incomes in the US, a country with a very weak social welfare system, a high concentration of private capital ownership and few nationalized industries when compared to Western Europe at that time.

It also seems likely that non-wage sources of income became more equal in the US at least up to 1980, because social insurance incomes rose during that time, and because the distribution of wealth tended to become somewhat more equal as inflation raised the value of houses relative to financial assets such as bonds whose ownership is highly concentrated (Wolff, 1994). Thus US wage and earnings inequality would have risen more rapidly than overall inequality in this period. The implication is that the dispersion of wage and salary earnings must have been quite low by international standards in the US at the end of 1969. This was a time of full employment, strong labour unions, recently installed trade protection in textiles, and a shooting war, all of which work to compress the distribution of earnings.

Since changes in social insurance coverage and in the wealth distribution are likely to have been less important in Europe than in the US in the decade of the 1970s, we think that the T'G estimates for Europe may be better reflectors of the trend in overall *family income* inequality than they are for the US. However, for both regions, the T'G indicators should provide fairly robust estimates of the trend in inequality of wage and salary *earnings*, since the cross-industrial dispersion of such earnings is what they actually measure.

In the case of the UK, several colleagues have noted that our measure of wage dispersion shows less increase since 1979 than other measures, notably the Gini coefficient for inequality of household incomes, and that the rise in inequality in the UK is nearly comparable to that in the US than our data show. We believe there are two explanations for this. Firstly, our variable-weighted T' deviates from the fixed-weighted measure in the UK case but not in the US case. When a fixed-weight T' is substituted, the rise in wage inequality in the UK approximately doubles, from 8.6 to 16.9 per cent, compared to 26 per cent for the US series. Secondly, we believe that the dispersion of non-wage incomes probably grew much more in the UK than in the US after 1979: the Thatcher regime was harsher on the welfare state than that of Ronald Reagan, partly because Reagan never controlled both houses of Congress. Thus a measure of inequality based on household income will grow more rapidly in this period in the UK, compared to a measure based on wages.

The absence of data on services from the STAN data set is another troubling issue. It is possible that a data set covering average wages in services would show a different rate of change of inequality than our restricted data set covering manufacturing. But would the rate be higher or lower? We can think of no clear *a priori* reason for bias in either direction. Some tentative evidence for the US suggests that a significant part of wages in the services sector in a large-market economy covary with manufacturing wages, so that our data on manufacturing wages represent a larger fraction of total employment than they actually cover. In smaller countries, solidaristic wage structures are likely to extend across manufacturing and services, further reducing the likelihood that inequality

Table 13.1(a): Estimated annual values of the Theil-Gini coefficient – 13 OECD countries

	Austria	Belgium	Canada	Denmark	Finland	France	Germany	Italy	Netherlands	Norway	Spain	UK	US
1970	0.248	0.311	0.255	0.408	0.251	0.200	0.203	0.318	0.342	0.261		0.331	0.200
1971	0.222	0.317	0.252	0.420	0.203	0.195	0.197	0.260	0.344	0.260		0.306	0.216
1972	0.208	0.325	0.256	0.414	0.222	0.176	0.189	0.245	0.326	0.231		0.319	0.231
1973	0.203	0.188	0.253	0.356	0.229	0.187	0.194	0.241	0.329	0.236		0.322	0.240
1974	0.224	0.191	0.243	0.356	0.211	0.197	0.210	0.229	0.342	0.240		0.289	0.238
1975	0.226	0.195	0.235	0.421	0.205	0.172	0.214	0.243	0.314	0.246		0.327	0.244
1976	0.224	0.193	0.240	0.353	0.198	0.193	0.218	0.233	0.275	0.233		0.267	0.266
1977	0.219	0.201	0.240	0.313	0.184	0.272	0.222	0.199	0.267	0.219		0.283	0.281
1978	0.215	0.199	0.238	0.318	0.184	0.275	0.211	0.200	0.265	0.208	0.308	0.290	0.278
1979	0.217	0.212	0.222	0.288	0.212	0.294	0.223	0.192	0.266	0.216	0.313	0.280	0.277
1980	0.215	0.214	0.225	0.271	0.188	0.301	0.223	0.197	0.258	0.222	0.295	0.297	0.287
1981	0.236	0.215	0.242	0.275	0.182	0.330	0.219	0.202	0.263	0.228	0.293	0.300	0.296
1982	0.228	0.213	0.272	0.301	0.168	0.325	0.225	0.202	0.257	0.217	0.286	0.310	0.301
1983	0.191	0.220	0.293	0.273	0.174	0.309	0.234	0.205	0.288	0.225	0.287	0.311	0.303
1984	0.208	0.226	0.305	0.261	0.193	0.296	0.250	0.197	0.299	0.246	0.304	0.301	0.298
1985	0.200	0.237	0.309	0.239	0.194	0.321	0.239	0.214	0.276	0.262	0.311	0.298	0.293
1986	0.200	0.230	0.313	0.247	0.202	0.312	0.229	0.221	0.256	0.245	0.306	0.304	0.293
1987	0.208	0.238	0.302	0.257	0.190	0.313	0.243	0.225	0.252	0.247	0.308	0.300	0.314
1988	0.182	0.237	0.287	0.274	0.164	0.315	0.232	0.254	0.273	0.257	0.321	0.308	0.340
1989	0.193	0.234	0.281	0.247	0.187	0.314	0.234	0.259	0.282	0.247	0.332	0.315	0.343
1990	0.184	0.224	0.266	0.260	0.199	0.315	0.234	0.255	0.282	0.227	0.315	0.317	0.340
1991	0.171	0.223	0.286	0.269	0.223	0.308	0.224	0.255	0.254	0.233	0.308	0.343	0.343
1992	0.159	0.230	0.342		0.214	0.313	0.231	0.269	0.244	0.226	0.259	0.322	0.365
1993					0.231			0.282	0.259				0.355

Note: Estimates based on Theil lower-bound estimates of the change in inequality computed across industry groups, benchmarked to values of the Gini coefficient for family incomes reported by the Luxembourg income survey.

measures taken on the manufacturing sector grossly misrepresent the larger picture. There is no reason to think that overall inequality measures could run counter to the trend within manufacturing, and the US case suggests that this need not be a concern. The issue posed by the absence of services data is one of magnitudes, not direction.

To compute a Gini coefficient for Europe as a whole, we would need to start by deriving an estimate of T for Europe, from equation (2) above, with both between-country and within-country components. The p_i are available in our relative employment weights, and these can be treated as though they were approximate population weights. The u_i/u can be taken from ratios of within-country per capita GDP to a cross-country employment-weighted average. We computed these from OECD Historical Statistics using a 1993 purchasing power parities.

Table 13.1 (b)   Estimated value of GT and CPS Gini

Year	European GT Estimate	US GT	US CPS-Gini
1970	0.265	0.200	0.353
1971	0.247	0.216	0.355
1972	0.241	0.231	0.359
1973	0.239	0.240	0.356
1974	0.236	0.238	0.355
1975	0.243	0.244	0.357
1976	0.230	0.266	0.358
1977	0.243	0.281	0.363
1978	0.247	0.278	0.363
1979	0.249	0.277	0.365
1980	0.251	0.287	0.365
1981	0.257	0.296	0.369
1982	0.261	0.301	0.380
1983	0.262	0.303	0.382
1984	0.264	0.298	0.383
1985	0.267	0.293	0.389
1986	0.264	0.293	0.392
1987	0.268	0.314	0.393
1988	0.272	0.340	0.395
1989	0.275	0.343	0.401
1990	0.271	0.340	0.396
1991	0.270	0.343	0.397
1992	0.270	0.364	0.403

Unfortunately this process founders on the fact that T' is only a lower-bound estimate of within-country inequality, so that we have no good proxy for the full within-country T_i. Our best guess, noting that the values of T_{US} estimated for the US by Grubb and Wilson (1992) are on the same order (about .35) as Gini coefficients, is that between-country variations in income have contributed fairly little (on the order of .02) to the overall inequality of European wage structures since 1970. These are all developed countries, and the relative incomes of the large countries are fairly close and change little, when PPP-adjusted. Ignoring the between-country variations, the tables provide a highly approximate estimate of trans-European inequality, basically a weighted average of within-country T'G estimates for 11 countries. This series is compared to the T'G estimate of earnings inequality in the US.

If the table is approximately right, both societies are markedly less equal in their wage structures than was the US, as recently as 1970, when the unemployment rate was last below 4 per cent. But the US has clearly lost its claim to being the middle-class, or classless society, in the intervening time. That distinction now belongs to Western Europe if it belongs anywhere at all.

14 Stabilization of economic fluctuation and commodity price by a commodity-based currency

John-ren Chen[1]

The wide and rapid fluctuations in the world market prices of primary products was described as one of the greatest evils in international trade by Keynes (see Singer, 1996a). In an article published in the *Economic Journal* (1938) Keynes has shown that the average annual price range of four representative commodities (rubber, cotton, wheat and lead) over the last ten years had been 67 per cent. He therefore proposed initially a world currency based on a bundle of 30 primary commodities to stabilize automatically their average price while not ruling out fluctuations of market prices of individual commodities against this average (Singer, 1996, p. 6). Singer pointed out 'A world commodity based currency would also have contributed to global macroeconomic stability; in slack times when commodity prices were low international buffer stocks would have been accumulated, thus injecting additional liquidity into the world economy, and vice versa in the case of inflationary demand pressures and high commodity prices' (*ibid.*, p. 2). Thus, though full employment is the main issue of the Keynesian Consensus, the stabilization of primary commodity prices was regarded to be very important by Keynes who was a fervent supporter of such stabilization as was appreciated by Singer.

In the Bretton Woods system proposed by Keynes there was in addition to the IMF and World Bank an essential third pillar: an International Trade Organization with commodity price stabilization as its major function (*ibid.*, 1996).

Economic policy measures, especially measures concerned with primary commodities, have been mainly designed and implemented in order to achieve other effects than to stabilize prices (for instance, support prices have been implemented to support the income of commodity producers; acreage allotment systems have been implemented to reduce the surplus of primary commodity production; sales taxes have been introduced to collect tax revenue for the government and so on.) Economic policy measures, however, usually also have effects on the volatility of commodity prices, even if they are implemented to achieve other effects than to influence the volatility of the commodity prices (Just, 1990; Chen, 1994).

This chapter studies the effects of a commodity based currency as proposed by J.M. Keynes to stabilize macroeconomic fluctuation and prices of primary products.

The harmful influence of wide fluctuation in commodity price is more serious since some irreversible effects cannot be avoided, for instance a strong price reduction may compel producers to give up the production of the primary product forever. It is true that price stabilization does not necessarily imply a stabilization of the revenue and even more of the income of the producers. This issue will not be discussed here.

This chapter deals with a simple partial equilibrium model with an additive stochastic error term for a competitive commodity market will be constructed to study the effects of economic policy measures on the volatility of commodity prices. Next it studies the buffer stock measure implemented to stabilize prices of primary commodities so as to allow an analysis of the effects of a commodity based currency and thus linking the buffer stock with the supply of money. In section three of this exposition, a basic macroeconomic model to study the Keynes proposal is constructed. The proposal of a commodity based currency by Keynes will be discussed in more detail in the following sections. The commodity based currency is studied in the framework of a macroeconomic IS-LM-model with a model for primary commodity. Throughout this chapter the volatility of a variable is represented by its variance.

A basic model for primary commodity
A simple basic model for a perfect competitive market of a primary commodity with stochastic demand and supply functions is constructed for discussing the influences of economic policy on the volatility of commodity prices. The contrast between perfect competitiveness on the market for primary commodities and imperfect competition for manufactures is argued by some economists to contribute to the long-run deterioration of terms of trade against primary commodities (Bloch and Sapsford, 1991). Therefore perfect competition seems to be a representative market form for most primary commodities, although elements of imperfect competition are found in at least some primary product markets.[2]

The stochastic elements in the model are introduced to capture the disturbances due to factors such as droughts, wars, natural disasters and so on. Both the disturbances on the demand and supply-side of primary commodity markets are assumed to be independent and not autocorrelated.

In applying the equilibrium approach a perfect competitive market of primary commodity can be modelled by the following linear demand and supply function with a stochastic additive disturbance term respectively:

$$Q = a_0 - a_1 P + a_2 Y + u \quad \text{(demand function)} \tag{1}$$
$$Q = b_0 + b_1 P + b_2 X + v \quad \text{(supply function)} \tag{2}$$

where Q: transaction amount

P: price of primary commodity

Y: an exogenous variable in the demand function, for instance, income and so on.

X: an exogenous influence factor in the supply function (for example factor price, technical change),

u, v: random disturbances on demand and supply of the commodity.

A linear partial equilibrium model is constructed because of its analytic tractability. With the exception of b_0 all parameters are specified as non-negative, that is $a_0, a_1, a_2, b_1, b_2 > 0$.

The equilibrium price, transaction quantity, and the volatility of commodity price of the above model are given by solving the above model as follows:

$$P^* = \frac{a_0 - b_0 + a_2 Y - b_2 X + u - v}{a_1 + b_1} \tag{3}$$

$$Q^* = \frac{a_1 b_0 + a_0 b_1 + a_2 b_1 Y + a_1 b_2 X + b_1 u + a_1 v}{a_1 + b_1} \tag{4}$$

$$\sigma_{p^*}^2 = E\left(P^* - EP^*\right)^2 = \frac{\sigma_u^2 + \sigma_v^2}{\left(a_1 + b_1\right)^2} \tag{5}$$

$$\sigma_{Q^*}^2 = E\left(Q^* - EQ^*\right)^2 = \frac{1}{\left(a_1 + b_1\right)^2}\left(b_1^2 \sigma_u^2 + a_1^2 \sigma_v^2\right) \tag{6}$$

The variances are calculated on the assumption that both X and Y are non stochastic exogenous variables and u and v are stochastically independent

and $\sigma_u^2 = E(u - Eu)^2$ with $Eu = 0$ and
$\sigma_v^2 = E(v - Ev)^2$ with $Ev = 0$

are the variances of disturbances in the demand and supply function respectively. E is used as expectation operator. The expectation of both random disturbances is assumed to be zero. Primary commodities like metals and cotton are bought by producers of final products. Thus the demand for primary commodities is a derived demand which is determined by price of product and factors as well as output. The same approach is followed by Bloch and Sapsford (1996). Most primary commodities can also be used by consumers. In this case the demand is determined by prices of primary commodities and income according to the utility maximization principle. Thus the demand function specified in the above basic model can be interpreted as intermediates bought by producers or as consumer goods bought by consumers.

The linear demand and supply functions specified in the basic model for primary commodities in this section do not fulfil all the properties derived for the utility maximization behaviour of consumers or profit maximization behaviour of producers for the demand and supply function, respectively. For instance both the demand function and supply function of primary commodity in the basic model do not fulfil the property of freedom from monetary illusion of the consumer and producer correspondingly, as the demand and supply function specified in the basic model are not homogeneous. The main reason for this simple model is the analytic ability of a linear model. Another form of demand and supply functions which are also easy to analyse is a logarithmical linear model. The latter case has two shortcomings; firstly, it implies a special stochastic property that the variance is no more constant as assumed in the basic model above; secondly, there are some problems for combining the basic model with a macroeconomic model to study the linkage effect (feedback effect) between the primary commodity sector and the macroeconomic sector.

Dynamic models like the cobweb model have been applied to study the cyclic fluctuation of commodity prices. The demand of primary products is, as a rule, a continuous process while production of these commodities is only periodic. Therefore cyclic fluctuation of the commodity prices, like the seasonal price changes, has usually been repeated. But the most rapid and wide fluctuations of commodity prices seem to be caused by random shock. The main issue of stabilization of commodity price is therefore how to reduce the volatility of the price fluctuation.

In this chapter random shock in the commodity production is modelled by an additive random variable to capture this feature. Throughout this chapter the active demand (D) and supply (S) are assumed to be non-negative. This assumption implies that the value of a random shock is limited, that is the absolute value of u and v is limited to be not higher than the expectation value of active demand and supply. This assumption can be easily explained by the fact that the least output cannot be less than zero, even if an acreage is fully destroyed by a typhoon nothing will be produced. A negative output cannot be realized. This assumption implies that

$$EP^* \geq 0 \text{ and } EQ^* \geq 0$$

As mentioned earlier, the fluctuation of commodity price can cause irreversible effects on the demand and supply of primary commodities and induce a change of the structure of an economy, if users or producers of the primary products are compelled to give up their business. To consider these effects a non linear model is needed. This will remain for further researches.

Buffer stock
Buffer stocks are one of the most discussed measures to stabilize commodity prices. There are different variants of buffer stock measures. In this section we consider the case that the buffer stock is used to stabilize the commodity price at a special level $\bar{q}$. The basic model is modified for this case as follows:

$$D = a_0 - a_1 q + a_2 Y + u \qquad \text{active demand function} \qquad (7)$$

$$S = b_0 + b_1 q + b_2 X + v \qquad \text{active supply function} \qquad (8)$$

$$I = S - D \qquad \text{buffer stock change}$$

$$\int_0^t I dt \geq 0 \qquad \qquad (9)$$

with q: target price; D: demand; S: supply; I: buffer stock change.
   The modified model represents the behaviour of active demand (7), active supply (8) and intervention of the buffer stock authority which is shown by the change of buffer stock to stabilize the commodity price at a target price. The condition (9) is given as a constraint for the intervention of the buffer stock authority that the buffer stock can be negative.
   To be able to stabilize the market price at the level T the authority should buy or sell the amount of commodity $I = S - D$ on the market, that is if the market price rises above the target price the authority should sell $D - S$ on the market to keep the price at q. If the market price is going to decrease the authority should buy the amount of primary commodity $S - D$ on the market.
   Therefore the buffer stock authority must have financial resources amount $\bar{q}(S - D)$ to be able to keep the market price at the target level q, if $S(\bar{q}) > D(\bar{q})$, and a quantity of the primary commodity $D - S$, if $D(\bar{q}) > S(\bar{q})$, where $D(\bar{q})$ and $S(\bar{q})$ are the active demand and supply at the price $\bar{q}$ respectively.

If the buffer stock authority can fulfil the above conditions the price of primary commodities can be stabilized at the target level.

In the implementation of buffer stocks many failures have occurred either because of insufficient stock accumulated for dampening the pressure of increasing price in the period of a negative random shock in the production of primary commodity or of insufficient financial resources to buy commodities on the market for damping pressure of increasing commodity price due to positive random shocks in commodity production. Therefore to provide sufficient financial resources for the implementation of buffer stocks has been an important issue (Singer, 1996, pp. 4–5).

A macroeconomic model of a commodity based currency

A commodity based currency combines the buffer stock measure with the quantity of money. The central bank has the obligation to buy and sell the primary commodities at the price set by the buffer stock authority from and to the private people who sells or buys primary commodities to or from the central bank. Due to this obligation (of a commodity based currency) the central bank can print (increase) money to buy primary commodities. Thus the problem of financing the buffer stock can be solved. The price of primary commodities can be stabilized at the level set by the buffer stock authority. In implementing the commodity based currency the central bank becomes the authority to run the buffer stock.

Summarizing this short description of the proposal for a commodity based currency by Keynes there are two main properties which have to be considered in the model:

1. The buffer stock is used to stabilize the price of primary commodities at a level set by the authority; and
2. There is a direct connection between the implementation of buffer stock measure and the quantity of money in the economy.

To consider the first point we modify the basic model for primary commodity, given the above, as follows:

$$D = a_0 - a_1 q + a_2 Y \tag{10}$$

$$S = b_0 + b_1 q + v \tag{11}$$

$$I = S - D \tag{12}$$

with D,S: demand and supply of primary commodity; q: target price of primary commodity set by the buffer stock authority; I: buffer stock change (increase if I > 0 and decrease if I < 0); Y: national income (endogenous variable); v: random disturbance on the supply side with Ev = 0.

In the above modified model there are two sorts of participant on the market for primary commodities, that is the producers and users of primary commodities and the buffer stock authority who has to keep the market price stable at the target price level. The former ones are called active and the later ones the passive participants of the commodity markets. To keep the model simple we consider only one commodity. The most important difference between the basic and the modified model for a commodity based currency is that the price in the first model varies to arrive at the equilibrium of demand and supply on the market. In the later model the price is set at $\bar{q}$. The usual market mechanism of the price to arrive at the equilibrium of active demand and active supply is removed. Therefore only in average will the market of the active demand and supply be in the equilibrium .

A further simplification in the modified model is made by assuming that random disturbances occur only on the active supply-side.

Now a macroeconomic model of the IS- and LM-type is attached to study the interdependence of a commodity based currency on primary commodity and national income.

$$Y = \alpha_{10} - \alpha_{11}r + \alpha_{12}G + \alpha_{13}q\,I \qquad \text{(IS-curve)} \qquad (13)$$

$$Y = \alpha_{20} + \alpha_{21}r + \alpha_{22}(\overline{M} + m) \qquad \text{(LM-curve)} \qquad (14)$$

$$m = I.q \quad \text{(link between buffer stock and money supply)} \qquad (15)$$

where Y is national income; r is interest rate; G is public spending; $\overline{M}$: is independent money supply m is change of quantity of money due to buffer stock activity of the central bank.

$I = S - D > 0$: commodity bought by the buffer stock authority
$I < 0$: commodity sold by the buffer stock authority with $\int_t Idt \geq 0$

$\alpha_{ij} > 0$ for i = 1,2; j = 0,1,2

Both the IS- and LM-curve are assumed to have the usual properties, that is $\alpha_{ij} > 0$ and $a_{11} + a_{22} \neq 0$

The buffer stock induces two links between the primary products sector and the macroeconomic sector, that is firstly, the link between buffer stock of primary product and investment which is shown by the last term of (13); and secondly, the link between buffer stock change and money supply.

The last equation shows the second link between the buffer stock activity of the central bank and the supply of money. This can be explained by 'Keynes's favourite idea of a linkage between commodity control and macroeconomic monetary control' (Singer, 1996, p. 6).

The first link between the primary product sector and the macroeconomic sector can be explained by the assumption in this chapter that primary products are used as inputs to produce final products therefore the production of primary products is already considered as a part of final product in the national income account, therefore the production of primary products need not to be considered in the IS curve except the change of storage induced by the buffer stock activities. The change of storage like an investment in the macroeconomic activity therefore has to be considered as a component of aggregate demand in the macroeconomic model.

A very popular way to see the effects of macroeconomic policies is the IS-LM model developed in 1937 by Hicks. The IS curve relates the level of aggregated demand to the level of interest rates while all other variables such as public spending are exogenous. A rise in the interest rate depresses aggregate demand through its effects on investment. A graphic representation of this relationship is known as the IS curve.

While the IS curve expresses the relationship between aggregate demand and interest rate at goods market equilibrium, the LM curve shows the graphic combination of these two variables consistent with money market equilibrium for a given level of real money balances.

The IS-LM model emphasizes interaction between the goods and money market and enables to study the effects of a commodity based currency in a very simple macroeconomic framework combining with a primary product sector. The relationship between the aggregate demand and interest rate of the IS and LM schedule is given by $-a_{11} < 0$ and $a_{21} > 0$; respectively.

The IS-LM framework is the first and most influential formal interpretation of the *General Theory* which received the approval of Keynes himself. In this chapter this framework is applied to clearly prove the effect of commodity based currency on the macroeconomic fluctuation expected by Keynes and Singer, though it has some limitations to represent the *General Theory*.

In an IS-LM model the price level is assumed to be constant therefore a stabilization of the price of primary products is also stabilizing the terms of trade between price of primary products and manufactures as final products.

Neutral buffer stock target price
The target price of the buffer stock is set by the authority. There are several ways of modelling the buffer stock measure particurlarly according to the types of target

price-setting measures by any authority. The first case to be considered is that the target price is set at the *expected equilibrium market price of the active demand and supply*. This price is called the neutral buffer stock target price since the authority will not influence the trend of the commodity price. The active demand and supply are demand of buyers and producers on the commodity market, respectively. In this case the target price can be determined at

$$E(D) = E(S) \text{ that is}$$

$$a_0 - a_1 q + a_2 Y = b_0 + b_1 q \tag{16}$$

Thus

$$q = \lambda_1 (\lambda_0 + a_2 Y) \tag{17}$$

$$\text{where } \lambda_1 = (a_1 + b_1)^{-1}; \qquad \lambda_0 = a_0 - b_0$$

Throughout this chapter the condition:

$$\int_t I dt \geq 0 \tag{18}$$

is assumed to be fulfilled since this is a necessary condition for stabilizing commodity price by buffer stock.

Now a complete commodity based currency macroeconomic IS-LM model with a neutral buffer stock target price can be given as follows:

$$Y = \alpha_{10} - \alpha_{11} r + \alpha_{12} G \tag{19}$$

$$Y = \alpha_{20} + \alpha_{21} r + \alpha_{22} (\overline{M} + m) \tag{20}$$

$$m = Iq \tag{21}$$

$$D = a_0 - a_1 q + a_2 Y \tag{10}$$

$$S = b_0 + b_1 q + v \tag{11}$$

$$I = S - D \tag{12}$$

Following the neutral buffer stock target price

$$\bar{q} = \lambda_1(\lambda_0 + a_2 Y) \qquad (22)$$

where $\bar{q} = Eq$

$$\lambda_1 = (a_1 + b_1)^{-1}$$

$$\lambda_0 = a_0 - b_0$$

$$I = -\lambda_0 + \lambda_1^{-1} q - a_2 Y + v = v \qquad (23)$$

$$m = \bar{q}v = \lambda_1(\lambda_0 + a_2 Y)v \qquad (24)$$

The solutions of the complete model are

$$Y^* = \frac{A_{11} + \lambda_0 \lambda_1(\alpha_{11}\alpha_{22} + \alpha_{13}\alpha_{21})}{B - Av} \qquad (25)$$

$$r^* = \frac{A_{21} - \lambda_1 a_2[\alpha_{13}(\alpha_{20} + \alpha_{22}\overline{M}) + \alpha_{22}(\alpha_{13} + \alpha_{12}G)]v}{B - Av} \qquad (26)$$

$$q^* = \lambda_1 \lambda_0 + a_2 \lambda_1 Y^* \qquad (27)$$

where $A_{11} = \alpha_{11}(\alpha_{20} + \alpha_{22}\overline{M}) + \alpha_{12}\alpha_{21}G + \alpha_{21}\alpha_{10}$

$$B = \alpha_{11} + \alpha_{21} > 0$$

$$A_{21} = \alpha_{12}G + \alpha_{20} - \alpha_{22}\overline{M} - \alpha_{10} - \lambda_1 a_2[\alpha_{13}(\alpha_{20} + \alpha_{22}\overline{M}) + \alpha_{22}(\alpha_{10} + \alpha_{12}G)]v$$

$$A = a_2 \lambda_1(\alpha_{11}\alpha_{22} + \alpha_{13}\alpha_{21}) > 0$$

To avoid a senseless solution we assume that $B - Av > T$.

To compare the solutions of the usual IS-LM model and the commodity based currency IS-LM model with neutral buffer stock target price the solutions of the usual IS-LM model are stated below:

(a) National income $Y^* = \dfrac{A_{11}}{B}$

$$\text{(b) Interest rate } r^* = \frac{A_{21}}{B}$$

The comparison shows that both the solutions for national income and interest rate in the commodity based currency IS-LM model have an additional random term not only in the denominator but also in the numerator, respectively.

It is easy to show the following results:

1. The multipliers of changing public spending and money supply in the commodity based currency model are equal to those of the usual IS-LM model if $v = 0$ (that is if there is no disturbance in the commodity sector).
2. A positive random disturbance (shock) in the commodity sector has positive effect on the national income (which implies also a positive effect on employment) due to the commodity based currency.

   A positive disturbance, that is $v > 0$, will have a negative effect on the commodity price due to increasing active supply in the usual case without commodity based currency. In the latter case the central bank who is responsible for the commodity based currency will buy the additional supply on the market to keep the buffer stock target price and due to this action an additional quantity of money is injected into the economy and induces therefore a multiplier effect for national income and employment.

   A negative random disturbance, that is $v < 0$ will have a negative effect on the national income and employment. In this case the central bank should sell commodity to keep the commodity price at the buffer stock target level.
3. A positive random disturbance in the commodity sector will have a negative effect on the interest rate in the commodity based currency model while there is no such effect in the usual IS-LM model.
4. Due to the commodity based currency the random disturbance in the commodity sector is passed through to the macroeconomics sector by changing buffer stock and money supply caused by the buffer stock activities of the authority.
5. There is a random disturbance factor on the buffer stock target price induced by the national income linked between macroeconomics activity and commodity sector by the commodity based currency.
6. The commodity based currency induces a built-in flexibility for the macroeconomics activities as well as a stabilization effect on the commodity price due to the buffer stock measures and its links to the supply of money, if a negative shock occurs in the commodity sector since the denominator of the solution for national income increases. But a positive shock will increase the multiplier of fiscal and monetary policy.

7. A positive shock in the commodity sector has a positive effect on the national income and vice versa due to a commodity based currency.

The buffer stock authority will only be active if a random disturbance (shock) occurs. Macroeconomic policy affecting the national income will also have an effect on commodity market. The causal relationship between economic fluctuations and commodity market has a clear structure as can be seen in Fig. 14.1.

(a) Macroeconomic fluctuation → always influences commodity price and
(b) Commodity sector → macroeconomic fluctuations only if a shock occurs.

A positive shock is represented by v > 0. This would have a negative influence on commodity price and induces therefore an intervention of the buffer stock authority to buy commodity. Thus liquidity is inserted into the economy and will have a positive influence on national income which increases the demand for money and commodity. A negative shock will have the opposite effect. The net effect of a shock is accumulated from the total effects induced by the shock. Since the effects can be classified in different rounds after the initial shock and in every round opposite effects can be induced therefore the total effect is not always clear.

Keynes originally proposed a basket of 30 primary commodities (both agricultural and metals) to supplement gold as part of the international currency reserves (Singer, 1996b, p. 4). As Singer explained 'in this way the average price

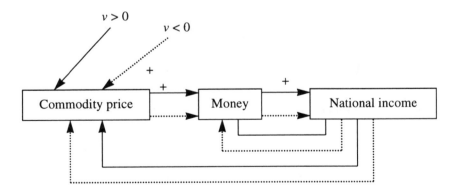

Note: → influence from . . . to... ; +: positive effect; –: negative effect.

Figure 14.1   Effects of a shock on macroeconomic fluctuations

(price index) of the thirty primary commodities would have been automatically stabilized while leaving the price of each individual commodity to fluctuate in relation to the average to specific market conditions, and maintaining neutrality between the commodities included in the basket'. A question open to be answered with a basket of commodities is the problem of the 'bimetal currency'.

Constant buffer stock target price

Keynes seems to have proposed a neutral buffer stock target price (Keynes, 1938). In this section a case of constant buffer stock target price will be studied. The commodity based currency model is modified for this case as follows:

$$Y = \alpha_{10} - \alpha_{11}r + \alpha_{12}G + \alpha_{13}qI \tag{19}$$

$$Y = \alpha_{20} + \alpha_{21}r + \alpha_{22}(\overline{M} + m) \tag{20}$$

$$m = Iq \tag{21}$$

$$D = a_0 - a_1q + a_2Y \tag{10}$$

$$S = b_0 + b_1q + v \tag{11}$$

$$I = S - D \tag{12}$$

where $\bar{q}$ is kept constant by the buffer stock authority.

For simplicity $\bar{q}$ is set at 1. Thus

$$m = I = (b_0 - a_0) + (a_1 + b_1) - a_2Y + v \tag{28}$$

After inserting the above equation for m into the macroeconomic model:

$$(1 + a_2\alpha_{13})Y + \alpha_{11}r \quad = \alpha_{10} + \alpha_{12}G + \alpha_{13}(\lambda_2 + v) \tag{29a}$$

$$(1 + a_2\alpha_{22})Y - \alpha_{21}r \quad = \alpha_{20} + \alpha_{22}[\overline{M} + \lambda_2 + v] \tag{29b}$$

$$\text{where } \lambda_2 = b_0 - a_0 + a_1 + b_1$$

The last equation is the LM curve under consideration of the links between the monetary and commodity sector due to the commodity based currency. The equilibrium solutions of the national income and interest rate of the above model are:

$$Y^* = \frac{\alpha_{21}(\alpha_{10} + \alpha_{12}G) + \alpha_{11}\alpha_{20} + \alpha_{11}\alpha_{22}[\overline{M} + (b_0 - a_0) + (a_1 + b_1) + v] + \alpha_{21}\alpha_{13}(\lambda_2 + v)}{(1 + a_2\alpha_{13})\alpha_{21} + \alpha_{11}(1 + a_2\alpha_{22})}$$

(30)

$$r^* = \frac{(1 + a_2\alpha_{22})(\alpha_{10} + \alpha_{12}G) - \alpha_{20} - \alpha_{22}(1 + a_2\alpha_{13})[\overline{M} + (b_0 - a_0) + (a_1 + b_1) + v] + \alpha_{13}(1 + a_2\alpha_{22})(\lambda_2 + v)}{(1 + a_2\alpha_{13})\alpha_{21} + \alpha_{11}(1 + a_2\alpha_{22})}$$

(31)

$$m^* = (b_0 - a_0) + (a_1 + b_1) - a_2 Y^* + v \qquad (32)$$

Now some comparisons between the multipliers in the usual IS-LM model and in the above model of a commodity based currency with a constant buffer stock target price can be easily shown:

1. The multipliers of public spending and money supply on the national income and interest rate are smaller in the commodity currency based model. Thus the commodity based currency with constant buffer stock currency has a built-in flexibility effect on the macroeconomic activities. This can be easily shown by the Figure 14.2.

   Since the target price is constant, a shock in the commodity sector has influences on the macroeconomic fluctuation which does not induce change in the commodity price.

2. There is a link from the random disturbance in the commodity sector to the macroeconomic sector due to the commodity based currency. The volatility of national income is equal to

$$\sigma_Y^2 = \left[\frac{\alpha_{11}\alpha_{22} + \alpha_{21}\alpha_{13}}{\alpha_{21} + \alpha_{11}(1 + a_2\alpha_{22})} \right]^2 \sigma_v^2 \qquad (33)$$

The volatility of national income will be higher if the multiplier of changing money supply on the national income is higher and vice versa.

3. The interest rate under the commodity based currency is also influenced by the random disturbances in the commodity sector. The volatility of interest rate is given as follows:

$$\sigma_r^2 = \left[\frac{(1 + a_2\alpha_{13})\alpha_{22} + \alpha_{13}(1 + a_2\alpha_{22})}{\alpha_{21} + \alpha_{11}(1 + a_2\alpha_{22})} \right]^2 \sigma_v^2 \tag{34}$$

4. The volatility of money supply linked by the commodity based currency is given:

$$\sigma_m^2 = a_2^2 \sigma_Y^2 + \sigma_v^2 - a_2\sigma_{Yv}^2$$

$$= \left\{ 1 - \frac{a_2\alpha_{11}\alpha_{22}(\alpha_{21} + \alpha_{11})}{[\alpha_{21} + \alpha_{11}(1 + a_2\alpha_{22})]^2} \right\} \sigma_v^2 \tag{35}$$

Since a commodity money based on primary product implies a constant exchange rate between the product and the currency therefore the model constructed in this section with a constant target price can better represent the case of a commodity money. Due to a constant target price and intervention of the buffer stock authority the price of the primary product is totally stabilized with a price volatility of zero. But a shock in the commodity sector cannot disappear without any effect. In a commodity based currency with a constant target price the effect of a shock on the volatility of commodity price has been substituted by an effect on the macroeconomic fluctuation. There is a similarity to the effect induced by the balance of payment surplus of deficit under a gold reserve currency.

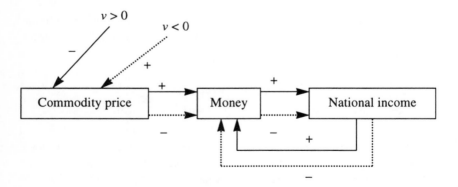

Note: → influence from . . . to . . . ; + : positive effect; − :negative effect.

Figure 14.2   Effects of a shock on macroeconomic fluctuations

Conclusions

The influences of economic policy on the volatility of commodity markets have been studied in this chapter. Many economists are concerned about the volatility of commodity development. But the influences of economic policies on the volatility of commodity prices have been rarely discussed though policy for stabilization of commodity prices has been intensively studied in the literature of development economics.

Policy measures implemented to achieve other effects also have influences on the volatility of commodity prices. The cases studied in this chapter show clearly the relevance of policy measure with respect to the volatility of price. Though the models constructed in this chapter are very simple, the results seem to be relevant for policy makers for their decisions.

To stabilize the strong fluctuation of commodity prices Keynes once proposed to introduce a commodity based currency. Due to the links between buffer stock activities and the money supply by a commodity based currency Keynes proposed that the commodity price would be stabilized and also the macroeconomic fluctuations.

To study Keynes's proposal a macroeconomic model connected with a simple model for a primary commodity is constructed in this chapter.

The links between commodity sector and the macroeconomic sector, especially the monetary sector, are explicitly considered in the model. Two cases of buffer stock measures are studied in combination with the macroeconomic activities.

The first case concerns a buffer stock target price which is set at an average equilibrium market price of active market demand and supply. In this case the commodity price is determined by fundamental market forces. This price of commodity should not be changed by buffer stock measure. Therefore the buffer stock is neutral with respect to the market price. The stabilization achieved by the buffer stock is restricted to the price fluctuations due to the random shock which occurs in the commodity sector.

The second case deals with a constant buffer stock target price for the commodity. In this case the commodity market will in general not be in equilibrium. The buffer stock authority has to intervene in the commodity market by buying or selling commodities to keep the price of the primary commodity at the constant target price. The links between buffer stock activities and the supply of money induce an indirect effect of the buffer stock activities on the commodity market.

The multipliers of public spending as well as supply of money in the model of a commodity based currency with a constant target price are lower than those in the usual IS-LM model. Thus the links of buffer stock activities and supply of money due to a commodity based currency has an implication of built-in flexibility for the macroeconomic activities. Therefore a commodity based currency in this case does not only stabilize the price of primary commodities but also makes the macroeconomic development occur more smoothly. A commodity based currency as the Keynes's proposal might have a problem like the bimetal currency known as the Gresham's law. Since in this chapter only one primary commodity is considered we don't touch on this point. But it seems to be relevant to consider this problem in more detail.

The very benefit of a commodity based currency as a policy measure to stabilize the price of primary commodity is that the problem of providing financial resources for implementing buffer stock measure is automatically solved since there is free convertibility between primary commodity and currency due to a commodity based currency.

In general, a built-in-flexibility effect cannot be achieved in a model with a neutral buffer stock target price. But this later case is not usually applied in a commodity based currency with only one primary product as currency reserve. This stabilizing effect of a commodity based currency on macroeconomic fluctuation has to be studied in a model with a basket of several commodities as proposed by Keynes in more detail.

In this chapter the effects of a commodity based currency on macroeconomic fluctuation and commodity prices have been studied in a very simple model. To implement a commodity based currency as well as a buffer stock measure a much more sophisticated model has to be constructed, especially to consider a basket of primary products. Also there are several different kinds of complications to implement a commodity based currency. They are objects of further researches.

Endnotes

1. I am indebted to Hans W. Singer and would like to thank him for his valuable comments. The topic of this chapter is mainly due to several earlier discussions with him and his cited publication. I also want to thank for their valuable comments: John Toye, E.V.K. FitzGerald, Richard Hule and Herbert Stocker.
2. Are prices of primary products more volatile on imperfect than on perfectly competitive market? Economists have discussed this point in general, but because of special properties of primary commodity markets it would be interesting to consider this problem in more detail.

References

Bloch, H. and D. Sapsford (1996), 'Prebisch and Singer Effects on the Terms of Trade Between Primary Producers and Manufacturers', Innsbruck Conference of Development Economics and Policy in honour of the 85th birthday of H.W. Singer.

Chen, John-ren (1994), 'Does Economic Policy Influence the Price Volatility of Commodities? An Econometric Investigation of the Rice Market in Taiwan', in D. Sapsford and W. Morgan (eds), *The Economics of Primary Commodities, Models, Analysis and Policy*, Aldershot: Edward Elgar; pp. 122–51.

Just, R.E. (1990), 'Modelling the Interactive Effects of Alternative Sets of Policies on Agricultural Prices', in L.A.Winters and D. Sapsford (eds), *Primary Commodity Prices: Economic Models and Policy*, Cambridge, UK: Cambridge University Press, pp. 105–33.

Keynes, John Maynard (1938), 'The Policy of Government Storage of Food-stuffs and Raw Materials', *Economic Journal*, 449–60.

Sapsford, D. and H.W. Singer (1996), 'The IMF and Commodity Prices: Some Recent Developments', Paper submitted to the World Development.

Singer, Hans W. (1996a), 'Commodity Stabilization: The Rounded Whole Policy'; Brighton: Institute for Development Studies.

Singer, Hans W. (1996b), 'How Relevant is Keynesianism Today for Understanding Problems of Development?', in S. Sharma (ed.) (1998), *John Maynard Keynes: Keynesianism into the Twenty-first Century*, Cheltenham: Edward Elgar, 103–14.

PART IV

MONEY MANAGEMENT

15 Some notes on 'standards' in Keynes's *Treatise* and the *General Theory*[1]

Jan A. Kregel

Economic discussion in the 1920s was dominated by the question of what domestic and international monetary system would replace the pre-war gold standard. Gold had provided an 'objective' standard, based on a commodity of unchanging characteristics. If the 'automaticity' of the gold standard were to be replaced by a 'managed money' system, a new 'standard' would be required to guide the management of money. From his *Tract on Monetary Reform* onwards, Keynes was preoccupied with this question of the appropriate 'standard' for monetary management in particular, and for economic analysis and economic stabilization in general.

The first draft of the Table of Contents for the book which followed the *Tract* (and which would become the *Treatise on Money*) had the title 'The Standard of Value' (July 1924), and argued in support of a 'managed' international standard of value, but which would still be based on gold. By October 1924 the proposed title of the book had been changed to 'The Monetary Standard', and the content had been expanded to deal with the theory and practice of an 'ideal' standard defined as requiring: (i) short-period adjustability, (ii) intrinsic value, (iii) long-period stability of intrinsic value, (iv) universal acceptability.

It reviewed various possible standards, including various types of composite commodity which had already been proposed. By March 1925 the book had become 'The Theory of Money with reference to the determination of the principle of an ideal standard', and three months later any reference to standards of value had completely disappeared from the title, which became simply 'The Theory of Money and Credit'. The final title, *A Treatise on Money*, was adopted sometime between August 1926 and June 1927.

During this period of transition to the final title, Keynes continued his historical study of money and Great Britain went back onto the gold standard. Just as Britain was returning to gold, Keynes seems to move away from it, and although he continues to support a managed international gold standard, the final version of the book no longer is an investigation into an ideal standard, but deals with an investigation into 'the theory and facts' of what Keynes calls in the Preface, 'Representative Money as it exists in the modern world'.

Representative money may be simply defined as private debt (such as bank money) created to serve as a means of transactions, or a public debt, such as the note of liabilities of a national bank, which is declared to be legal tender in discharge of public and private debt, thereby eliminating a commodity from the role of discharging the debt.

Keynes now considers the ideal standard in relation to the problem of managing 'Representative Money' which, he now argues, actually preceded the introduction of the gold standard in England. Indeed, the gold standard is defined as a 'mixed managed system' (Keynes, 1930, p. 16), which was not a pure commodity money stabilized with respect to an objective standard, gold, but which retained 'the uses of Representative Money' that 'had become so familiar and acceptable to the public, and so profitable to the Treasury and the Bank of England'. (Keynes also noted the existence of an alternative system which used another country's exchange rates as a standard, the 'Exchange Standard'.)

Keynes criticizes the operation of this mixed system because it erred in the attempt to 'make Representative Money behave exactly as though it were Commodity Money' (*op. cit.*, p. 17). On the other hand, he considered that the success of a 'mixed managed system' depended on the recognition of the 'connection between bank-rate policy and the maintenance of the standard'.

Thus the problem, not a new one in economics, is to define a standard which serves as a reference point for the management of Representative Money. In a gold standard, this is the commodity content of the monetary unit (which is also often the unit of account): the mint ratio. In a Representative Money system this cannot be the case, since debts are discharged by the same debts, not by a third asset; thus the error of operating the mixed system as if Representative Money were Commodity Money such as gold. 'When, however, what was merely a debt has become money-proper, it has changed its character and should no longer be reckoned as a debt, since it is the essence of a debt to be enforceable in terms of something other than itself' (*op. cit.*, p. 6). Such a system thus has no natural standard 'in terms of something other than itself' in which it can be enforced, and thus the search for the ideal standard, which may be either subjective or objective.

Keynes reviews possible candidates for ideal standards in Book II, 'The Value of Money', starting with the Purchasing Power of Money or the Consumption Standard:

> Since the Purchasing Power of Money in a given context depends on the quantity of goods and services which a unit of money will purchase, it follows that it can be measured by the price of a composite commodity, made up of the various individual goods and services in proportions corresponding to their importance as objects of expenditure. Moreover, there are many types and purposes of expenditure... corresponding to each of which there is an appropriate composite commodity. The price of a composite commodity which is representative of some type of expenditure,

we shall call a Price-level; and the series of numbers indicative of changes in a given price-level we shall call Index-numbers (*op. cit.*, p. 53).

This leads Keynes into a long digression on index numbers (it is interesting that many of the national accounting questions which surface in the *General Theory* are already present here, for example the need to use only final goods and services, eliminating double counting for intermediate goods and so on.).

But there is no reason to restrict the standard to purchasing power over commodities. There is also a 'Labour Power or Money Earnings Standard', representing the power of money to purchase units of human effort (or labour of standard efficiency). Further, if one divides the Purchasing Power of Money over Commodities (1/P, where P is an index of commodity prices) by the Purchasing Power of Money over Labour (1/W, where W is an index of efficiency wages), the result is what may be called the Standard of Life, an index of real earning power (W/P) or what would be called real wages when applied to the appropriate index of the cost of living and of wages for labour. These two standards, or their combination, Keynes considers as the most appropriate for the new monetary standard.

Before analysing the usefulness of these standards for the management of Representative Money, Keynes notes that none of them are equivalent to those to be found in the then existing economic theory, in particular in the various versions of the quantity theory which are instead based on what Keynes calls 'Currency Standards'. These 'Currency Standards' 'weight different articles, not in proportion to their importance to consumers, but to their importance in connection with the volume either of cash-transactions or of cash-balances'. Keynes thus rejects both Irving Fisher's 'Cash-transactions standard' and Alfred Marshall's 'Cash-balances standard' because they are not 'objective' in the sense of being the 'object' of an actual economic decision. They are simply theoretical constructions, as opposed to the

'Purchasing Power Standard' or the 'Labour Standard', which 'are fundamental in a sense in which price-levels based on other types of expenditure are not. Human effort and human consumption are the ultimate matters from which alone economic transactions are capable of deriving any significance; and all other forms of expenditure only acquire importance from their having some relationship, sooner or later, to the effort of producers or to the expenditure of consumers. I propose, therefore, to break away from the traditional method of setting out from the total quantity of money irrespective of the purposes on which it is employed, and to start instead ... with its twofold division (1) into the parts which have been earned by the production of consumption-goods and of investment-goods respectively, and (2) into the parts which are expended on consumption-goods and on saving respectively (*op. cit.*, p. 76).

The *Treatise* conditions for price stability are thus given as the equivalence of these two proportions: consumption-good sector earnings relative to investment goods sector earnings, and investment sector expenditures relative to savings. If the ratio of income earned in the production of consumption goods to total output is equal to the expenditures on consumption goods out of total income 'then the price-level of consumption-goods will be in equilibrium with their cost of production' (*op. cit.*, p. 134).

Keynes elaborates this proposition in terms of the fundamental equation for the price of consumption goods,

$$P = (1/e)W + (I' - S)/R.$$

When $I' = S$, $P = (1/e)W$, where W is the rate of earnings per unit of human effort, and e is the efficiency wage or productivity of labour and $(1/e)W$ the rate of earnings per unit of output, R; in short, unit labour costs.

Thus, if the purchasing power standard is measured by $1/P$, and the labour standard is $1/W$, both reduce to the same thing when $I' = S$. Another way of viewing this proposition is to say that managing money to produce stability will make the 'purchasing power of money over labour' and 'purchasing power of money over commodities' equivalent when corrected for the differences in the efficiency of labour effort, 'e', such that $1/e = P/W$. Thus $WN = PR$ and $W/P = R/N$, which is the 'Standard of Life'. There is no difference between the three standards. This means that money wages have the same amount of purchasing power over goods for labourers (W/P) as the money wage buys producing power over goods for the entrepreneurs (R/N). Keynes thus concludes that for the purchasing power of money to be stable 'efficiency earnings should be constant and ... the cost of new investment should be equal to the volume of current savings' (*op. cit.*, p. 136).

Since Keynes has chosen both standards (which means all three) as objectives for monetary stability, the problem of the management of money will also have to be concerned to keep the relation between these standards stable. The impact of money on them is thus of crucial importance. It is here that Keynes takes another major step away from the Quantity Theory when he argues that since the quantity of money cannot influence any of the elements of this relation directly, it has no effect on the labour or purchasing power standards: managing money will not keep the chosen standards equivalent. It thus also follows that money is redundant as an explanation of prices for it has no effect on the 'effort of producers or the expenditure of consumers'. It thus follows that the quantity of money will not have any direct effect on output or employment for, if it does not have any influence on the relation between costs and prices, it can create no incentive to change normal levels of operations. Any impact which money might have comes indirectly through the impact of money on interest rates and of interest rates on the relation between I' and S. The behaviour of wages remains independent, only influenced by technology as embodied in 'e', and any spill over effect from I' > S on W.

This result stems from the fact that the determination of prices is given in terms of the decisions of two groups, households and firms as they influence the two proportions: the proportions in which earnings are divided into expenditure on consumption goods and saving; and the proportions in which entrepreneurs' expenditures on labour are divided into employment in the production of consumption and investment goods. Only factors which change the decisions of households and firms over these proportions will have an effect on prices, and given wages, on profits as well as on output and employment decisions. Thus Keynes's insistence on the importance of central bank rate as influencing interest rates, and thus keeping I' equal to S in the process of stabilizing purchasing power and labour power.

In the *General Theory* Keynes's perspective shifts from managing money to curing the persistent level of unemployment; the emphasis on two independent decision-making centres: the expenditure by households on goods and services, and the composition of employment in the production of consumption and investment goods by firms, is replaced by a single decision maker taking two decisions, entrepreneurs deciding on the level of operation of existing capacity and the increase in capacity through the decision to make net investment expenditures. The decisions of the households have been incorporated into the rather mechanical consumption function which is of importance not for the factors which determine consumption decisions, but for the fact that its marginal value is less than unity. Keynes vacillated between treating the consumption function as one of the 'independent' psychological variables, and taking it as a constant or 'given' whose changes were not directly relevant to the analysis of the problem at hand.

The question Keynes is trying to answer has thus changed in the *General Theory*. Keynes is no longer looking for the ideal standard which may be used for monetary management, but rather to explain the determinants of the level of output and employment. With only the entrepreneur taking decisions, it was natural to adopt the standard which was of greatest relevance to the decision taken by entrepreneurs, the decision to hire labour. This is the 'Labour Power of Money or the Earnings Standard' which measures 'the purchasing power of money over units of human effort.' Keynes recognized in the *Treatise* that

> ...the chief obstacle in the way of computing this standard is to be found in the difficulty of finding a common unit in which to compare different kinds of human effort. For even if we agree – as we must – that it is proper to ignore degrees of skill in this connection and to mean the rate of earnings per unit of effort averaged over all grades of skill actually prevailing in the community, we ought still, theoretically at least, to take account of variations in the intensity, distastefulness and regularity of work (Keynes, 1936, p. 63).

The adoption of this standard in the *General Theory* thus required the assumption of a constant distribution of skill levels and an associated set of constant wage differentials, 'the best that can be achieved ... is to take as our index of the labour power of money ... the average hourly money earnings of the whole body of workers of every grade' (*ibid.*).

From this it would seem that the adoption of the 'wage-unit' as the standard in the *General Theory* was not so much intended to provide a consistent method of aggregation or a means of translating from real to nominal values, as to provide an adequate standard for the entrepreneur's management of the firm in order to produce maximum profitability. Since the 'wage-unit' or the 'labour standard' is a 'real' or 'objective' value (in the sense used above in the discussion of the *Treatise*) as far as the entrepreneur is concerned, it does not necessarily follow that the wage-unit must be either rigid or constant if it is to be used as a standard, although it is necessary that wage differentials should be constant and independent of the level of output if it is to be used for the management of the level of employment. The fundamental assumption for the application of the 'labour standard' is constancy of wage differentials, not rigid money wages.[2]

There is some evidence, however, to suggest that this is an assumption which Keynes did take from experience (cf. *General Theory*, pp. 13–14); his insistence that labour would attempt to use money wage bargaining to protect their relative real wages earned the criticism that he assumed that labour suffered from money illusion when he was in fact assuming that labour recognized, as he did, that real wages were determined by factors which were outside their direct control.

There was, however, a loss in the passage from the 'two-standards' system of the *Treatise*, to the single standard system of the *General Theory*. As already noted, equilibrium in the *Treatise* could be expressed in terms of an equivalence between the labour and purchasing power standards: $1/P = e/W$ or $WN = PR$ or $W/P = R/N$. These conditions, it should be noted, are similar to the income-expenditure equality of the *General Theory*. Out of equilibrium, when two standards are no longer equivalent with $1/P$, and thus W/P, falling or rising relative to W/e depending on whether I' is greater or less than S. For example if $I' > S$, the producing power of money over labour for entrepreneurs remains unchanged while the purchasing power of money earned as wages over commodities falls, the difference giving rise to 'windfall profits'. Thus the relative movement of the two indices will indicate the movement of prices and total profits (normal profits, included in the normal remuneration of entrepreneurs, plus windfall profits).

If we write $e = R/N = A$ (average product of labour) and if $(I' - S)/R$ are the windfall profits or losses per unit of consumption goods output, then the fundamental equation for the prices of consumption goods can be written as $P = k(W/A)$ if k is defined as $1 + K$ and $K = [(I' - S)/R]/(W/A)$ and $k = 1 + K$

then $P = k(W/A)$ and k becomes the measure of divergence of the two standards. Written in this way, k can be recognized as the factor more commonly known as 'the degree of monopoly' or the 'mark-up of prices over costs'. On Weintraub's definitions (1959) k is Z/wN so that 1/k becomes a measure of labour share in national income (but note that W as used in the *Treatise* sense covers full costs, including entrepreneurs' remuneration, overhead labour and so on).

In 'normal' conditions of monetary stability A is constant and $k = 1$, so that an alternative way of viewing the equivalence of the standards is in terms of constancy of the degree of monopoly or of the distribution of income. Changes in prices are then seen to be determined by changes in those factors which determine the distribution of income. This highlights the relative nature of the standards employed, for there is nothing which explains the base or normal distribution of income, that is the price level relative to wages, which is implicit in the equilibrium position $k = 1$, or the changes in the level of efficiency wages themselves.

Since K is a function of investment decisions relative to savings, the mark-up' on consumption goods, k becomes a function of the rate of interest (which makes consumption goods prices similar to capital goods prices which are also determined by interest rates). Changes in distribution are then caused by divergence of the interest rate from its 'natural' value. But since the natural rate is that which preserves the normal distribution, there is no objective way to determine the natural rate. As Nell (1973) has forcefully observed, there is no objective basis upon which to base earnings, either absolute or relative. Put simply, a technological relationship such as marginal productivity simply will not do.

In such conditions it would seem appropriate to extend Chick's (1985) suggestion that Keynes's use of the wage unit represents reference to historically given circumstances governing wage levels to include reference to historically given skill and wage differentials. The base or 'normal' distribution of income between wages and profits is then historically determined, as is the natural rate of interest which produces $I' = S$ and $k = 1$. Alternatively, one could specify full employment as the point at which to determine $k = 1$. It would appear that this is one of the reasons for the existence of the employment function in the *General Theory*, to fix the standard.

We can thus conclude by trying to provide an explanation for the sympathy which Keynes reiterated in his writings for the pre-classical doctrine that

> everything is produced by labour, aided by what used to be called art (cf. Walras!) and is now called technique, by natural resources which are free or cost a rent according to their scarcity or abundance, and by the results of past labour, embodied in assets, which also command a price according to their scarcity or abundance. It is preferable to regard labour, including, of course, the personal services of the entrepreneur and his assistants, as the sole factor of production, operating in a given

environment of technique, natural resources, capital equipment and effective demand. This partly explains why we have been able to take the unit of labour as the sole physical unit which we require in our economic system, apart from units of money and of time (Keynes, 1936, p. 214).

The inclusion of the earnings of entrepreneurs is a clear reference to the definitions of the *Treatise*, where in equilibrium P = W/e, and prices reflect labour costs. While I' = S does not necessarily imply that the rate of interest is equal to zero, the above passage occurs in Keynes's discussion of the fact that capital earns a return only because of positive liquidity preference, not because it is productive (or smelly, or risky). If liquidity preference is driven down to the point required for full employment, and this point drives interest rates to the pure risk rate, which at full employment should be near zero, then the relevant standard is the labour standard. It is interesting that in an earlier version of this passage, Keynes makes reference to the Marshallian equilibrium condition of zero profits:

In so far as we can identify prime costs with labour costs, the modern doctrine according to which prices tends to equal marginal prime costs is, in a sense, a return to the old conception of the wage unit as the ultimate standard of value (Keynes, 1973, p. 454).

Endnotes

1   This chapter develops themes first raised in Kregel (1989).
2.   John Hicks has also noted that Keynes's theory employs a 'labour standard', in difference from, for example, a 'gold standard', but reaches the opposite conclusion that the nominal wage level be not only constant, but rigid (a brief exposition of this idea is found in Hicks, 1985). Hicks suggests that Keynes assumed rigid wages as the result of his observations of the movement of wages during the return to the gold standard (the implicit reference is to the General Strike in 1926).

References

Chick, V. (1985), 'Time and the Wage-unit in the Method of The General Theory: History and Equilibrium', in T. Lawson and H. Pesaran (eds), *Keynes' Economics: Methodological Issues*, London: Croom Helm.
Hicks, J.R. (1985), 'Keynes and the World Economy', in F. Vicarelli (ed.) *Keynes's Relevance Today,* Philadelphia: University of Pennsylvania Press, pp. 21–7.
Keynes, J.M. (1930), *A Treatise on Money*, London: Macmillan.
Keynes, J.M. (1936), *The General Theory of Employment, Interest and Money*, London: Macmillan.
Keynes, J.M. (1973), *The Collected Writings of J.M. Keynes*, vol. XIII, *The General Theory and After*, part I Preparation, London: Macmillan.
Kregel, J.A. (1989) 'Keynes, Income Distribution and Incomes Policy', in *Macroeconomic Problems and Policies of Income Distribution: Functional, Personal and International*, Upleadon, UK: Edward Elgar, pp. 42–55.
Nell, E.J. (1973), 'The Fall of the House of Efficiency', in S. Weintraub (ed.), *Income Inequality*, The Annals of the American Academy of Political and Social Science, pp. 102–11.
Weintraub, S.A. (1959), *General Theory of the Price Level*, Philadelphia: Chilton.

16 'Global' saving and interest rate behaviour: why don't international capital markets clear?

E. V. K. FitzGerald

In the opinion of the International Monetary Fund (IMF), which in this case as in others is representative of the academic and policy making orthodoxy as well as of the global bond market, there does exist a global 'savings shortage' which lies at the heart of international macroeconomic instability:

> The critical importance of saving for the maintenance of strong and sustainable growth in the world economy, for external adjustment, and for the amelioration of the international debt problem is well recognized. Consequently, the declining trend in the saving rates of many countries, industrial as well as developing, has been a major source of concern. This decline has been associated with lower rates of capital accumulation and growth in the world economy. In addition, the substantial divergence of saving rates among countries has contributed to the emergence of large current account imbalances, especially among the major industrial countries.[1]

The Keynesian view is, of course, diametrically opposed to this essentially Ricardian view, seeing investment demand as ultimately generating the required level of saving if only liquidity problems can be overcome by appropriate extra market intervention. The prevailing orthodoxy, however, sees the imminent surge of investment demand – including cyclical technological absorption in the OECD (Organization for Economic Co-operation and Development) countries, infrastructure requirements in the NICs (newly industrialized countries), industrial renovation in the transition economies and human capital backlogs in the LDCs (less developed countries). This surge encounters impenetrable savings constraints generated by structural budget deficits and demographic trends, thus driving up world interest rates.

In the Ricardian tradition, savings out of profits provide a constraint on investment because the saving and investment decision are the same, so that *ceteris paribus* growth is constrained by the rate of profit. Strict neoclassical theory suggests that the capital market is like any other, with the interest rate clearing the demand and supply of funds both nationally and internationally unless constrained by extra-market forces. None the less, Ricardian tendencies frequently reappear in mainstream economic theory either in the form of the theoretically attractive life-cycle models of household saving or in that of the inverse relationship between public and private savings. Such a tendency evidently informs the view of the IMF cited above.

In the *General Theory*, of course, the principle of effective demand itself is a theory of how the demand for investment and the willingness to save are brought into equilibrium with each other, the equilibrating force being the level of aggregate income and not the rate of interest. This level would not necessarily correspond to full employment, and 'savings equals investment' simply because investment induces a like amount of savings. Although individual countries would face additional balance of payments constraints which could prevent equilibrium being achieved at any particular level of activity, the global unemployment problem would only arise if the propensity to save were too high, rather than too low – which could be rectified by appropriate demand expansion by the surplus economies.

However the Keynesian model is not entirely plausible either because of the fixed savings coefficients implicit in its consumption function. The redefinition by Hicks of saving in terms of changes in net worth allows for wealth effects in the consumption function,[2] and allows for an attractive ambiguity about the net effect of interest rates on saving. This is also much more convincing empirically[3] than the post-Keynesian attempts to endogenize the savings rate in the Ricardian manner by making it contingent on income distribution. However, a major shortcoming of the Keynesian model (and by extension the theory of effective demand) is that it assumes that capital markets intermediate between saving households and investing firms. In fact, of course, firms largely finance investment out of retained profits and households are major borrowers.

Determinants of global savings

The standard view is that declining savings rates are 'associated with lower rates of capital accumulation and growth in the world economy', while 'changes in inflation and interest rates seem to have had relatively small effects on saving behaviour'.[4] Most empirical work on savings behaviour has been undertaken under an agenda driven by the life-cycle model[5] where changes in demographics, income growth, interest rates and inflation are assumed to be the main determinants – although the econometric results indicate that differences in age structure and income growth appear to be the only significant variables.[6] In this context, it is interesting to note that empirical explanations focus on household saving and neglect profit retention by firms, despite the fact that this is a major component of gross saving (before depreciation) and the source of almost all the funds for fixed investment by business.[7] The neoclassical assumption that the modern corporation is merely a 'veil' for household savings decisions exercised as shareholders does not bear serious examination as an explanation of firms' behaviour.[8]

Moreover the empirical evidence[9] on determinants of private savings behaviour is in fact widely divergent. Such tests, which all seem to be in the neoclassical tradition, not only indicate that real interest rates are not a significant determinant, which is hardly surprising once the ambiguous implications for wealth and income in the overlapping-generations model is taken into account,[10] but also the effect of demographic factors on saving varies greatly across countries for no readily explicable reason.[11] Factors to which the decline in private savings in industrial countries (IEs) during the 1970s and 1980s – see Table 16.1 – have been attributed include improvements in the relative position of older groups in the population, the revaluation of the stock of wealth (in particular equities and housing) and financial liberalization.[12] It is not clear how relevant such explanations might be in the 1990s, but the imminent ageing of OECD populations, and that of the high-saving Japanese in particular, is clearly a source of major concern.[13]

Table 16.1   Sources of world saving (per cent of GDP)

	1975–9	1980–4	1987	1990	1993
World	24.8	22.8	23.2	23.3	20.5
IEs					
Total	22.8	21.4	20.5	21.7	19.4
Private	21.1	20.8	19.6	19.2	20.2
Public	1.7	0.6	0.9	1.5	-0.7
US					
Total	20.3	19.9	16.0	15.2	14.9
Private	19.0	19.2	16.1	15.4	16.1
Public	1.3	–0.3	–0.1	–0.2	–1.3
EU					
Total	22.1	20.0	20.3	21.1	18.7
Private	20.7	20.0	20.7	21.5	21.9
Public	1.5	–	–0.4	–0.4	–3.2
Japan					
Total	32.4	30.8	32.3	34.0	33.5
Private	29.1	26.7	25.8	23.6	25.4
Public	3.3	4.1	6.5	10.4	8.1
LDCs	26.5	23.2	24.5	26.2	24.0
FCPEs	41.9	32.8	28.7	27.0	17.8

Source: IMF (1992b, 1995)

Table 16.2 The structure of global capital accumulation

	No.	% world GDP	% world exports	% world saving	% world investment	S/Y	I/Y	(S-I)/Y
World	183	100.0	100.0	100.0	100.0	23.1	23.7	-0.6
Industrial Economies	23	54.6	70.2	47.0	45.8	19.9	20.0	-0.1
USA	1	21.2	13.2	14.3	14.0	15.6	17.4	-1.8
Japan	1	8.4	8.4	11.5	11.2	31.7	28.8	2.9
EU	15	21.1	40.4	20.1	19.6	22.0	19.0	3.0
Rest of world	160	45.4	29.8	53.0	54.2	26.6	27.9	-1.3
Net creditors	7	2.1	3.9	1.9	2.0	20.8	22.2	-1.4
Net debtors	125	38.0	22.2	46.6	47.4	28.0	29.2	-1.2
Mkt Borr	23	23.0	16.5	33.5	33.2	33.3	33.8	-0.5
Div Borr	33	10.3	4.0	10.0	10.3	n.a.	n.a.	n.a.
Off Borr	69	4.8	1.7	3.0	3.9	14.4	18.9	-4.5
Transition Economies	28	5.3	3.7	4.4	4.5	19.0	20.0	-1.0
Developing countries	132	40.1	26.1	48.5	49.5	27.6	28.9	-1.3
Africa	50	3.3	1.7	2.5	3.1	17.3	21.7	-4.4
Asia	30	23.1	16.6	34.4	34.1	34.0	34.5	-0.5
ME & E	18	4.8	3.9	4.4	4.3	21.1	20.8	0.3
W. Hem.	34	8.9	3.9	7.1	8.1	18.2	21.4	-3.2
Balanced Accounts								
World	183	100.0	100.0	100.0	100.0	23.6	23.6	0.0
Industrial Economies	23	54.6	70.2	46.3	43.6	20.0	18.8	1.2
Rest of world	160	45.4	29.8	53.7	56.4	26.6	27.9	-1.3

Source: IMF (1995) for shares of world GDP (on a PPP basis) and exports of goods and services, and for saving/investment rates (that is shares of current GDP) by country groupings.

Notes: The estimates of country group shares in world investment and saving have been made by weighting the respective rates for each country grouping by their share in world GDP. As the IMF estimates for world investment and saving are not in balance (as they must be by definition), 'balanced accounts' are also shown where the error (some 0.6 % of world GDP – mainly attributable to unreported investment income) is allocated to industrial economies' income and saving, and then recalculating the resulting shares, following the methodology in Vos and de Jong (1995).

In the standard model (which forms the basis for IMF stabilization policy) the public sector deficit is at the discretion of the government. Public sector savings can result in larger private savings due to the increased public sector borrowing requirement driving up interest rates or, if these are constrained in a closed economy, by increasing the money supply and forcing private savings through a real balance effect. In the small open economy, the effect is felt through an inflow of foreign savings in the monetary approach to the balance of payments.

Public saving behaviour[14] is mainly seen in published studies as reflecting the fiscal stance of governments which is partly endogenized through the differential effect of tax receipts and welfare entitlements of the position of the economy in the business cycle. Over the longer term, these welfare entitlements have a demographic dimension, while tax pressures are limited by the international mobility of factors of production. Debt in turn becomes endogenized too, as the accumulation of fiscal deficits. In principle 'Ricardian Equivalence' theory suggests that these fiscal deficits will be balanced by increased private savings in order to provide for future tax burdens[15] – but the downward trend in public savings in the OECD countries has in fact been accompanied by declining private savings rates.[16] The strong evidence that the scale of this 'crowding in' is very limited in practice is complemented by indications that origin of the deficit – whether from changes in tax or expenditure rates – is also a determinant of private sector response.[17] The particular composition of the expenditure and tax structure is crucial: tax reductions appear to generate offsetting private savings but increased expenditures do not.

The downward trend in saving in non-OECD economies (see Table 16.2) is partly explained by the loss in income to oil-exporting countries, but it is interesting to note that the reduced budget deficits and enhanced private savings (from higher real interest rates and profit shares) expected from structural adjustment have not been forthcoming. Finally the formerly centrally planned economies have, not surprisingly, seen a decline in savings as constraints on consumption and direct state access to profits were both removed.

Global capital markets

In principle, the level of investment in an open economy need not be constrained by savings (nor would savings have to come into line with investment) because the resultant current account balance could be financed by matching international capital flows. Under the Bretton Woods system of fixed exchange rates such flows were relatively small,[18] so that savings and investment moved together in most large economies. However, from the late 1970s onwards, capital became much more mobile and the US itself suddenly shifted from a net surplus to a net deficit position – and its fiscal deficit was essentially financed by Japanese householders.

Empirical analysis of trends in long-term international capital flows is impeded by the fact that the data for such flows (and by extension, global asset/liability positions) does not balance.[19] Broadly speaking, investment income flows are badly recorded (particularly the under-reporting of returns on financial assets), while the observed global excess of recorded liabilities over assets and the relative reliability of various sources means that most of the required adjustment falls on the reduction of the initial estimates of liabilities.[20] None the less it is clear that such capital flows have grown much more rapidly than global output, investment or trade.

Interest rates within the OECD became broadly equalized for similar dollar bonds in the 1980s, while exchange rates adjusted in response to domestic interest rate differentials which in turn allowed for a modest risk margin.[21] The flexible exchange rates had originally been expected to permit some autonomy to domestic demand management but in practice the bond markets have come to enforce a uniform monetary policy irrespective of the divergent cyclical position of the national economies.

None the less careful studies continue to reveal a close correlation between domestic saving and investment in the IEs,[22] which cannot simply be explained by a spurious correlation[23] or regulatory restrictions. It is more likely that the 'home bias' in the acquisition of financial assets arises from factors such as currency risk, agency problems and asymmetric information. In other words, it is endemic to market structures themselves.

In other words, interest rates do not act so as to clear the international capital market and bring savings and investment into line on a global scale,[24] while exchange rates do not appear to affect trade flows sufficiently to adjust current account deficits rapidly enough to avoid asset adjustment. In effect, a systemic rationing system exists based on market perceptions of 'sovereign risk', expressed as an assessment of the 'quality' of that country's bonds and thus its longer-term growth potential and fiscal solvency.

In the case of flows between the IEs and the RoW (rest of the world) there is a clear segmentation between portfolio flows, foreign direct investment (FDI), bank credits and official development assistance,[25] each of which form of asset acquisition appears to be driven by different institutional behaviour but where country 'quality' appears to be a determinant factor. This is true even when the investment and savings decisions are the same, in the case of FDI, where externalities prevent profitability from reflecting factor scarcity[26] and infrastructure and skills are central to the choice of location.[27]

There is also a clear segmentation between country groupings. The decline in bank credit flows from the IEs to the RoW since the debt crisis of the early 1980s, and the rise of portfolio flows in the early 1990s, has been confined to a small group of upper middle-income countries: both have been essentially concerned with public sector finance. FDI flows have similarly been confined to relatively few NICs, and are largely financed by the firms concerned. Aid flows are focused on the poorest countries, and determined by non-economic factors. The effect of an increase in autonomous capital flows from the IEs towards the RoW – sometimes seen as a means of generating greater global aggregate demand – depends crucially on how this is financed. To the extent that this is done by increased tax or reduced investment in the 'north', then reduced northern demand for exports from the 'south' can have a counterbalancing effect; while monetary expansion can raise interest rates and affect both commodity prices and debt burdens.[28]

In consequence, it would seem to be the case that if investment rises autonomously in one country, it is not necessarily possible to tap a savings investment surplus in another country because of the portfolio preferences of asset holders.[29] This is broadly true within the IEs (at least as between the US, Japan and the EU) and *a fortiori* between IEs and the RoW. In a sense, of course, this is a global form of liquidity preference which the SDR issues are supposed to overcome.

The current orthodox position on global savings is thus essentially Ricardian and not neoclassical at all, although it shares with Keynesian theory the strength of wealth effects and the weakness of ignoring saving by firms. Work on international capital flows clearly indicates that although interest rates are broadly equalized between OECD countries and make exchange rates subject to monetary policy, they do not clear the market for savings and investment. This conclusion holds *a fortiori* for flows to the RoW, where access to global capital markets is highly segmented and the 'quality' of financial assets relates to investors' perception of country characteristics. These propositions would imply that some sort of international portfolio approach[30] is necessary in order to understand global savings, where the reconciliation of desired asset positions between economies determines the global macroeconomic equilibrium.

Global interest rates
The globalization of capital markets in the early 1990s has generated a 'global' long-term interest rate which has become a key anchor for both national monetary policies and multinational business strategies. While nominal short rates are essentially a policy variable in the hands of national monetary authorities, affecting both exchange rates and consumer credit demand, long rates are largely determined by the capital market. Real (that is inflation adjusted) long rates affect corporate investment decisions, the fiscal solvency of governments and the return on personal pension schemes.

What is more, long rates have become an essential anchor for the world economy, affecting both the stability and growth of global capital markets and the sustainability of domestic monetary policies – when these become 'misaligned' huge short-term capital flows are generated and exchange rates come under immense pressure until short rates are adjusted accordingly. Resulting lack of independence in domestic monetary policy can be seen as a good or a bad thing – depending on one's view of the ability of governments to make macroeconomic judgements – and has led to the anomaly of autonomous central banks with little real room for manoeuvre.

The long-term global real interest rate (that is the G7 mean) averaged about 3 per cent per annum adjusted for inflation between 1960 and 1972 – which has been the usual peacetime level for almost two centuries. However real rates collapsed in the subsequent inflationary splurge and the collapse of the Bretton Woods system, becoming negative in the late 1970s, and then returning to historically high levels of 5 per cent in the 1980s – led by US fiscal deficits and tight monetary policy. Despite falling world inflation in recent years, real long-term rates are still around the 5 per cent level and show no signs of falling despite sustained declines in short rates. Long rates in leading industrial countries are increasingly converging on this high 'global rate' (see Table 16.3).

Table 16.3   Global interest rate trends

	1977–84	1985–92	1993–96	1997–2000
Industrial countries				
GDP deflator	7.9	3.9	2.2	2.4
Real 6m LIBOR	4.4	3.7	3.0	3.5
Implicit NIR-s	12.3	7.6	5.2	5.9
Developing countries				
Debt/exports	n.a.	154.3	119.0	89.4
Service/exports	n.a.	19.0	8.3	5.5
Implicit NIR-l		12.3	7.0	6.2
Change in ToT	2.9	–2.2	0.1	–0.1
RIR-l (borrower)		14.5	6.9	6.3
RIR-l (lender)		8.4	4.8	3.8

Source: Calculated from IMF (1995).

Despite the crucial importance of long-term interest rates, there is little agreement as to their determination, an ambiguity which is reflected in conflicting market opinions which in turn result in wide swings of sentiment in response to particular incidents. Broadly, there are two analytical approaches to long-term interest rates:

- long-term real rates are determined by the balancing of personal savings supply and corporate investment demand, while any increases in government deficits are balanced by private savings rises in anticipation of future taxes (so-called 'Ricardian Equivalence'); so long-term nominal rates are this fundamental equilibrium rate *plus* the market's expectation about inflation;

- long-term nominal rates reflect market expectations about the global liquidity situation, and thus about the borrowing strategies of major governments and the monetary policies of their respective central banks on the one hand, and the demand of portfolio managers for bonds as against equities on the other; so long-term real rates are this market equilibrium *less* the inflation which eventually occurs.

The implications of these two approaches for the determination of interest rates are quite different. The first would take into account the apparently falling rates of personal saving in OECD economies due to demographic factors, and the rising demand for funds from emerging economies – particularly the infrastructure requirements of Eastern Europe, Asia and Latin America – and thus lead to a forecast rise in long real rates. The second, in contrast, would focus on factors such as the efforts to reduce government deficits in the G3 and the implications of the EMU (European Monetary Union), both of which would lead to a reduction of nominal rates by the opening of the next decade.

The policy implications are also quite different. The first view would imply that the only way to bring long rates down – other than by reducing investment demand, which would harm world growth prospects – would be to raise saving in the major economies, by radical reductions in fiscal deficits and by the privatization of pension schemes. The second, in contrast, would place more emphasis on the reduction of the debt overhang and improved policy co-ordination, in order to improve market sentiment.

Research by the IMF staff[31] suggests that while the growing level of debt to GDP among the G7 since the 1980s has put pressure on short rates, long rates are less affected by monetary and fiscal policy. The rising level of return on new investment due to global deregulation and the falling level of savings in industrial countries (which has declined steadily from 24 per cent of GDP in the 1970s to 21 per cent in the 1980s and 19 per cent in the 1990s) are seen as the main causes, suggesting that a new equilibrium relationship has now emerged on global capital market fundamentals.

In contrast, research by OECD staff suggests that G7 fiscal deficits and balance of payments difficulties continue to generate considerable risk premia, which in turn are reflected in long rates. About one half of the higher-than-historical level can be explained by fiscal and monetary policies, while the remainder is probably due to the effect of financial deregulation since the 1980s, which has reduced the authorities' ability to contain long rates for specific market segments such as government bonds and mortgages.

In addition, while the IMF believes that a single global interest rate has emerged, the OECD suggests that the 'convergence' is largely confined to EU members, and that the G3 dissonance has not been reduced significantly.

This lack of clarity as to the underlying determinants of long-term interest rates is a major problem for business strategists. On the one hand, major technological investments in a multi-country strategy require corporate planners to take a view on the long-term cost of capital which cannot be reversed once the projects are undertaken. On the other hand, uncertain capital market sentiment on global bond prices implies a corresponding instability in long-run key exchange rate relationships and thus the profitability of production in different locations. The lack of clarity is not just a problem for private sector planners, but also for the G3 monetary authorities in their efforts to keep short rates down and sustain economic activity.

Figures for benchmark bond yields indicate the wide divergence in monetary policy between the three centres of the global capital market, which largely affects short rates as inflation-adjusted long rates have converged on a global average during recent years:

- US official policy appears to be to keep short rates as low as possible through the elections and only to raise them if there is an apparent danger of wage inflation from near capacity utilization, while relying on eventual budget balancing to bring down long rates eventually; a policy which the market clearly does not yet fully believe, which is why short rates remain above 5 per cent and the long rates of over 7 per cent contain an expected inflation rate of some 4 per cent.
- The recent reduction in short German rates towards 2 per cent despite signs of economic recovery still leaves long rates at over 6 per cent – again approximating the global rate once expected inflation is taken into account; the short rate will be maintained in the medium term in order to depreciate the Deutschmark substantially by 1998 so as to allow the EMU to lock in at a competitive overall rate, although uncertainty as to the eventual membership will keep the differential for other EU members quite high.
- Japanese short rates are now as near zero as is technically possible, with monetary and fiscal expansion continuing despite the fact that output is now growing at the fastest rate for a decade; nevertheless, long rates have recently risen to nearly 4 per cent which approximates the global real interest rate – Japanese investor uncertainty about corporate solvency is expressed more in the declining Nikkei than in bond prices.

However behind these essentially transitional issues lie deeper ones of the role of interest rates in the key poles of the world economy.[32] It would apppear that the emergence of an orderly international bond market is blocked by the very different political economies of the G3, which not only make co-ordination difficult but also create uncertainty for institutional fund managers – which in turn generates destabilizing capital movements as portfolios are continually adjusted to reflect the expected moves by the three key authorities.

Global macroeconomic co-ordination

G7 meetings to discuss global economic issues are currently expected to tackle several serious problems in the governance of international capital markets. The World Trade Organization (WTO) is beginning to build up useful precedents in settlement of disputes but the forthcoming trade agenda of services trade and intellectual property rights will require another gruelling round of negotiations – designed particularly to control emerging Asian high-tech exporters such as India and China – which no one is to eager initiate at present.

International capital market reform poses a much greater problem for G7 leaders than trade, for at least three reasons:

1. Unlike trade, full liberalization of financial flows is not possible because of the implications for the fragility of financial institutions of volatile capital flows and the lagged adjustment of asset and liability positions.
2. Financial markets, being based on assets whose value depends on expectations, are inherently unstable and integration of markets is not just a matter of eliminating barriers to entry, but one of integrating jurisdictions.
3. Government debt is a large part of international securities trade, and thus the fiscal stances of government become a determinant of, and subject to, international financial flows.

International regulatory reform could develop[33] along three different tracks in order to eliminate the current overlapping and gaps between regulatory authorities in different countries – it is precisely these inconsistencies (or 'fault lines' as the Bank of International Settlements in Basle calls them) where both large profits and potential disasters are spawned:

1. The extension of a dominant regulatory system from a major national market to cover the world – not surprisingly this is the preferred US option, although the Federal Reserve is reluctant to take on the implicit monetary responsibilities this implies in the wake of the Mexican debacle, and this approach can lead to difficult issues of extraterritorial jurisdiction.
2. The UK proposal to establish a 'convening regulator' for each international financial business group, which would be responsible for initiating and co-ordinating the response of all affected regulators in the event of the crisis; this would put the Bank of England in a commanding position for a number

of key groups and reflect the dominance of the City of London within Europe.

3. The creation of a supranational regulatory body out of the existing capabilities of the BIS (Bank of International Settlements), the IMF and the OECD; this would not suit the US or the UK but would have considerable advantages for the other players in system in terms of clear rules and participation in the regulatory body – not only Japan and France but also emerging regional powers such as Brazil, India and China.

The other financial topic discussed without great success has been the question of debt relief for the poorest counties. The problem arises because successive attempts at debt relief over the past 15 years have not involved an orderly workout, but rather the replacement of debt coming due by longer-term loans from the World Bank and the IMF. There has also been some success in cancelling bilateral debt for poorer countries (under the so-called 'Naples terms' at the Paris Club negotiations) but this is limited by the declining aid budgets against which debt cancellations must be charged as current expenditure. What is more, both the Fund and the Bank are precluded from multilateral debt cancellation, so their proposals are in fact an attempt to lengthen repayment schedules in the hope that LLDC (least less developed country) exports recover sufficiently in the future to pay them back.

The UK – supported by the US and France – are pressed for US$2 billion sales from the IMF gold reserves of US$40 billion in order to provide further long-term roll-overs, which would then be supported by a further US$1 billion from the World Bank over five years – the Bank is at present in a very liquid position due to repayments from some of its major clients. Japan and Italy acquiesced – albeit reluctantly. Germany, in contrast, is pressed for further bilateral support on the grounds that IMF gold sales form an undesirable precedent in the light of the Mexican debacle and the risk of similar events in Russia; it also points out, correctly, that the US is over US$1 billion in arrears to international institutions and that the other two G3 members are carrying the greater part of the burden.

No compromise has been reached (apart from a commitment to extend 'Naples terms' from 67 to 80 per cent of eligible bilateral debt) but the gold sales would have been no real solution to the LLDC problem as it only defers repayment and, by not reducing the debt overhang, prevents these economies from acquiring the creditworthiness that would stimulate both domestic and foreign investment. The failure to commit further G7 resources to international poverty resolution through the UN was not disguised by the commitment to explore the rationalization of aid efforts – although this is indeed long overdue.

The problem of reaching agreements at G7 level is not just a geopolitical one. Even if the leaders had come to a major new agreement on debt or – more importantly – regulatory co-ordination, there remain three outstanding difficulties:

1. G7 leaders cannot necessarily carry their own legislatures, central banks or major financial institutions with them in implementing decisions.
2. Global financial stability requires greater fiscal discipline and co-ordination of monetary stances within the G3;
3. In global financial emergencies (as Russia may soon become) there is a need for rapid and autonomous action by a tasked agency with the resources and the ability for rapid intervention.

Meanwhile there is an increasing tendency for financial problems to be dealt with on a regional level, which is probably easier in terms of institutional harmonization and intergovernmental co-ordination, but can create even greater tensions between the resulting 'tectonic plates' in view of the ability of capital markets to exploit gaps between regulatory areas.

In the US the principle of countervailing powers makes coherent economic policy extremely difficult to achieve, and in any case the principle of the supremacy of a dispersed corporate enterprise means that capital markets rather than the authorities are seen as the arbiters of what the most desirable economic strategy might be. This system has the benefits of considerable flexibility to changing business circumstances, but the variability in interest rates and exchange rates that result strongly prejudice the management of the world economy, given the enormous political and economic weight of the US and its very low savings rate. There is a continuous downward pressure on short nominal rates from political sources, and an upward pressure on long rates from capital markets due to the budget deficit.

In Germany, in contrast, both corporate power and policy-making capacity are highly concentrated; this is articulated through the banking control of industry – which requires stable long-term interest rates – and a centralized incomes policy – which requires low inflation. Economic strategy is thus 'negotiated' with business and labour, but once chosen can be firmly applied and supported by a strict monetary policy, which implies relatively high long-term interest rates. The government does not attempt to plan the economy, but rather to control the conditions under which strategy is negotiated between banks, firms and labour. This gives great stability to German policy (and thus considerable predictability) but little flexibility.

Japan has a similar concentration of economic power to Germany, but has a higher degree of planning as the authorities directly administer capital markets, and maintain real interest rates at low levels through market segmentation and relatively tight monetary policies. The results in terms of weak asset portfolios are now well known, but it has permitted the export drive upon which much of Japan's economic strength is based.

These three very distinct political economies attempt to generate long term interest rate policies derived from national needs which have strong international effects and require frequent modifications to prevent the resulting exchange rates and capital flows from becoming uncontainable. At the global level, there is a double confrontation: the confrontation at summit meetings of the leading countries regarding the economic policies of the three currency areas, and the confrontation between the policy line expressed at these summits and the world financial system that is increasingly integrated and liquid.

Conclusion

In sum there is no global savings shortage but there is a liquidity preference problem in the strict Keynesian sense of uncertainty about global asset values. Long rates will probably stay up at their present historically high real levels despite low short rates, until the new institutional conventions emerge . This is due to the risk premia involved in the lack of a solid basis for capital market expectations, rather than any global shortage of capital as such.

High real interest rates clearly affect private investment prospects as well as government debt solvency. In addition the reluctance by institutional investors to commit long-term capital – rather than a shortage of saving as such – works against large investment projects. This is a particular difficulty for global companies facing major technological investment programmes, but not (unfortunately) for those planning takeovers or speculative operations on financial markets. The problem is not so much the interest cost of funds as such but the terms upon which they are offered – which increasingly involve an unacceptable dilution of management control or repayment schedules which do not recognize the long lead times involved.

The enormous infrastructure requirements of Asia, Latin America and Eastern Europe will generate large bond offerings from governments and regulated private utilities in the next few years. Again the problem is not so much the real interest rate charges (which rarely exceed 5 per cent after inflation) but rather the risk evaluation process undertaken by overseas investors, which is highly volatile and reliant on incomplete information. In consequence, market sentiment about a particular country or region can swing sharply, making an efficient medium-term financing programme for infrastructure almost impossible to construct.

The ultimate solution for the problems of high real interest rates and lack of long-term investment funds in a global economy would presumably be a global monetary authority. This is a long way off, if only because it would have to be able to deal in key currencies and government bonds and thus effectively constrain G3 macroeconomic policy. As will the EMI.

Endnotes

1. Aghevli (1990, p. 3).
2. Measured savings differ from changes in net worth because changes in asset values are not included in standard definitions of income, and thus are implicitly excluded from savings once consumption is subtracted. The definition in Hicks (1946) of income equates it to the maximum value that a household (or other economic unit) can consume during a given period while remaining as well off as it was at the beginning of the period. For a discussion of the application of national accounting procedures at the global level, see Vos and de Jong (1995).
3. Because saving rates vary widely over space and time.
4. Aghevli (1990: 3). It is interesting to note that all discussion of national savings is conducted in terms of *rates* (that is domestic saving as a proportion of GDP), which implies acceptance of Ricardian (or perhaps even Keynesian) savings propensities rather than the strictly neoclassical funds market, which would imply tracking the absolute amounts.
5. Where individuals are assumed to maximize the present value of their utility subject to a budget constraint equal to their current net worth plus the present value of their expected income over the rest of their life.
6. Dean *et al.* (1989).
7. Goldstein *et al.* (1993).
8. Fazzari *et al.* (1988).
9. See, for instance, Aghevli (1990), Hutchinson (1992) and Bosworth (1993) for surveys.
10. Blanchard and Fischer (1989).
11. Hutchinson (1992).
12. Aghevli (1990).
13. Although as Barro (1989) points out, the US savings rate in the 1980s is not really low if measured as the change in the real market value of assets, and thus the current account deficit is an illusion once capital gains on direct investment are included. Much the same might be said, in reverse, of the Japanese surplus in the 1990s.
14. See Buiter (1988).
15. Barro (1989), but see also Buiter (1988).
16. Dean *et al.* (1989); see also Table.
17. See Hutchinson (1992), who also points out that the concept of a long-run 'balanced budget' should go beyond the simple cross-cyclical view to include contingent liabilities such as welfare entitlements, which implies that existing measures of the private savings offset overstate the extent to which the private sector in fact incorporates the government sector's budget constraint in its decision making.
18. As Keynes, mindful of the experience of the gold standard, had intended them to be (Moggridge, 1992) – as well as assuming that they would take place between central banks.
19. The global current account discrepancy, which approximately equals the current account discrepancy in the IMF balance of payments statistics, is of the order of US$100 billion in 1990 (IMF, 1992a). This is relatively small in comparison with estimated global saving of US$5 trillion in 1991 (IMF, 1992b), but large in comparison with the investment savings balances (that is the current account balances) of major economies such as the US or Japan, thus making empirical discussion of international capital flows difficult. On this accounting problem, see Vos (1989) and de Jong (1993).
20. See de Jong (1993) for the 'World Accounting Matrix' methodology, developed from Vos (1989) on the basis of Stone's original proposals for SAM matrix balancing according to the relative reliability of statistical sources. Such balancing has the effect, in the case of the US and the UK, of producing a major reduction in the current account deficit once the flows are reconciled.
21. Of no greater than five percentage points in practice.
22. Turner (1991), Frankel (1992), Obstfeld (1994).
23. In the neoclassical view (which forms the basis for IMF stabilization policy) a fall in public sector savings can result in larger private savings due to the increased public sector borrowing requirement driving up interest rates or, if these are constrained in a closed economy, by

increasing the money supply and forcing private savings through a real balance effect. In the small open economy, the effect is felt through an inflow of foreign savings in the monetary approach to the balance of payments.

24. This is explicitly admitted by the IMF (Goldstein, *et al.* 1993).
25. World Bank (1995).
26. Lucas (1990).
27. UNCTC (1992).
28. See Vos (1994) for a model of international debt adjustment that traces the effect of source of aid finance.
29. This is central to Tobin's international portfolio model (Brainard and Tobin, 1992).
30. Brainard and Tobin (1992) provide some of the elements for this, particularly the concept of 'home bias' as a form of liquidity preference, but this is still a theory of one country's capital account and does not allow for interaction between the portfolio preferences of various countries.
31. IMF (1995).
32. Ciocca and Nardozzi (1996).
33. FitzGerald (1996).

Bibliography

Aghevli, B.B., J.M. Broughton, P.J. Montiel, D. Villanhera and G. Woglom (1990), 'The Role of National Saving in the World Economy', *IMF Occasional Paper No. 67*, Washington DC: International Monetary Fund.

Barro, R.J. (1989), 'The Ricardian approach to budget deficits', *Journal of Economic Perspectives*, **3** (2), 37–54.

Blanchard, O.J. and S. Fischer (1989), *Lectures on Macroeconomics,* Cambridge, MA: MIT Press.

Bosworth, B.P. (1993), *Saving and Investment in a Global Economy*, Washington, DC: Brookings.

Brainard, W.C. and J. Tobin (1992), 'On the internationalization of portfolios', *Oxford Economic Papers*, p. 44.

Buiter, W.H. (1988), 'Death, birth, productivity growth and debt neutralitys', *Economic Journal*, p. 98.

Ciocca, P. and G. Nardozzi (1996), *The High Price of Money: An Interpretation of World Interest Rates*, Oxford: Clarendon Press.

Dean, A. *et al.* (1989), 'Saving Trends and Behaviour in OECD Countries', *OECD Working Paper No. 67*, Paris: Organization for Economic Cooperation and Development.

Fazzari, S.M., R.G. Hubbard and B.C. Petersen (1988), 'Financing Constraints and Corporate Investment' *Brookings Papers on Economic Activity*, Washington DC: Brookings.

FitzGerald, E.V.K. (1994), 'International Finance', in P. Arestis and M. Sawyer (eds), *The Elgar Companion to Radical Political Economy*, Aldershot: Edward Elgar.

FitzGerald, E.V.K. (1996) 'Intervention versus Regulation: The Role of the IMF in Crisis Prevention and Management', *Discussion Paper No. 115*, Geneva: UNCTAD.

Frankel, J. (1992), 'Measuring international capital mobility: a review', *American Economic Review*, **2** (82).

Goldstein, M., D. Folkerts-Landau, P. Garber, L. Rojas-Suarez and M. Spencer (1993), *International Capital Markets*, Washington, DC: International Monetary Fund.

Hicks, J.R. (1946), *Value and Capital: An Inquiry into Some Fundamental Principles of Economic Theory*, Oxford: Clarendon Press.

Hutchinson, M.M. (1992), 'Budget Policy and the Decline of National Saving Revisited', *BIS Economic Paper No. 33*, Basle: Bank for International Settlements.

IMF (1991), 'Determinants and Systemic Consequences of International Capital Flows', *Occasional Paper No. 77,* Washington, DC: International Monetary Fund.

IMF (1992a), *Report on the Measurement of International Capital Flows*, Washington, DC: International Monetary Fund.

IMF (1992b), *World Economic Outlook*, Washington, DC: International Monetary Fund.

IMF (1995), *World Economic Outlook*, Washington, DC: International Monetary Fund.

Lucas, R. (1990), 'Why doesn't capital flow from rich to poor countries?', *American Economic Review*, p. 80.

Moggridge, D.E. (1992), *Maynard Keynes: An Economist's Biography*, London: Routledge.

Obstfeld, M. (1994), 'International Capital Mobility in the 1990s', *Discussion Paper Series No. 902*, London: Centre for Economic Policy Research.

Turner, P. (1991), 'Capital Flows in the 1980s: A Survey of Major Trends', *BIS Economic Papers No. 30*, Basle: Bank for International Settlements.

UNCTC (1992), *The Determinants of Foreign Direct Investment: A Survey of the Evidence*, New York: United Nations Centre on Transnational Corporations.

Vos, R. (1994), *Debt and Adjustment in the World Economy: Structural Asymmetries in North-South Interactions*, Basingstoke: Macmillan.

Vos, R. and N. de Jong (1995), 'Trade and Financial Flows in a World Accounting Framework: Balanced Matrices for 1985–90', *Review of Income and Wealth*.

World Bank (1995), *World Debt Tables 1994–5*, Washington, DC: World Bank.

17 Financial constraints on Keynesian macroeconomic policies

Malcolm C. Sawyer

Keynesian macroeconomic policies can be variously defined. In this chapter, a narrow definition is adopted, namely the use of fiscal and monetary policies in pursuit of high levels of economic activity (notably full employment) which may involve substantial budget deficits. Keynesian policies are broader than that, and specifically can involve the stimulation of investment through, for example, seeking to reduce uncertainty or to lower the cost of finance.[1] More generally, Keynesian policies should be seen to include the construction of institutional arrangements which are supportive of high levels of demand.

Two strands of objections to the potency and possibility of Keynesian reflationary policies stand out. The first comes from the notion of a supply-side determined equilibrium level of employment (and corresponding levels of unemployment and output) summarized in the phrase the Non-Accelerating Inflation Rate of Unemployment (NAIRU). The second comes from a variety of financial constraints, whether on the ability of a government to run a budget deficit through to the reactions of financial markets. For reasons of space, our focus in this paper is on the latter, whereas we have discussed the former elsewhere (see, for example, Sawyer, 1997).

It should be made clear that a high level of aggregate demand (however generated) is seen here as a *necessary but not sufficient* condition for the achievement of high levels of economic activity (including employment) (for a discussion on the constraints on the achievement of full employment see Sawyer (1995a, 1995b). The achievement of full employment requires a wide range of policies including a sufficient level of aggregate demand.

Budget deficits
We begin by considering the limits on the use of budget deficits for the creation of sufficient aggregate demand to underpin full employment. Even with significant levels of unemployment most Western governments are running budget deficits though in many cases the deficit can be attributed to a combination of interest payments on government debt. It is thus likely that full employment would involve a substantial budget deficit in most industrialized countries.

A budget deficit is unsustainable in two ways: namely if it leads to a spiralling national debt to GDP ratio (and hence to rising interest payments on the debt relative to GDP) and, secondly, that the level of interest payments while not rising (relative to GDP) may nevertheless constitute what is seen as too heavy a burden on taxpayers through perceived adverse incentives from the tax rates and from the general transfer from the relatively poor to the relatively rich which the interest payments on national debt often represent (and these issues are addressed below).

The algebra relating to the budget deficit can be readily laid out. Define D as the outstanding public debt, B the primary budget deficit (that is excluding interest payments on debt and taxation paid on any such interest payments), g the growth rate of the economy and r the (post tax) rate of interest, then it is well known that the debt to GDP ratio will not rise when $(g - r).D = B$ (which can also be written as $g.D = r.D + B$) (with the primary deficit to GDP ratio being held constant). Any size of primary deficit (relative to GDP) will not lead to the overall deficit rising (relative to GDP) provided that the growth rate exceeds the post tax rate of interest (either both expressed in nominal terms or in real terms) (see also Pasinetti, 1997). The difficulty for budget deficits which has arisen in recent years is simply that real rates of interest have been at historically unprecedented high levels while economic growth has been sluggish.[2] We would attribute these higher interest rates to the pursuit of tight monetary policies in the belief that tight money and high interest rates will (eventually) dampen down inflation (see also next section). There is a clear conflict of view between the prevailing orthodoxy which sees the interest rate as set by loanable funds considerations, and the post-Keynesian perception that interest rates are set by liquidity considerations. In the former case, a budget deficit is seen to raise interest rates through adding to the demand for loanable funds, whereas in the latter case, attempted monetary constraint raises interest rates which makes budget deficits less manageable.

In so far as government face the 'principle of increasing risk' (Kalecki, 1937) then higher deficits (relative to GDP) would entail higher interest rates: if we knew the relationship between the interest rate which had to be paid by government and the size of its budget deficit we could calculate the nature of the barrier presented by the condition $g - r \geq 0$.

Since if $(g - r)$ is positive it is likely to be rather small, that is of the order of 0.01 or 0.02, the debt to GDP ratio will stabilize at a large multiple of the primary budget deficit to GDP ratio (clearly with numbers given previously at multiples of 100 or 50). But perhaps more significantly, the interest payments would stabilize at $(r/g - r) B/Y$. The overall budget deficit (including interest payments) would be much larger than the primary deficit and that those payments would appear to constitute a large transfer of income to the holders of government debt. The transfer is an apparent one in that the financing of those interest payments comes from further borrowing and represents a transfer within the rentier class. Further, the government is, by running a deficit, in effect permitting the savings to occur and then absorbing them. If investment were higher, thereby reducing the need for public expenditure, savings would again occur and profits flow to the wealthy. If the rate of interest on government bonds is lower than the rate of profit, then the income distribution with a substantial budget deficit may not be more unequal than the income distribution with higher investment but a lower budget deficit.[3] It can be noted that a high proportion of the government bonds may be held by pension funds and so on. For the UK, life assurance and pension funds held £133 billion of British government securities and Treasury Bills (as at March 1996) out of a total £262 billion, compared with financial liabilities of £400 billion and net liabilities of £250 billion. With debt interest payments by general government of nearly £26 billion in 1995/6, we could hazard a guess that £11 to £12 billion was being paid out to life assurance and pension funds. At least for the UK, the budget deficit and the resulting interest payments are acting as a set of pension arrangements. In 1995, contributions to pension funds and life assurance companies were over £33 billion of which nearly £18 billion were lent to the government to finance the budget deficit; on the other side, interest payments of £11 to 12 billion can be compared with nearly £66 billion paid out as pensions and life assurance benefits and contributions of £31 billion and life assurance premiums of some £36 billion.

What then should be the rule for government deficits ? We adopt the position that the balance between expenditure and taxation should be struck to provide the highest level of aggregate demand consistent with constraints on the economy, which include the balance of trade, inflationary pressures, capacity and availability of labour.

A number of distinct cases then arise:

1.   A relatively small primary deficit (or a surplus) arises, and the rate of growth is greater than the post-tax real rate of interest. Then the debt to income ratio will stabilize (at $(1/g)$ times the total deficit equivalent to $(1/g-r)$ times the primary deficit). Interest payments relative to national income will stabilize at (r/g) times the deficit to income ratio or $(r/g-r)$ times the primary deficit to income ratio respectively. In either case, interest payments are only a proportion of the total deficit (since r/g is less than unity). The debt to income ratio may also be deemed relatively small.

2.   A relatively large deficit arises and/or the difference between the rate of interest and the growth of growth is rather small, which has the effect that the stabilized debt to income ratio would be rather high and the corresponding interest payment to income ratio also rather high.

What is meant by high or low in this context? There is little economic analysis which helps here, and we would hazard the guess that when the interest payments to income ratio exceeds 10 per cent, political pressures build up to reduce the budget deficit and the national debt. We would also guess that interest payments relative to national income are more significant than the debt to income ratio (for example the UK had a debt to income ratio of over 300 per cent after World War II without it appearing to cause any political or economic difficulty, perhaps because interest rates were low).

It appears that a substantial part of taxation is going to finance interest payments, though this would not actually be the case if the primary deficit is held constant for then in effect interest payments are met by further borrowing. Then, by definition tax rates are held constant and there is no rise in taxation to fund the deficit.

3. The rate of interest is greater than or equal to the rate of growth. This may well be the present position for a number of countries including the UK. For that country if we take the underlying rate of growth of GDP at $2\frac{3}{4}$ per cent (the figure used by government in its public expenditure projections, which is rather optimistic in light of growth averaging 2 per cent per annum since 1980), then for interest rates (on government securities) around 8 per cent nominal, inflation around 3 per cent, and assuming an effective tax rate on interest of around 25 per cent then the relevant post-tax real interest rate would be around 3 per cent. The precise figures are a matter of conjecture, but this order of magnitudes suggests that the stability condition that the rate of growth exceeds the post-tax real rate of interest is not readily met. Assuming that this is to be the prevailing norm, then any deficit will grow (as interest payments mount) as will the national debt to income ratio. While the time period over which the deficit and debt/income ratio can grow without causing major difficulties may be quite substantial (that is if the deficit is initially relatively small and/or the difference between the growth rate and the interest rate is small), nevertheless the difficulties will come sooner or later.

In this case, there are two relevant policy responses. The first is to seek to reduce interest rates (or the much more difficult task of raising the growth rate). If high interest rates are viewed to be a consequence of the pursuit of tight monetary policies, then this constitutes an additional reason for lowering interest rates. However, international financial markets place severe limitations on the ability of national governments to vary domestic interest rates out of line with prevailing interest rates elsewhere (though paradoxically low domestic interest rates would be associated with an expected appreciation of the currency).

The second response relates to the initial cause of the deficit. Note that the deficit was seeking to raise aggregate demand: another way of putting the same point is to say that private aggregate demand was insufficient. The appropriate response is then to seek ways of reducing private savings and/or raising private investment (more accurately profit generating investment). The national accounts identity provides $S = I + (G - T) + (X - M)$, where S is savings, I investment, G government expenditure (in total), T taxation, X exports and M

imports. Applying the identity at full employment makes the obvious point that a budget deficit corresponds to some combination of excess of private savings over investment and foreign trade deficit. In so far as the budget deficit is in effect mopping up the excess of private savings over investment, then the Keynesian alternative to running a deficit would be the stimulus of investment and the discouragement of savings. If it is considered politically or otherwise infeasible to run budget deficits, then action should be taken to reduce net private savings. This recalls some arguments of Kalecki and Keynes. Kalecki (1944) saw limits to the stimulation of private investment (essentially that such stimulation would lead to rising capital output ratio and declining profit rate), and advocated deficit spending by government and a redistribution of income from higher to lower income groups to stimulate consumption. Keynes foresaw a time 'when investment demand is so far saturated that it cannot be brought up to the indicated level of savings without embarking upon wasteful and unnecessary enterprises', and at such a time '[i]t becomes necessary to encourage wise consumption and discourage saving, – and to absorb some part of the unwanted surplus by increased leisure, more holidays (which are a wonderfully good way of getting rid of money) and shorter hours' (Keynes, 1980, p. 321 and p. 323; see also Arestis and Glickman,1997, for further discussion of this idea).

Thus we are advocating that governments only run deficits when it is necessary to do so for aggregate demand reasons. Hence, if a deficit is unsustainable, then other means to sustain aggregate demand have to be found.

Government borrowing and interest rates

It is possible that interest rates rise with a budget deficit thereby limiting the government's ability to borrow. It can here first be noted that in the international financial markets any government is still a relatively small borrower. Thus the bidding up of price against oneself, which can arise when there is a dominant buyer, may not arise here. But the operation of the 'principle of increasing risk' can still arise. It could be argued that the high interest rates arose from high levels of government borrowing. But the evidence linking budget deficits and interest rates is weak. For example, in a paper which is generally hostile to Keynesian macroeconomic policies, Cunningham and Vilasuso (1994/5) have to concede that '[u]nfortunately, empirical studies examining the relationship between interest rates and fiscal deficits are far from conclusive' (p. 90) and that 'whether fiscal deficits are associated with higher interest rates has yet to be resolved in the economics literature' (p. 91). And in a similar vein, '[t]he lacking of supporting empirical evidence linking interest rates to budget deficits is troublesome' (Wyplosz, 1991). Further 'the empirical results on interest rates support the Ricardian view [that there is no effect on budget deficits on real interest rates]. Given these findings it is remarkable that most macroeconomists remain confident that budget deficits raise interest rates' (Barro, 1989, p. 48).

While Barro has approached the matter from a rather different theoretical perspective, these results support our more Keynesian perspective that one of the supposed crowding-out routes, namely that budget deficits raise interest rates and thereby depress private investment, is not empirically supported. These quotes are indicative of a general conclusion that budget deficits do not raise interest rates.

Financial markets

The financial markets are often viewed as placing limits on the use of fiscal policy (notably budget deficits). Adverse reactions (or the threat of such) by the foreign exchange markets to particular policies leading to a fall in the value of the currency, and higher domestic interest rates, are often viewed as placing limits on policy. In this section we briefly explore how much of a constraint the financial markets impose.

The distinction, utilized by Sayer (1992) in his discussion of the power of the City of London, as to 'whether market prices are based on economic fundamentals or bubbles, fads and herd behaviour' is useful here. Clearly if it is the former then the financial markets may perform a useful service by providing early signals that an economic policy is unsustainable in the longer term. As Sayer (1992) argues fundamentally unsustainable 'policy strategies [include those] that give rise to accelerating inflation, a worsening balance of trade or rapidly growing public sector deficit. Sooner or later such policy strategies would have to be abandoned in response to underlying fundamental constraints such as the disruption caused by hyperinflation, balance of payments constraints and the 'fiscal crisis of the state' (p. 141). In such a case, the financial markets do not pose any threat to the range of policies (Keynesian or otherwise) which we would wish to advocate (but no one is going to admit to advocating unsustainable policies). However the difficulty arises that any fiscal expansion of the economy is likely to involve some elements of rising inflation, worsening balance of trade and growing budget deficit. The advocates of fiscal expansion would argue that such effects may be short-lived and do not lead to hyperinflation and so on. There are likely to be differences of view as to whether or not certain policies are sustainable.

However, even when financial asset prices reflect fundamentals, the operation of financial markets may still pose a constraint on the economic policies pursued. The 'fundamentals' of interest to the financial markets may be quite different from the 'fundamentals' of concern to others: for example, the financial markets may focus more on the rate of inflation while others may feel that unemployment is of more importance. Market participants will be concerned over the rate of inflation (in foreign exchange markets specifically expectations on the differential inflation rates between countries, in domestic financial markets expectations over domestic inflation relative to the nominal rate of interest). Inflation affects the returns which participants in financial markets receive. Unemployment and the level of economic activity are of no immediate concern to operators in financial markets since they do not directly affect the financial returns in the way in which inflation does (and indeed if some form of Phillips' curve analysis is accepted, reductions in unemployment, which are associated with higher inflation, are unwelcome to financial markets). In addition the implicit economic model to which the financial markets adhere may be quite different from the economic model which underlies a government's policies and both may be quite different from reality. It is clearly quite possible that a policy may be seen as sustainable and desirable when judged against one economic model but not against another. A simple illustration of this point arises with regard to the Phillips' curve with some short-term but no long-term trade-off between unemployment and inflation. If (as often appears to be assumed) the financial markets accept that model, then any fall in unemployment (below the 'natural rate') would be seen as involving higher inflation and being unsustainable. In contrast, the view that there is a long-run trade-off or that any trade-off is between changes in unemployment (or level of unemployment relative to its recent history) and inflation, would imply that the inflation rise may only be temporary and the decline in unemployment may be sustainable. Yet if the financial markets adhere to the former view (or government ministers believe that they do) then attempts to reduce unemployment may not be undertaken.

The use of the term 'fundamentals' carries, we would suggest, two implicit suggestions. Firstly, the fundamentals give rise to a unique set of (equilibrium) prices whereas there are theoretical reasons for thinking that there may be multiple equilibria.[4] If there are multiple equilibria, then the expectations of the financial markets may be an important element in which equilibrium is selected even though the chosen equilibrium may not be the socially preferred one. Secondly, the term suggests a separation between the real side of the economy ('the fundamentals') and the financial side akin to the classical dichotomy. In contrast our view would be that of mutual interdependence. Specifically we would view the influence of the financial sector through interest rates and willingness to grant credit as constraining the development of the real sector. Clearly, if the fad raises interest rates, investment may be thereby affected and hence the fundamentals of the economy changed. Similarly a falling exchange rate would stimulate domestic inflation which would change the fundamental value of the (nominal) exchange rate.

The financial markets pose a different type of constraint on the pursuit of sustainable fiscal policies when the 'bubbles, fads and herd behaviour' come to determine movements in prices (notably interest rates and exchange rates). There is now an extensive literature which indicates that financial market prices are 'excessively volatile' (and casual observation of the movements in the exchange rates in the past 20 would be supportive of that view).[5] Further there are theoretical literatures (surveyed by, for example, Camerer, 1989) which show that individual rational behaviour can generate 'bubbles'. In a world of uncertainty, where knowledge of the economic 'fundamentals' is given to few, it is inevitable that asset prices will fluctuate and follow fads and fashions. The significant question here is whether the adoption of say a Keynesian demand reflation (especially if pursued by a left-of-centre government) would set off adverse reactions in the financial markets. These reactions may be individually rational in the sense that if each (or most) individuals believe that others believe that such a reflection would be harmful and mark down prices then doing so themselves is rational. This is not to evoke conspiracy theories but rather to indicate that people having the perception that others think that some policy or events will lead to a deterioration in 'fundamentals', whether or not it would actually do so, would be sufficient to lead to a fall in price. Expectations and beliefs are important driving forces behind price movements in financial markets, and expectations have a self-fulfilling element to them. Expectations that the price of a particular currency is going to fall set up forces which lead to a fall in that currency's price.

If, as we would argue is the case, financial markets behave closer to the 'bubbles' representation than the 'fundamentals', then financial asset prices are essentially unpredictable, and further the way in which markets react to particular information or policies may also be unpredictable. This has two implications for our line of argument. Firstly, it enables those opposed to a particular policy to pontificate that if that policy is followed the financial markets will react in an adverse manner. A recent notable example of this arose in the dispute between the Chancellor of the Exchequer and the Governor of the Bank of England in May 1995 over interest rate changes. The Governor argued that the financial markets would react adversely if interest rates did not rise: rates were held constant and nothing happened. Secondly, significant changes in asset prices (and here of particular concern in interest rates and exchange rates) occur for essentially random reasons, and any government whatever policies it pursues faces the prospect of a 'run on the pound'. For example, Coakley and Harris, (1983, p. 193) report a fall in value of the pound against the dollar of 5.6 per cent in a fortnight in November 1982 despite the monetarist policies being pursued by the Thatcher government. The sterling crisis of 1976 which led to the IMF visit to the UK and imposition of conditions on public expenditure is a further example of an exchange rate crisis which owed more to 'fads and bubbles' than to 'fundamentals'. For 'there is also evidence to support the view that the convulsion in the foreign exchange market [during 1976] was in part a "confidence crisis" unrelated to the "fundamentals". For, indeed, all the obvious fundamentals – the inflation rate, the money supply, the current account –

were moving in a favourable direction at the time and there were the additional factors that by 1976 the prospective value of North Sea oil to the exchanges was understood and the government's hand had been strengthened politically by the results of the Common Market entry referendum.' (Artis and Cobham, 1991, p. 271).

This brief discussion would suggest that the financial markets pose constraints for the pursuit of macroeconomic policies in two ways. Firstly, policies which are sustainable and/or desirable from the perspective of a government may not be from the perspective of the financial markets. In that context financial markets may react adversely to policies which might otherwise be successful. Secondly, the financial markets may be influenced by fads and bubbles, and a movement in the exchange rate can be set off by what are effectively random factors. This in itself may not act as a constraint on policy, but rather that governments feel obliged to respond to such movements in the exchange rate.

Conclusions

We have argued that budget deficits may have to be incurred to attain full employment, but that budget deficits would not be sustainable in the face of post tax real interest rates which exceed the rate of growth. Policy measures would then have to focus on reducing interest rates and/or stimulating investment and depressing savings. We have also discussed some of the ways in which the financial markets may place limitations on fiscal policy. In the absence of Say's law, adequate aggregate demand to underpin full employment is not assured, and government action to secure it is required. But there are many other constraints on the achievement of full employment which also have to be addressed. Specifically the reactions of the financial markets may impose a significant constraint on the pursuit of reflationary macroeconomic policies.

Endnotes

1. See, for example, papers in Arestis and Sawyer (1997) and in Symposium on Keynesian Policies, *International Review of Applied Economics*, vol. 10.
2. 'Since modern capital markets came into existence, there have never been such high long-term rates as we recently have had all over the world' (Homer and Sylla, 1983, p. 1 quoted in Pasinetti, 1997). The recent high levels of real interest rates are indicated by the estimates of Tease *et al.* (1991). They estimate the long-term real rate of interest for the UK as 2.86 per cent in the 1960s, −1.34 per cent in the 1970s and 5 per cent in the 1980s: corresponding figures for France were 1.72 per cent, −3.79 per cent and 4.07 per cent; for Germany 3.85 per cent, 3.16 per cent and 5 per cent and for the US 2.60 per cent, 1.31 per cent and 6.20 per cent.
3. It being assumed that property income is more unequally distributed than labour income, and such that the distribution of property income reinforces the inequality of the distribution of labour income. The comparison being made here is for an equivalent level of savings and income.
4. The reasons are, in general, theoretical ones (rather than empirical ones) since the conditions for equilibria (unique or multiple) are properties of particular theoretical models.
5. The work of Shiller (Shiller, 1990, and the paper collected together in Shiller, 1989) has strongly suggested that there is excessive volatility in the stock and bond markets.

References

Arestis, P. and Glickman, M. (1998), 'The Modern Relevance of Post Keynesian Economic Policies', in S. Sharma (ed.) (1998), *Keynes Fifty Years After and Beyond*, Cheltenham: Edward Elgar, 51–60.

Arestis, P. and Sawyer, M. (eds) (1997), *John Maynard Keynes: Keynesianism into the Twenty-first Century*, London: Macmillan.

Artis, M. and Cobham, D. (1991), 'Summary and Appraisal' in M. Artis and D. Cobham (eds.), *Labour's Economic Policies, 1974–79*, Manchester: Manchester University Press, pp. 266–77.

Barro, Robert J. (1989), 'The Ricardian approach to budget deficits', *Journal of Economic Perspectives*, 3, 37–54.

Camerer, C. (1989), 'Bubbles and fads in asset prices', *Journal of Economic Surveys*, vol. 3, 3–42.

Coakley, J. and Harris, L. (1983), *The City of Capital*, Oxford: Basil Blackwell.

Cunningham, S.R. and Vilasuso, J. (1994/5), 'Is Keynesian demand management policy still viable?', *Journal of Post Keynesian Economics*, vol. 17, 187–210.

Homer, S. and Sylla, R. (1983), *A History of Interest Rates* (3rd edn.), New Brunswick: Rutgers University Press.

Kalecki, M. (1937), 'Principle of increasing risk', *Economica*, vol. 4, 440–46.

Kalecki, M. (1944), 'Three Ways to Full Employment', in Oxford University Institute of Statistics, *The Economics of Full Employment*, Oxford: Blackwell, pp. 39–58.

Keynes, J.M. (1980), *Activities 1940–1946 Shaping the Post-War World: Employment and Commodities, Collected Writings*, vol. XXVII, London: Macmillan.

Pasinetti, L. (1997), 'The Social "Burden" of High Interest Rates' in P. Arestis, G. Palma and M. Sawyer (eds.), *Capital Controversy, Post Keynesian Economics and the History of Economic Theory : Essays in Honour of Geoff Harcourt*, vol. 1, London: Routledge, pp. 161–68.

Sawyer, M. (1995a), 'Obstacles to the achievement of full employment in capitalist economies', in P. Arestis and M. Marshall (eds) *The Political Economy of Full Employment: Conservatism, Corporatism and Institutional Change*, Aldershot: Edward Elgar, pp. 15–35.

Sawyer, M. (1995b), 'Overcoming the barriers to full employment in capitalist economies', *Economie Appliquée*, 48, 185–218.

Sawyer, M. (1997), 'What are the Constraints on the Pursuit of Keynesian Macroeconomic Policies' in P. Arestis, G. Palma and M. Sawyer (eds.), *Markets, Unemployment and Economic Policy: Essays in Honour of Geoff Harcourt*, vol. 2, London: Routledge, pp. 419–30.

Sayer, S. (1992), 'The City, power and economic policy in Britain', *International Review of Applied Economics*, vol. 6, pp. 125–51.

Shiller, R.J. (1989), *Market Volatility*, Cambridge, Mass.: MIT Press.

Shiller, R.J. (1990), 'Speculative Prices and Popular Models', *Journal of Economic Perspectives*, vol. 4, 55–66.

Tease, W., Dean, P., Elmeskov, J. and Hoeller, P. (1991), 'Real interest rate trends: the influence of saving, investment and other factors', *OECD Economic Studies*, No. 17 (Autumn 1991).

Wyplosz, C. (1991), 'Monetary Union and Fiscal Policy Discipline' in *European Economy*, The Economics of EMU: Background Studies for European Economy, *OECD Economic Studies*, No. 44 (Winter 1991).

18 Free currency markets and systematic devaluations in developing countries: the legacy of Keynes

Pan A. Yotopoulos

Keynes has left a long legacy on exchange rates. Some parallels between his ideas and what follows in this article are too obvious to deserve further comment. An indirect part of his legacy that has failed to attract much attention thus far relates to the potential transcendence of his innovation on interest rates into the field of exchange rates and the global capital flows. The *General Theory* (1936 (1973), Chapter 13) extended the determination of the rate of interest into the 'liquidity-preference' approach that depends on: (i) the transactions motive; (ii) the precautionary motive, that is, the desire for security as to the future moves of interest rates; and (iii) the speculative motive, that is, the float around the price of a bond that represents transactions between the 'bears' and the 'bulls' – those who expect interest rates to be higher in the future than the organized market indicates in comparison to those who expect them to be lower, respectively. The role of the transactions motive in the determination of the nominal exchange rate is obvious through the balance of payments equation. The precautionary motive and the speculative motive play as important a role in determining the exchange rate, especially in a global economy with free currency markets, as they do in Keynes's application of the liquidity approach to the rate of interest.

What follows is that in open capital markets with free exchange rates the precautionary motive in specific assumes paramount importance in determining the nominal exchange rate as individuals in soft currency (developing) countries substitute the foreign exchange (hard currency) for their liquid holdings. This leads to a systematic tendency for the domestic currency to devalue, contingent on the transaction and the speculative demand for foreign exchange. In the case of the free juxtaposition of a reserve currency and a soft currency, it will be argued that the free currency market instead of 'setting prices right' tends to set them wrong. Moreover a trade bias is created that leads developing countries to misallocate resources systematically, at great cost to growth and to the detriment of development. The same process also changes the distribution of income in favour of the wealthy.

In what follows the focus on Mexico and the December 1994 devaluation of the peso will provide the real world motivation for the rest of the chapter. The peso had been previously pegged (at 3.5 pesos to 1 US$) and it was initially devalued by roughly 20 per cent. Within a week the efforts to support the peso had failed and a free exchange rate was adopted that settled for a while (at 6 pesos to 1 US$) and has systematically devalued since then. The discussion on Mexico applies equally well to the economy of any other developing country that has opened the capital account and afforded to residents unrestricted access to foreign exchange. These characteristics qualify most 'emerging market economies' that are undergoing stabilization and structural adjustment for the future 'peso fiasco' scenarios.

Finally the issue is generalized by focusing on the adverse effects on growth that devaluations and excessive trade bias may have for developing countries. The empirical evidence is from panel data for 80 countries, covering the period 1970–75.

The Mexican peso fiasco: welfare for the wealthy

There have been two (largely complementary) views of serious observers on what went wrong with the peso. The one is the fundamentals story, and the other the story of the onslaught of foreign speculative capital.

The fundamentals story has certain merit. There has been a persistent current account deficit – the difference between what Mexico takes in from exports and what it pays out for imports and for servicing the foreign debt. By the end of 1994 it had grown to 7.6 per cent of GDP. Liberalization of a repressed economy was bound to contribute to the deficit. Dismantling of long-standing restrictions on imports, reducing tariffs and opening up the economy into a world market system drove imports up. The consumerist drive is reflected in the decrease in the rate of personal savings from 15 per cent of GDP in 1988 to 7.4 per cent in 1994. How was the Mexican penchant for consuming more and saving less financed? Enter the second story, the flood of foreign finance.

The net foreign capital streaming into Mexico in 1994 rose to US$30 billion. Little of that was in equity capital of corporate investment in plants and equipment. And little was in long-term government debt, which actually had been drastically reduced from its pre-crisis peaks. Some of the foreign capital went to plug the trade deficit. This is what Keynes had called transactions demand for foreign exchange.

Keynes distinguished also a second motive for dealing in foreign exchange – speculation. Most of the capital streaming into Mexico represented an excessive inflow of short-term financial and portfolio capital that fit the speculative motive. Thus the second story focuses on the lemming-like march of multinational banks and mutual funds bearing loans to emerging markets. This supply side of the Mexican crisis also has merit.

But the import binge cannot explain the total debacle, and the supply of foreign financial capital was certainly not forced on non-consenting adults and on unwilling Mexican clients. What has been left out of both stories is the demand side. It is Keynes's third motive for holding foreign exchange, the *precautionary* demand.

The financial integration aspect of the liberalization agenda included the comprehensive deregulation of financial institutions and the abolition of restrictions on capital movements and exchange transactions. Opening up the capital market sounds like a good idea, and in many cases it is. But a premature opening, as in the case of Mexico (and most other 'emerging markets'), can signal a catastrophe that waits to happen: *asymmetric* financial integration. The word in emphasis has nothing to do with the size or the wealth of the US economy. It refers to the status of the dollar as a reserve currency, a hard currency, as opposed to the peso that is soft.

Hard currencies are treated as a store of value internationally. This quality is based on 'reputation,' which means that there is a credible commitment to stability of relative hard currency prices (towards other hard currencies, or say, gold). The soft currency, in contrast, is expected to devalue in a free currency market since it lacks reputation as a safe haven. Under these conditions, and with international financial intermediation present, there is an asymmetric demand from Mexicans to hold dollars as a store of value – a demand not offset by Americans holding pesos as an asset. This asymmetry tends to increase the price of the dollar in Mexico – to depreciate the peso. This will encourage currency substitution, a flight from the peso, which will precipitate further depreciation. Expectations of devaluation feed unto themselves to become self-fulfilling prophesies. The fault is not with the peso as such. In free currency markets, without restrictions on foreign exchange, devaluation of the soft currency is inevitable and it becomes a political economy bubble: a set of reinforcing expectations. This gradual devaluation scenario represents closely the present situation of the peso when the exchange rate is allowed to float freely. Devaluation shall also occur if the exchange rate is fixed, the regime that held in Mexico before the crisis.

The variant of exchange rate policy that held before the 1994 devaluation focused on the stability of the peso as policy objective. The fixed exchange rate had to hold against the tide of peso asset holders in Mexico who wanted to hedge their wealth against future depreciations of the currency by buying dollars. This was done by offsetting this precautionary demand through increasing the supply of speculative short-term capital that the banking system borrowed in the international market. The dollars of the Central Bank were thrown into the market to flush out pesos, thus providing for currency substitution without disturbing the equilibrium of the foreign exchange at 3.5 pesos to the dollar. When the dam burst on 20 December the diagnosis was that the exchange rate had appreciated.

The new thesis being proposed is that with free currency markets and unrestricted access to foreign exchange the precautionary and the speculative functions of money become the tail that wags the dog of the transactions demand for money. Over and above the demand for dollars to pay for imports and for servicing the debt, there is also dollar demand as an asset to substitute for peso-asset-holding as an attempt to pre-empt the expected depreciation of the domestic currency. The official data that came out months later (*The Economist*, 26 August 1995) confirmed this scenario built around currency substitution, as opposed to the imbalance in fundamentals or to the foreign capital exit thesis. In the three weeks of December 1994 leading up to the devaluation Mexican Central Bank reserves fell by US$2.8 billion. In the same period foreign investors sold US$326 million worth of Mexican debt, leaving roughly US$2.5 billion to be accounted for. The situation worsened in the final week of December, after the initial modest devaluation. For the month as a whole the Central Bank lost US$6.7 billion in reserves. Foreign investors sold only US$370 million worth of debt and equity, and another US$1.7 billion of the loss in reserves can be accounted for by Mexico's trade deficit for the month. The balance remaining for currency substitution is US$4.6 billion, up US$2.1 billion for the final week as a minimum (after considering the trade deficit portion of the first three weeks for which data are unavailable). This is a hefty amount that is attributed to Keynes's precautionary motive for holding foreign exchange. The unravelling of the 'orderly' devaluation followed.

The evidence on the Mexican experience confirms that there is a reverse Gresham's law, in which the good currency, the dollar, drives out the bad. The absence of exchange restrictions that leads to currency substitution in effect constitutes a form of insurance that protects peso asset holders against capital losses. Moreover since it is mostly the wealthy who can afford to hold liquid assets, the process also works as an indexation for the well off against future currency depreciation. Free currency markets in developing countries provide welfare relief for the wealthy whether the exchange rate is fixed, flexible or pegged – only that with the fixed exchange rate the windfall becomes more generous, courtesy of the Central Bank that supports the price of the peso.

Blaming the crisis on the appreciation of the peso in the past, or for that matter on its further depreciation subsequently, is no more convincing than the drunk driver's complaint on smashing up his car that the roads are unsafe. Both depreciation and appreciation are the symptoms of the same disease: currency substitution away from the soft peso.

A parable of systematic misallocation of resources

There are winners and losers when there is unrestricted access to foreign exchange in soft currency countries. But the more important question is how currency substitution, which relates to financial flows, is transmitted to the real economy and how it translates into prospects for economic growth.

In answering this question it helps to distinguish between tradables (*T*) and non-tradables (*N*) – commodities that enter the current account of a country as exports and imports and those that do not. The distinction is in part only an issue of the physical characteristics of a commodity, say wheat versus haircuts. In great part it becomes a question of what a country can afford to pay for in foreign currency. The distinction becomes immaterial for hard currencies, as is the case with most developed countries (DC). But it becomes hugely important for developing countries (LDC) that have soft currency. One way of understanding this is to compare a DC and an LDC along the continuum of possibilities for transforming non-tradable output, or the resources that produced it, into tradables.

To enhance the intuition suppose both countries are overindebted, for example the US and Mexico. With the peso being a soft currency and the Mexican debt being denominated in dollars (because the peso is soft currency), Mexico cannot service its foreign debt from the proceeds of producing non-tradables. These are traded in pesos. It has instead to shift resources away from the non-tradable sector to produce tradable output to procure the dollars for servicing the debt. In the US, on the other hand, the debt is serviced in dollars whether the output produced consists of tradables or non-tradables.

A parable can help enhance understanding of the process that leads from currency substitution to resource misallocation in developing countries. Consider an equilibrium allocation where a bundle of resources produces T and N, measured so that one unit of each is worth US$1. Entrepreneurs should be normally indifferent between producing one unit of the former or one of the latter. But in the case of Mexico the soft currency may be devalued and it becomes risky for entrepreneurs to produce (or hold) one unit of N that could not be converted for later spending into US$1. Expressed in another way, entrepreneurs are attracted to producing T because that is the only way they can acquire US$1 they wish to hold for asset purposes. Production then is biased excessively toward T, despite the fact that the relative productivities of the bundle of resources have remained unchanged. This represents misallocation of resources that produces inefficiency and output losses. It originated in free currency markets setting prices wrong, not right, for the soft peso. This dilemma does not exist with the developed countries that have hard currency. For their entrepreneurs US$1 of T will always be worth US$1 of N in hard currency, contrary to the soft currency case where the expectation of devaluation becomes a self-fulfilling prophecy.

The intuition behind the parable is simple. Distortions inherent in free currency markets lead to systematic depreciation of soft currencies of developing countries – to high nominal exchange rates. Devaluation of the exchange rate leads to increased exports. But not all exports are a bargain to produce compared to the alternative of producing non-tradables. For instance some countries without a climatic or resource advantage in producing grapes are known to export wine. Other countries graduate from being exporters of sugar and copra to exporting their teak forests, and on to systematically exporting nurses and doctors, while they remain underdeveloped all the same. If this happens, it may represent competitive devaluation trade as opposed to comparative advantage trade. Competitive devaluation trade is misallocating resources against non-tradables at great cost to growth and to the detriment of development.

The empirical evidence on exchange rate parity and development outcomes

Yotopoulos, (1996) re-examines some of the conventional wisdom of the Washington consensus, especially with respect to 'setting the prices right' for trade and development. It so turns out that when there is market failure, even more so when markets are 'incomplete' (that is, they 'do not span time, space, and uncertainty'), the market clearing price where supply is equal to demand does not produce Pareto-optimum outcomes. Government intervention and rationing become necessary in these cases. To make things worse, there is no presumption that government intervention will be successful.

This section relates to the dynamics between real and nominal exchange rates under free currency markets in developing countries. It is intended to provide a test and quantification of the losses in GDP and welfare in developing countries when the price of T becomes 'too high' by means, as an example, of devaluation-induced high nominal exchange rates (NER).

The theoretical framework is an adaptation of the Australian model that distinguishes T and N (Salter, 1959; Corden, 1977). In a non-Hicksian world where the two are not perfect substitutes, the production of N can become a binding constraint for economic development. This situation arises when the prices of T are 'high' relative to those of N, with resources moving 'excessively' from the latter to the former.

The operational framework of the research utilizes purchasing power parity data. Micro-ICP (International Comparisons Project, Kravis, Heston and Summers, 1982) data provide price information for a complete set of outputs of an economy, appropriately normalized by the international prices of the same commodities. Data from international trade statistics are used to define T ('tradeds') and N on a country-by-country basis. The ratio of the prices of the two is an index of the real exchange rate (RER). The meaning of 'setting the prices right' is precisely setting this RER at its equilibrium value. Although the index computed cannot be used to measure the deviation of the RER from its equilibrium value, it can clearly tell whether one country has higher prices of tradables relative to non-tradables than another, that is, it has a more undervalued RER, always in relative terms. An example appears in Table 18.1 that ranks 33 countries by the value of their RER index in 1985. Cursory examination suggests that developing countries are crowded at the top of the table, having relatively high prices of T.

Table 18.1   Countries ranked by the value of the RER index, 1985

Country	RER	Country	RER
Ethiopia	1.967	Kenya	1.070
Rwanda	1.962	Morocco	1.069
Pakistan	1.747	Norway	1.013
Malawi	1.713	Netherlands	1.009
Sri Lanka	1.546	Turkey	0.998
Yugoslavia	1.542	Denmark	0.980
Greece	1.417	Australia	0.969
Ivory Coast	1.329	Belgium	0.963
Portugal	1.230	Jamaica	0.949
New Zealand	1.208	Sweden	0.933
Nigeria	1.196	Canada	0.928
Thailand	1.193	Japan	0.923
Hungary	1.192	Ireland	0.918
Egypt	1.186	Finland	0.879
India	1.178	Italy	0.831
Germany	1.155	Poland	0.829
France	1.095		

Source: Yotopoulos (1996), Chapter 6, Table 6.2.

The RER index has been related to the rate of growth of real GDP per capita in an endogenous growth framework that otherwise includes the conventional explanatory variables (for summary and examples see Levine and Renelt, 1992; Romer, 1994; Solow, 1994; Pack, 1994). Such variables are: the ratio of investment in GDP, the openness of the economy, the direction of trade towards more or less advanced partners, the change in the rate of inflation, the share of government consumption in GDP, the secondary school enrolment ratio, the rate of growth of population, plus time, regional and income dummies. For simplicity, Table 18.2. reports only two of the many models and the various country/year permutations that are presented in the original research (Yotopoulos, 1996: Chapter 7): the simple regression result of the real GDP growth per capita on RER, and the multiple regression that besides RER includes also variables for time and for income per capita regime. In both cases – and in all regression reported in the original research – the coefficient of the RER is significant, robust, and negatively related to the real rate of growth of GDP per capita. How are such empirical results to be explained?

Table 18.2   A preview of the relationship between growth and real exchange rate

	RER 1	RER 2
Test 1 All countries: 1970, 1975, 1980, 1985		
Coefficient	−0.021	−0.024
T-statistic	−2.708	−2.947
Constant	0.040	0.068
Standard error of Y est.	0.025	0.024
Number of observations	123	123
Adjusted R^2	0.049	0.139
Test 2 All countries: 1980, 1985		
Coefficient	−0.025	−0.021
T-statistic	−2.720	−2.051
Constant	0.040	0.042
Standard error of Y est.	0.024	0.024
Number of observations	86	86
Adjusted R^2	0.070	0.064
Test 3 All countries: 1985		
Coefficient	−0.031	−0.022
T-statistic	−3.290	−1.963
Constant	0.051	0.033
Standard error of Y est.	0.019	0.017
Number of observations	37	37
Adjusted R^2	0.214	0.322
Test 4 All countries: 1980		
Coefficient	−0.021	−0.021
T-statistic	−1.270	−1.165
Constant	0.032	0.045
Standard error of Y est.	0.027	0.028
Number of observations	49	49
Adjusted R^2	0.013	0.000
Test 5 All countries: 1970, 1975		
Coefficient	−0.023	−0.034
T-statistic	−1.995	−2.533
Constant	0.056	0.096
Standard error of Y est.	0.023	0.022
Number of observations	37	37
Adjusted R^2	0.076	0.123

Table 18.2   continued

	RER 1	RER 2
Test 6 Low and middle income countries: 1970, 1975, 1980, 1985		
Coefficient	−0.019	−0.025
T-statistic	−1.851	−2.416
Constant	0.035	0.073
Standard error of Y est.	0.030	0.029
Number of observations	74	74
Adjusted R^2	0.032	0.112

Source: Yotopoulos (1996), Chapter 7, Tables 7.1 to 7.6.

Note:
The dependent variable is annual rate of growth of real per capita GDP for a five-year period, centred on the year of observation.
RER is defined as the ratio of relative prices of tradables to non-tradables appropriately normalized by international prices and aggregated using expenditure weights.
RER 1 reports the coefficient of the simple regression.
RER 2 reports the coefficient of the RER after controlling for time (the slowdown of growth in the 1980s), DC-LDC status, and trade regime.

Within the RER framework, observations of relatively high prices of tradables (RER *under*valuation) can be generated through aggressive devaluation of the NER that increases the price of exports and import substitutes relative to the price of non-tradables, both expressed in units of national currency per international dollar. Such NER policies can lead to overshooting the comparative advantage of a country by extending the range of tradability to commodities that are produced at 'high' resource cost relative to non-tradables. This bias towards trade can lead to exporting (or import-substituting) commodities that may earn (or save) foreign exchange in the short run, but they can compromise the prospects of self-sustained growth in the future. If this happens, it may represent non-comparative advantage trade. No country can become rich with competitive devaluation trade. Such trade simply misallocates resources against non-tradables, which may explain the negative relationship between the RER and the real rate of growth in GDP.

The intuitive explanation offered above can be fleshed out into two analytical components. Firstly, it implies that there is an inherent distortion in free currency markets that makes LDCs have high RER. Secondly, this distortion leads LDCs to a systematic misallocation of resources. If so this line of reasoning leads to another paradox. It implies that it is *undervaluation* of the NER – or wanton depreciation of the home currency – that causally relates to low rates of growth. Conventional wisdom, on the contrary, sees the problem as NER *overvaluation* – which is considered both endemic among LDCs and responsible for inferior development outcomes. The two views can be reconciled if the NER and RER, while covariant, do not fully correspond: setting the one at an equilibrium value does not necessarily imply equilibrium for the other. In fact the parable of resource misallocation that was mentioned earlier makes an even stronger statement. Allowing the NER to find its equilibrium value in a free currency market leads to a high (undervalued) RER that systematically misallocates resources in LDCs in favour of excessive tradable production. Moreover this situation of 'incompleteness' in the foreign exchange market is systematically related to the level of underdevelopment. This argument for market incompleteness in foreign exchange is symmetrical to the economics-of-information approach to credit markets (Stiglitz and Weiss, 1981; Floro and Yotopoulos, 1991); only that the origins in this case lie with issues of *reputation*.

Summary and implications
The devaluation of the peso has been dissected by scholars and policy makers in terms of weak fundamentals and by resorting to the rapaciousness of international bankers who pressed their credits on hapless Mexico. While there is some merit in each of the propositions, taken together they are deficient in providing a convincing story. The drama of the peso without the demand side is like Hamlet without the Prince. Short-term financial and portfolio capital flooded the country because there was a huge demand by peso asset holders to currency-substitute into dollars and thus index their wealth against inflation and future peso devaluations. In free currency markets with unrestricted foreign exchange transactions devaluation becomes a sequential self-fulfilling prophecy. It is bound to transpire, whether or not it is temporarily arrested through draconian fiscal and monetary policies and the inflow of foreign capital.

The tendency of soft currencies of developing countries to devalue under free currency markets is due to asymmetry in reputation. The benefits from currency substitution accrue to the upper strata in the distribution of income because there reside the liquid assets that are being hedged. The costs, on the other hand, permeate the economy through systematic misallocation of resources. The remedy for asymmetric reputation lies down the road as development occurs and the fundamentals of the economy improve. Financial integration, therefore, should be the last act in a slow and deliberate process of sequential liberalization.

The most direct way of dealing with depreciation of the domestic currency that is induced by reputation deficit is to control the nominal exchange rate. Foreign exchange restrictions are inevitable, and these involve some control of trade also. This may sound like turning the clock back. But premature liberalization in LDCs amounts to adopting summer-daylight-saving-time in the middle of financial winter. The 'dirty little secret' in international economics is that the costs of intervention are commonly much lower than the people who talk about these issues would have one believe. They can certainly not explain the difference between Brazil and South Korea. Perceptive scholars and policy makers are cautiously promoting the view that the evidence does not add up to a case that free trade is unquestionably good for development (for example, Edwards, 1993; Bruno, 1994). At the end it turns out that the redistribution gains, the rectangles, are greater than the efficiency gains, the triangles. In the specific case of incomplete markets, as the one relating to foreign exchange discussed above, the triangles totally disappear.

Intervention in incomplete markets in developing countries can provide an immediate pay-off in terms of growth. The big caveat, of course, is that the success of intervention depends on the agent of intervention. Good governance, therefore, is a basic ingredient for economic development (which is further discussed in Yotopoulos, 1996, Chapters 3 and 9–11).

References

Bruno, M. (1994), 'Development issues in a changing world: new lessons, old debates, open questions', *World Bank Economic Review*, Supplement 9–19.

Corden, W.M. (1977), *Inflation, Exchange Rates, and the World Economy*. Chicago: The University of Chicago Press.

Edwards, S. (1993), 'Openness, trade liberalization, and growth in developing countries', *Journal of Economic Literature*, 31,1358–93.

Floro, S.L. and P.A. Yotopoulos (1991), *Informal Credit Markets and the New Institutional Economics: The Case of Philippine Agriculture*, Boulder: Westview Press.

Keynes, J.M. (1936), *The General Theory of Employment, Interest, and Money*. New York: St. Martin's Press (1973), *The Collected Writings of John Maynard Keynes*, vol. VII.

Kravis, I.B., A. Heston and R. Summers (1982), *World Product and Income: International Comparisons of Real Gross Product*, Baltimore: Johns Hopkins.

Levine, R. and D. Renelt (1992), 'A sensitivity analysis of cross-country growth regressions', *American Economic Review*, 82, 942–63.

Pack, H. (1994), 'Endogenous growth theory: intellectual appeal and empirical shortcomings', *Journal of Economic Perspectives*, 8, 55–72.

Romer, P.M. (1994), 'The Origins of Endogenous Growth', *Journal of Economic Perspectives*, 8, 3–22.

Salter, W.E.G. (1959), 'Internal and external balance: the role of price and expenditure effects', *Economic Record*, 35, 226–38.

Solow, R.M. (1994), 'Perspectives on Growth Theory', *Journal of Economic Perspectives*, 8, 45–54.

Stiglitz, J.E. and A. Weiss (1981), 'Credit rationing in markets with imperfect information', *American Economic Review*, 71, 393–410.

The Economist, London, 26 August 1995.

Yotopoulos, P.A. (1996), *Exchange Rate Parity for Trade and Development: Theory, Tests, and Case Studies*. New York and London: Cambridge University Press.

PART V

MISCELLANEOUS

19 How Keynes came to Croatia?
Zvonimir Baletić

John K. Galbraith's well-known article *How Keynes Came to America?* (1975) has inspired me to write this chapter. I am sure that in view of the distant events that took place under complex conditions of a small country – Croatia, which was involved in a bitter ideological and political feud, it is interesting to learn as to how Keynes came to this country. The 1920s and 1930s did have a deep imprint on the intellectual life of Croatia, the full extent of which could be properly judged only now, when the country is finally free from totalitarian rule.

Croatian economic thought has a long tradition, from Benedict Kotruljević, an outstanding precursor of the mercantile doctrines in the fifteenth century, Juraj Križanić, a missionary and social reformer in Russia in the seventeenth century, to Josip Šipuš, an early admirer of Adam Smith in the eighteenth century. In the nineteenth century and in the first quarter of the twentieth century Austrian cameralists (for example Sonnenfels), and later the German historical school had the dominant influence. The Anglo-Saxon tradition of economics was partly known, but never had a distinct following.

Among Croatian economists the first who was familiar with the professional activities of Keynes was Đuro Račić, who already in his handbook (1929) made reference to Keynes's theoretical work (notably to his *Tract on Monetary Reform*) in support of stable currency and better regulation of the reparations and war debts. Later (1955) in his book *Financije* (Finance), he stated that Keynes left the strongest impact on contemporary economic debates. He devoted much space to presenting and commenting on Keynesian views on monetary problems. But he did not consider himself as a Keynesian.

With the appearance of a group of young economists well educated in monetary economics, the change came about in the early 1930s. Their spiritual leader was Mirko Lamer, who had worked for his doctoral research (1933) in international economic problems at the Institute of the World Economy in Kiel (Germany). His doctoral thesis was on integration of Yugoslavia into the world economy. In 1935 and 1936 he stayed in Washington and New York in order to prolong his studies. He also was a driving force in launching an economic monthly, *Ekonomist*, published from Zagreb for which he regularly contributed articles and reviews on topical issues. Very often Keynes's name appeared in his writings that concerned the debates on current, especially American, economic issues. In his article *Stabiliziranje američke privrede putem regulacije cijena* (1935b) he speaks of stabilizing the American economy through price control. Referring to Keynes's *The Means to Prosperity*, Lamer wrote: 'In this respect, theories of Keynes have a marked influence on Washington's circles. [Keynes] maintains that the industrial prosperity is characterized by the fact that investments exceed savings, and that during depression the contrary holds. Therefore, he considers that during depression the state should with its own investments set in motion the wheels of industrial process, and in respect of the secondary effects of those investments draws some interesting theoretical calculations'. Later (1935b) he wrote on the constitutional aspects of Roosevelt's New Deal, as well as an article about Roosevelt's reform of the Federal Reserve System, making echo of the Keynesian theoretical propositions. He also contributed several reviews of books, pertaining to the same theoretical and practical debate.[1]

After his return to Croatia, Lamer extensively wrote on Keynesian themes (public works, credit creation, war and war economy, forms of economic policy, principles of a planned economy and similar), much in a spirit of Keynes, with numerous references to his works. He very well noted the change in Keynes's theoretical foundations, which took place in the *General Theory of Employment, Interest and Money* in comparison to Keynes's earlier works. In 1938 he undertook great efforts to set up a research institute in Zagreb. With a few other enthusiasts he succeeded in convincing the authorities to establish the Institute of Economics of Croatia (the present Institute of Economics, Zagreb). He directed the research work of the Institute, until 1941, when he moved to the government. Soon after he emigrated to Switzerland. After the war he stayed abroad and joined FAO (Food and Agriculture Organization) as an expert.

The story of Croatian Keynesianism was not a one-man story. Lamer had several followers and friends. The most prominent among them was Jozo Tomašević, a financial expert of the National Bank of Yugoslavia. He studied economics and obtained a doctoral degree from Basle (Switzerland), writing a dissertation on the Yugoslav debts. He extensively contributed on issues of public finance (for example investment budget as a means of promoting business; public debts in France, England, US; public works and similar) for the journals in Zagreb and Belgrade. More important were his two books: *Financijska politika Jugoslavije* (1935) and *Novac i kredit* (1938). Although in his first book he discussed Keynes's monetary views, it is only in his later book that his intimate knowledge of all major Keynes's works from *Indian Currency and Finance, A Tract on Monetary Reform*, to *A Treatise on Money* and *The General Theory of Employment, Interest and Money* came to full expression. This book is an extensive scholarly treatise, where Keynes's views occupy the central place. Keynes is quoted more than any other author, and if his views are not always fully accepted, they are always considered with high appreciation. The foreword to the book was written by Ivo Belin, another prominent economist and Vice-governor of the National Bank of Yugoslavia, who wrote in the Keynesian trend and shared much of Keynes's views (1924, 1935).

Without going into details of Tomašević's exposition and appraisal of Keynes's views, I will only mention the presence of his ideas in topics included in the book (for example functions and nature of money, bank money, deposit money, money and gold, Indian monetary system, circulation of money, theory of purchasing power of money, savings and investment equilibrium, quantitative theory of money, psychological aspects of business fluctuations, theory of multiplier, Keynes on inflation and deflation, his advocacy of a stable currency in the *Tract* and modified views in the *General Theory*, managed money as a means of achieving full employment, influence of international monetary flows in determining exchange rates, rejection of exchange rate determination based on metal reserves of central banks, problem of transnational bank money and so on). Keynes is presented as the highest authority on all issues, as author of an authoritative treatise on the subject. Tomašević's work did not fail to have a strong impact among students and professional circles.

In 1938 Tomašević was awarded a two-year Rockefeller Foundation fellowship. He went to the US and after the outbreak of war in Europe he stayed on there as a professor at the City University, San Francisco.

More dramatic was the destiny of the third prominent Keynesian in Croatia, Milan Fišter. In 1936 as a young student he enrolled in economics at Cambridge, where he attended lectures of Keynes. After three years of studies he graduated and returned to Zagreb, where Lamer employed him at the Institute of Economics. He published his first book review of Colin Clark's *The Condition of Economic Progress* (1940), stressing the connection between Clark, Pigou and Keynes.

When the war broke out and the pro-nazi regime was established in Croatia, the range of issues which could be publicly discussed was severely reduced. Topics pertaining to democratic societies and personalities representing their values were practically excluded, so the *Ekonomist* could at best publish only about 'neutral' Swedish economists (for example Cassel). Under such circumstances Fišter continued to work on 'the use of buffer stocks in commercial policy' for his doctoral dissertation. At the same time he also prepared for publication the selected works of Keynes. What was surprising is that not only did he prepare them, but he actually published them under a mysterious title *Problemi novca izmedju dva rata* (Problems of money between the two wars) (1944), but still with the subtitle 'selection from works of Keynes'. The publisher was Matica Hrvatska, a leading national cultural association, that made the event even more curious and significant.

Fišter indeed made a representative selection from Keynes's writings on money. He included part of *A Treatise on Money, The Economic Consequences of the Peace, A Tract on Monetary Reform, The End of Gold Standard, The End of Lassez-Faire, The Economic Prospects of Our Grand-children, How to Pay for the War, Robert Malthus, Alfred Marshall.* The largest part was devoted to *The General Theory of Employment, Interest and Money.* The criteria of money was obviously not fully respected, and the inclusion of essays on Malthus and Marshall clearly indicated that he wanted to present a larger account of the Cambridge School.

In his introduction to the book Fišter was explicit in indicating his intention: to present, 'within the framework of present possibilities', 'economic or monetary problems in one of centres of the world economic and social crisis' through a selection of works of Keynes, who 'attempted a reform of the classical theory of political economy'. He presented Keynes as nobody else did. At the same time he discussed the theoretical economic and political problems based on his own practical experience. To him monetary problems are most common and have an international significance, he concluded.

Lamer aimed far beyond his objective of promoting Keynes as he added his own comments to Keynes's writings, appendices (for example lending among allies, gold in the international monetary system, British financing of war, international management of money, transition from the war to the peace economy and so on). This gave him opportunity to present to the Croatian public the full text of the Bretton Woods agreement on International Monetary Fund, as well as the account of the British policy of full employment (the *Beveridge Report*) and economic recovery. The way those texts were presented and amended conveyed a message to the public, that the Allies were going to win the war and establish a new international order. No doubt that his sympathies were with the allies.

The message was well understood by the authorities as well, and they were alarmed. They seized the edition and destroyed it. Only a small number of copies were saved. Fišter was put under custody. But even the end of war did not bring him relief. It seems that he was equally suspected by the new communist regime. In 1946 he was arrested and vanished without a trace. Ironically, while Keynes was becoming triumphant in the US and the Employment Act was being promoted under his shadow, he was being replaced by Marx and Lenin and officially banned in Croatia.

None the less the fact remains that the Keynesian message succeeded in reaching the public during the occupation, and, more important, that it somehow survived under the new totalitarian regime. Although the main protagonists of the Keynesian revolution were not active any more in Croatia, many others who understood the message managed to stay active and expanded the new economic doctrines. To mention a few: Rudolf Bićanić, Marijan Hanžeković, Zlatko Gašparović, Slobodan Štampar, Ivo Vinski and others. Most vocal of them was Rudolf Bićanić, who persisted in challenging openly the official views on political and economic issues. During World War II he lived in the UK and was engaged in preparatory works for Bretton Woods, and he probably knew

Keynes personally. Another important person was Rikard Lang, who spent some time in the Economic and Social Council of the UN and for years was director of the Institute of Economics. He made it a centre of modern economics in Croatia. In the 1950s a number of young economists went abroad to study, especially to the US and the UK. Among them the most prominent was Branko Horvat. In the 1960s the new generation of Croatian economists were educated abroad, mainly in the US, and they followed the world trends in their own theoretical and applied research. Two most distinguished Keynesians, Joan Robinson and Alvin Hansen, were among the first to visit Zagreb and the Institute of Economics in 1950.

To conclude, as it is now becoming more difficult to recognize what in modern economics is Keynesian and what is not Keynesian, we could easily side with Milton Friedman's claim that we are all Keynesians. But the Croatian economists today cannot forget that modern economics came to Croatia with Keynes.

Endnotes

1. He reviewed among others the following books: CUNY (1934), *Report of the Columbia University Commission on Economic Reconstruction*, New York: Columbia University Press; Brown, D.V. (1934), *The Economics of the Recovery Program*, New York: McGraw Hill; Slichter, (1934), *Towards Stability,* New York: Holt and Co.; Strachey, T.S. John (1935), *The Nature of Capitalist Crisis*, New York: Harcourt; Ryan, John A. (1935), *A Better Economic Order*, London; and Pigou, A.C. (1937), *Practical Questions of Political Economy* (translation from German), Jena: Verlag von G. Fischer.

References

Belin, Ivo (1924), 'Problemi naše valute' (The problems of our currency), Zagreb: Nove Evrope.
Belin, Ivo (1935), 'Financiranje javnih radova' (Financing public works), *Ekonomist*, 4, 145–202.
Clark, Colin (1940), *Conditions of Economic Progress*, London: Macmillan.
Fišter, Milan (1944), *Problemi novca izmedju dva svjetska rata* (Problems of money between the two world wars), Zagreb: Matica Hrvatska.
Galbraith, John K. (1975) 'How Keynes Came to America?', in Milo Keynes (ed.), *Essays on John Maynard Keynes*, Cambridge, UK: Cambridge University Press, pp. 132–41.
Lamer, Mirko (1933), *Weltwirtschaftliche Verfleuchtungen Südslawiens*, Kiel: Doctoral Dissertation.
Lamer, Mirko (1935a), 'Stabiliziranje američke privrede putem regulacije cijena', *Ekonomist*, 1. 171–258.
Lamer, Mirko (1935b), 'Američki ustav protiv Roosevelta: National Recovery Program protuustavan' (American constitution against Roosevelt: national recovery act – unconstitutional), *Ekonomist*, 6, 259–64.
Račić, Đuro (1929), *Fiancijska znanost* (Financial science), Zagreb: Kultura.
Račić, Đuro (1955), *Nauka o novcu* (The Science of Money), Zagreb: Školska knjiga.
Tomašević, Jozo (1935), *Financijska politika Jugoslavije* (Financial policy of Yugoslavia), Zagreb: own edn.
Tomašević, Jozo (1938), *Novac i kredit* (Money and Credit), Zagreb: own edn.

Index